HOW TO HYPNOTIZE YOURSELF AND OTHERS

by Rachel Copelan

Frederick Fell Publishers, Inc.
New York

Library of Congress Catalog Card Number 80-70951
ISBN 0-8119-0418-0

Copyright © 1981 by Rachel Copelan

For information address:

Frederick Fell Publishers, Inc.
386 Park Avenue South
New York, New York 10016

PRINTED IN CANADA

1 2 3 4 5 6 7 8 9 0

Contents

CONTENTS

Preface

Hypnosis is at last coming into its own after centuries of being dismissed as theatrical magic or the practice of "quacks." Ignorance and superstition have combined to create a veil of mystery obscuring the nature and benefits of this valuable technique. In the past few years, millions of people have seen examples of hypnotic phenomena on prime-time television. There is a tremendous popular curiosity about them and very few books to answer the need. Those books that are available are mainly written for professionals working in the fields of psychology and medicine. The few books that have been written for the layman tend to be limited to the uses and techniques of a decade ago.

The purpose of this book is to acquaint both the beginner and professional with most up-to-date methods and uses of hypnosis. With simplified techniques that anyone can quickly learn, it is possible to harness a dynamo of mental energy more productive than any oil well in the Middle East. If you are like most of us, you will use only ten percent of your brain's capacity in your lifetime. Imagine the potential for good if we could learn how to tap some part of the remaining ninety percent! WELL, WE CAN! Hypnosis is not only effective as a key to the mind, it can also help to direct the mind's energy to alter our concepts and sensations.

During hypnosis, applied suggestion causes changes to take place in the message system that leads from the brain through the spinal cord. and on through countless branches of nerves, large and small, short and long. The twitch of an eye, the motion of a finger, a puff on a cigarette, the lifting of a beer bottle, all are controllable through hypnotic thought. Nerve responses are complex and multitudinous, yet respond to simple reconditioning techniques when receptivity is established during induced hypnosis. Pain, pleasure, boredom, and joy are all reactions to a passing thought. For this reason, thoughts sometimes will enslave an individual and the power of his mind will turn against him, magnifying his problems instead of helping him solve them. Hypnosis is the facilitator that helps you to tap the brain's resources and efficiently use its energy in a most positive, controlled manner.

Hypnosis is the wedge with which we can enter and stretch the mind to enhance the human potential for personal and professional growth. There is no other single therapeutic technique that holds out so many possibilities for exploration.

Part One
For Beginners

Habits and Hidden Hypnosis

We have all been secretly hypnotized. Yes *you* probably have, too, unless you are one of those rare individuals who has never watched a television program. Most people drift into a common, everyday trance when they gaze into the light of the TV tube. Indirect hypnosis manipulates the minds of millions of unsuspecting viewers everyday. Surreptitiously, subliminal persuasion leaves its mark upon the collective subconscious. Ideas implanted by commercials affect the health and behavior of all of us. We eat, drink, dress, and make love based on what we see and hear. Television has the power to lull the mind into a state of exaggerated suggestibility, opening it up to behavior control from the outside.

Billions of dollars are spent each year in the United States to push products we could live better without. Intelligence notwithstanding, we allow ourselves to be coerced into consuming products dumb animals would run from: sleep inducers, fat reducers, uppers, downers, pain killers for every part of the body. TV, in fact, can train the brain to anticipate pain even when you feel fine.

Advertisers are well aware of the basic principles of hypnosis: (1) Relaxation, (2) Concentration, and (3) Suggestion. It's simple. As we sit relaxed and concentrate on the light, we absorb the suggestions directed at us. During such periods we are extremely vulnerable because we enter a hypnotic state of consciousness (Alpha). Have you noticed how often a commercial is repeated? This is another principle of hypnosis. Repetition enforces suggestion and finally engraves the behavior into the reflexes of the nervous system. The dictionary defines habit this way: "An act or practice so frequently repeated as to become relatively fixed in character and almost automatic in performance."

Every moment of the day and night, newspapers, billboards, radio announcers, and television commercials are implanting harmful habits

3

deeply into the mind. Inevitably, *we become outer-directed instead of inner-protected.*

The average person spends fifteen years of his life immobilized, gazing at the television tube with childlike faith in what he is told. Periodically, every few minutes, day after day, specially-trained voices, ringing with sincerity, assure us that their pills and potions are *the* panaceas. Some people become so convinced by this colossal put-on that they buy things they never heard of.

Surveys estimate that U.S. pharmaceutical companies spend billions of dollars each year to promote over-the-counter drugs. Headache soothers, nerve smoothers, uppers, downers, sleep inducers, and weight reducers are incessantly pushed on the unwary consumer. We are psychologically tricked by motivational researchers, social scientists, and psychological consultants to lose control of our appetites. Substances we could live longer without, such as alcohol, cigarettes, and fattening foods, come to seem indispensable.

Why do we deliberately do harm to our health?

Obviously, one's instinct for self-preservation becomes confused by the steady bombardment of the ad men. Our senses are assaulted by psychological devices which our conscious minds cannot detect, secret in-depth language is used to subconsciously stimulate our tastes, and the result is that bad habits are implanted and reinforced without our suspecting it.

Eventually, masses of people are convinced problems have easy, superficial solutions. The persuaders evoke more than physical appetite. They also appeal to the emotions: fears of rejection, guilt, and loneliness.

Instead of helping us to use our innate abilities to cope with the challenge of daily living, the media has been converting the human mind into catatonic dough. To some extent, most of us have fallen prey to the huckster's pitch, letting ourselves be channeled into unthinking habits custom-built to serve industry's motive to make a profit even if the product promotes death.

If the advertising media doesn't get to you, you may become influenced by the bad habits of the people around you. Only the rare, self-aware person manages to remain untouched by the behavior of others. For most, it's easier to succumb to the lure of the piper who sings, "Dance to the tune or become a social misfit." Rather than be ostracized, we fall into step—team players for free enterprise.

Eventually the indoctrination becomes ingrained as the victim begins to react with neurotic compulsion. This weakening of will leads to behavior even more harmful than the original stimuli promoted. Milder drugs escalate to stronger dosages. The alcoholic's "one drink" may graduate into "one bottle", the pot smoker's one joint into dependency. Addiction is reinforced as addicts are accepted into some of the highest social circles, where being "spaced out" is the "in thing". Try attending a party where most people are smoking pot. Refuse to participate and you may be treated like a "square" and not invited back. Yet, unless we are able to reject being programmed, we face not only the prospect of dehumanization, but also "moronization" as we come to behave more and more like brainless robots.

YOU CAN BREAK THE SPELL

Fortunately, the human brain is able to change. Learn to think for yourself! Habits are adjustable. Behavior is malleable. Areas of the mind marred by years of unhealthy thinking can become areas of growth and improvement through the utilization of positive programming. We can outgrow learned limitations and achieve the highest degree of innate potential.

Hypnosis helps in focusing on the inner reality of who you really are and what you want from life. Moreover, hypnosis is dynamically helpful in achieving those ends. You don't have to remain a cooperative puppet assisting in your own demise. You can stand on your own feet, take over your own controls and snip the strings of manipulation by others.

Self-enhancement requires systematic *deconditioning*, followed by *reconditioning*. Habits tend to cling like the tentacles of an octopus unless you are determined to free yourself from their grasp. The process is mental and it helps to know that, where your behavior is concerned, the most powerful mind involved is your own.

FROM THE WOMB TO THE TOMB

From the moment a baby is born, society's molding begins. The infant leaves its mother's womb and becomes a separate individual. Soon he is the recipient of suggested behavior that influences all of his future habits. He experiences sensations, which are stored in his memory bank. As he hears and feels, impressions that result form images for future reference.

It is interesting to note that children are in a trance state about fifty percent of their waking time. Their spongelike vulnerability explains their superior ability to absorb and retain information.

From the womb to the tomb, a persistent contest for control prevails between the "other world" and one's inner world of intelligence. Most of us allow the outside to take over the inside and so we travel from birth to old age, acquiring one habit after another. Some habits are, of course, useful and necessary, while others are so dreadfully addictive and destructive they lead to illness and premature death. If some of your habits disturb you, consider yourself normal, for we are all creatures of habit. Like a soft bed, habits are easy to get into and hard to get out of.

Once our power over the selection and rejection of habits has vanished, desire surpasses logic because the user has lost his ability to evaluate objectively. From the richest to the poorest, everyone is hooked to at least one bad habit. Fact is, most of us have more than one. A network of harmful behavior takes over as one habit interlaces with another. Finally, a destructive lifestyle evolves.

Overeating	Uppers	Cocaine
Smoking	Downers	Negative Thinking
Alcohol	Marijuana	

Some people, collecting bad habits like a hobby, are burdened with all of these. Combinations are limitless and uniquely individual. Periodically, the routinized person may attempt to alter his fixed conduct. He may give up cigarettes, but in most cases he drifts back. If able to stay off cigarettes, he may substitute fattening food or alcohol. Instead of smoking himself to death, he's eating or drinking himself to death. And it matters little to the undertaker which bad habit did him in.

IMITATION IS A POWERFUL FORCE

We know that human social conduct is reinforced through emulation. Your senses feed your habits. The input to habit comes from *sensory perception*. Our thoughts and actions respond to:

What we see	What we smell
What we hear	What we touch
What we taste	

The human mind works like a computer, absorbing information through the senses. Reactions are fed back to the muscles, nerves and reflexes.

As a child grows, he learns that certain words evoke specific responses. Throughout the rest of his life, each word he hears, each sight he sees, every event his senses absorb elicits images and reactions. This response is called output.

Your mind is constantly concerned with input and output.

For example, the word "animal" might bring to mind a positive or negative image, depending upon previously acquired impressions. To a child once frightened by an angry dog, it would present a negative image, while to another child it might recall a pleasant memory of a playful pet.

Reflexes are trained to behave in a ritualized pattern by the process of image-recall. Our brain is constantly flashing images for our consideration. Not only old images, but those we pick up from our immediate environment. This is why it's important to develop the ability to sort out the wanted from the unwanted impressions.

HOW SUGGESTION WORKS

We have noted that television is a prime example of mass suggestion. These days, a person cannot hang out the laundry without worrying about "Tattle-tale gray," "Ring-around-the-collar," and so on.

Fears of acid-indigestion, cancer, and heart attack bombard the television viewer as he sits transfixed, open-mouthed and blank-minded. The more a person absorbs, the more he suspects something must be wrong with him. Many psychologists believe worrisome commercials can cause the very problem the announcer warns against. No wonder people are confused.

Take, for example, Mrs. Gullible. Mrs. Gullible watches television night and day. She begins to imagine she has every ailment described. Before long, filled with anxiety, she makes an appointment to see a doctor for a checkup.

By the time Mrs. Gullible arrives in the doctor's office, she is a bundle of nerves, expecting bad news. After a thorough examination, the doctor assures her that there is nothing physically wrong with her. But Mrs. Gullible won't take no for an answer. The power of television suggestion has left its mark in her mind.

"Look me over again, doctor," she persists. "I must have a lump somewhere."

Her complaints continue. Headaches, backaches, sleeplessness, anxiety. As a result, not only has she been conned into buying useless products, but she harbors a fear that no matter what the doctor says, something must be wrong. She travels from doctor to doctor in search of one who will confirm her fears. As long as Mrs. Gullible persists in her negative expectations, she may eventually develop a symptomatic ailment. *This syndrome is responsible for a great number of psychosomatic illnesses.*

Hypochondriacs are people who, like Mrs. Gullible, have fallen into the habit of imagining ailments that exist only in their fantasies. These people are highly suggestible because of their impressionable imaginations.

Scrutinize your own behavior. Do your negative habits override your positive ones? Are you propelled by a force over which you have no control? Keep in mind problems are not solved by pills, puffs of smoke, sniffs of powder, or chocolate cream pie. Problems can only be solved by facing them squarely and by taking the proper action to eradicate them. Hold a mirror up to the innermost workings of your mind. You may find some of your thinking habits just to be someone else's, implanted while you were least suspecting it.

The first step against bad conditioning is *deconditioning*, which erases the old imprint so you can start with a clean slate. The next step is *reconditioning*, which imprints new and better thoughts for healthier behavior. Hypnosis accomplishes this through retraining the reflexes.

A conditioned reflex can be defined as a reflex which is activated by a new signal as the result of new connections being formed within the brain. It exists in every person, is produced by repetition, and will tend to deteriorate unless regularly reinforced. (This last characteristic can be useful or detrimental.) The conditioned reflex is involved in the development of athletic skills, too. *Thought initiates specific movement.*

THE CONDITIONED REFLEX

The conditioned reflex is at the root of every habit pattern. This is the automatic response that makes you get out of bed in the morning, walk to the bathroom, wash your face, brush your teeth, dress, eat breakfast, go to work, and follow your usual routine.

We are products of our environment. Every experience we have leaves a mark on the cortex of the brain. This works in very much the same way as a tape recorder does. Like a recorder, imprints are played and replayed. Each time an experience is repeated, the markings on the cortex of the brain are strengthened. Repeating a habit makes this engraving penetrate deeper.

Dr. Ivan P. Pavlov was a Russian physiologist. He received the Nobel prize for physiology and medicine in 1904 for his outstanding contribution in tracing patterns of human behavior based on laboratory research with animals. He was the first authority on the development of conditioned reflexes. In his experiments with dogs, he not only discovered how habits originate, but what makes them repetitive.

Using the following test, Dr. Pavlov discovered a reflexive habit could be firmly established in a dog. He would ring a bell and then offer the dog food. After this procedure had been repeated several times, whenever Dr. Pavlov rang the bell the dog would salivate in eager anticipation. Eventually the dog began to salivate if he heard the bell ring *even when he was not hungry.* The bell had become a signal to the brain which started the flow of digestive juices. In other words, the brain told the glands, "Secrete! Food's coming," even after the dog's belly was full.

How does the Pavlov experiment with a dog compare to human behavior?

PEOPLE ARE ALSO TRAINED ANIMALS

Human beings respond to stimuli in very much the same way as animals. In spite of their superior intelligence, sensory signals set off reflexive behavior.

For example, take the plight of Rosemary Jones. Rosemary weighs two hundred and sixty pounds. Whenever she passes a bakery window, her mouth begins to water. Her body doesn't need the calories, yet she "can't help herself."

"Should I or shouldn't I?" she agonizes. "Oh, just this one last time," she tells herself. "One more cream puff won't make that much difference."

The moment she swallows, Rosemary wishes she hadn't.

"Oh, why did I do it?" she scolds herself. "It doesn't make sense. I'll never do such a stupid thing again," she promises and means to keep her promise, too. She does, until the next temptation. Like Pavlov's dog, her salivary glands responded to her senses even when there was no hunger. Just as the experimental dog reacts, so do we when the bell in our mind rings.

The mere mention of the word "food" will tickle the palate of a habitual overeater, even if he's already stuffed. Drinkers of alcohol, cigarette smokers, and drug addicts behave in the same programmed way, responding to signals like trained animals in a circus act.

Bob T., one of my clients, said, "Every time the telephone rings, I automatically reach for a cigarette, even if I've just finished one." He paused and smiled sadly. "Even if it's not my telephone."

Another habit-hooked client, Harry P., described himself as "totally dependent on one martini to pick me up before dinner and a couple afterward to settle me down for the evening."

Habit-addicts associate their habit with emotional satisfaction. Thus, when feeling signs of distress, they reach for a pacifier.

Dr. Pavlov not only demonstrated that habits become entrenched by repetition; he also discovered something else. CONDITIONING IS STRONGER AND FASTER WHEN THE EMOTIONS ARE INVOLVED.

Whenever Pavlov's laboratory dogs were irritable or anxious, they reacted with increased tensions and salivated more. Keep in mind that appetite is often not based on hunger or real need, but rather on emotions because emotions spur physical reactions.

HOW EMOTIONS AND HABITS INTERRELATE

Dr. Pavlov proved that a conditioned reflex (habit) could be established even from *just one input if strong emotion is present*. Because this is true, traumatic shocks can bring on reflexive behavior which may last a lifetime. The following example illustrates how this principle works both for a man and an animal:

A new mailman approaches a house. The dog living on the premises barks. The inexperienced mailman kicks the dog. The dog becomes frightened and snaps at the mailman's trousers.

The conflict persists as long as the mailman and the dog continue to react to each other with fear, and the habit extends beyond this particular situation. The mailman reacts with fear when he sees *any* dog and the dog barks at *every* mailman.

Let's see how this sort of automatic reaction applies to people in the ways they relate to each other. A woman molested by a man when she was a child may forever after tremble with fear at the advances of *all* men. Her automatic withdrawal may keep her from marrying, raising a family, and enjoying male-female intimacy.

The same may hold true for men who have had a disturbing experience with a woman early in life. Have you ever heard a man say: "All women are alike!" Such a person is reacting with conditioned emotions.

A black man may have been treated badly by a particular white employer, yet suppressed his hatred in order to keep his job. The power of that suppressed hatred can cause him to later react with strong distrust and hatred toward every white man who reminds him of his earlier boss.

The problem of reacting automatically and without logic has significance beyond the distrust it can create between two individuals. Conditioning affects entire nations and races. There are people who dislike all Jews, all Blacks, all Catholics, all Protestants, all Russians, even if they have known only one person in that category.

The habit of prejudice can become a barrier between people on many levels, involving even such simple things as physique or hair color. Some people cannot stand redheads; others, short people; others, tall people, or fat people, or thin people. Most habit reactions of a prejudicial nature have their root in some emotional experience of the past.

HABITS CAN BE BROKEN

Every human being comes into this world equipped with the necessary mental machinery to adjust to the harsh conditions of life and change them. This is not difficult if the desire is strong enough. When a person is motivated to change, he can do so. The hypnotic process is similar to the one which gave him the habit in the first place. Instead, however, absorbing of negative, harmful suggestions in the relaxed, receptive state, he uses positive, helpful ones and reverses the effect.

The most encouraging characteristic of a habit pattern is that the repetitive activity can be interrupted when the mind is turned to other interests. Hypnosis causes a break in the continuity of a habit, thereby acting as a wedge to weaken its hold on the mind. This is the key that can help change a harmful habit into a helpful one, because if the interruption can happen once, it can happen again and again.

PERSONALITY AND HABIT PATTERNS

Habits not only affect the body, but form the foundation of one's personality and character. People who chain-smoke or bite their nails are saying something about how they relate to life. Physical habits are merely ripples on the surface. Deep in the mind's riverbed, stress rocks and shocks the psyche. Emotional responses tend to become habitual. For example, some people, if given a choice between reacting with a smile or a frown, will invariably frown. Who decides whether you will feel happy or unhappy? Only you. Happiness is a habit. Abraham Lincoln said, "People are just about as happy as they make up their minds to be."

The point is, some people look at life with cheerful expectations while others expect everything to go wrong. Those anticipating the worst get what they're looking for. They also reinforce a very prevalent personality habit: self defeat. The habitual "loser" reveals his feelings about himself in his "body language." He may glue his eyes to the ground and walk with rounded shoulders or his body in a slump. If he would lift his head, arch his chest, and draw in his abdominal muscles, he would not only look like a winner, but reflect a winning personality.

Physical habits are the flip side of the way we feel toward ourselves. Emotional habits color not only the surface personality, but the deeper character as well. People are habitually depressed, habitually evasive, habitually late, habitually disorganized, habitually dishonest. The list is endless. Each individual combination of physical and emotional habits shapes you into the particular person you are.

Remember, hypnosis doesn't just take away your habits. Rather, it is a tested method for exchanging bad habits for good ones. It trains you how to maintain a relaxed body and tranquil mind, prerequisites for a strong and attractive personality.

The "wish to fail" is also a habit. People fall into the habit of unconsciously handling their affairs improperly. By so doing, they subconsciously make sure not to succeed.

Disaster-prone people fall into an automatic pattern in which they are always expecting failure. And every negative thought, no matter how fleeting, carries an anticipation of defeat.

The habit of negativism can actually turn some people into serious neurotics, according to a recent news release. Headed "Bad Habits That Drive You Crazy," it quotes Dr. Joseph Wolpe: "Neuroses are emotional bad habits. A neurosis results from a fearful response to

things or situations which offer no real threat. Therapists now use their
knowledge of learning processes to weaken and eliminate these bad
habits. At the same time, they teach patients how to respond reason-
ably to a situation."

WINNERS AND LOSERS

There are winners and there are losers. I'm not talking about betting on
a horse. I'm talking about betting on yourself. You can't control the
horse's mood, but you can control your own.

Negative people tend to put off making decisions. This traps them
into another bad habit: procrastination. One of the worst human failings is resistance to facing up to responsibility. We push unpleasant
tasks into the background, waiting for "some other time," postponing
while hoping the problem will simply disappear. For some procrastina-
tors, tomorrow never comes. Days, months, and years may go by and
they don't "get to it". Before they realize, their lives have passed by and
they haven't fulfilled their dreams.

One interesting aspect of personality is that other people notice
our failings more and sooner than we do. Traits can become so im-
bedded we do things automatically without knowing it. Routinized behavior is a giveaway to others as to what is going on in the deeper
mind. For example, a salesman who wants to project confidence yet
nervously interrupts his client is revealing rather than concealing his
insecurity.

A self-proclaimed "loser," Gregory R., complained of his inability
to close a sale. "I never seem to get the breaks," he said. "Other men
have good luck. They get ahead of me and I'm always left behind. I
don't understand why I'm so unlucky."

Do You Believe It's Really Luck that Makes a Person Succeed?
Or Is It His Pattern of Thinking?

Gregory had not yet learned the sales power of his own mind.
Eventually, he learned to apply self-hypnosis to change his self-image
from low to high. The result was remarkable. Once he had lifted his
self-esteem, his life took a turn for the better. Confident behavior
invites and paves the way for success. Gregory also found he had to

eliminate additional habits which had grown out of his self-denigrating attitude.

Here are the personality habits which interfered with Gregory's sales success. This was his "formula for failure."

The Procrastination Habit

Gregory was a chronic putter-offer. Slow to make decisions, fearful of making mistakes. He allowed things to slide. Bills piled up. Down to his last clean shirt in the drawer. Phone calls remained unanswered. Visits to his dentist postponed.

Gregory lived in a world of disorder and neglect. His life was swamped with unfinished business. But putting things off was only *one* of his problems. He also had:

The Fear of Success Habit

This is a common hangup affecting millions of people. Because with success once attained, one must live up to its responsibilities. In order to avoid success, he postponed and developed:

The Self-Pity Habit

This is a pattern of thinking that habitual losers suffer from and that perpetuates their defeatist behavior, which eventually carries over into most areas of their lives.

The Alcoholism Habit

In Gregory's case, this led him straight to the nearest saloon where alcohol was used as a cop-out. And of course, then he had another habit to cope with.

HABITS HAVE ROOTS

Most of us are like Gregory. We develop a complex of physical and emotional habits which "branch out" from the "main trunk" of our daily behavior. While habits are sprouting, we may not notice them.

Eventually they force themselves on our consciousness and we are amazed at their overpowering strength.

Sources of compulsive conduct can be traced back. Once you discover and uncover the "soil" and the "roots" of your "tree of behavior," you will better understand the "blossoming" that occurs on the surface. When the problem becomes clear, and you face up, you are ready for the next steps: how to dig it out, snip it off, reseed, replant, and grow healthy and meaningful habits.

Some capricious behavior stems from imitation. We tend to fall into a reaction pattern through parental indoctrination. Well-meaning parents, filled with love and "do-goodness," often train their children to follow in their footsteps. "Step into my shoes," says Dad hopefully, even if the shoes are uncomfortable; living through one's children is a bad parental habit. How often do we hear, "I've been teaching Junior how to run the button business since he was fourteen years old. Someday when I'm ready to retire to Florida, he'll take over for me and build it bigger and bigger."

While listening to this spiel year in and year out, Junior is secretly hating buttons. What Senior does not realize is: his shoe may not fit Junior's foot. Junior might prefer to be a ball player, an astronaut, or a rock musician. Torn between loyalty to parents and a desire to stand on one's own feet causes resentment and anger which becomes self-destructive.

Oral compulsiveness, such as eating, drinking, and smoking, can often be traced to early experiences. Habits feed on childhood memories, which are linked to emotions. The earliest moments of life can play a part. When a baby is loved and treated in a consistently warm and understanding way, he has stronger resistance to negative behavior in adult life.

Unless we use the mind's capacity for erasing past influences, we may remain forever linked to behavior suited to the infantile needs of childhood. An understanding of the nature of personality comes when we examine the attributes a child assumes as he or she matures.

During the first six years of life, we develop:

1. Trust in or distrust for other people.
2. A general sense of self-confidence or self-doubt.
3. Initiative to try or fear of failure.
4. Sexual identity or gender confusion.
5. Friendliness toward or alienation from others.
6. Creative expression or destructiveness.

These habit patterns are more or less integrated into an individual's personality for life. However, one is never too old to improve, in spite of a bad beginning.

In reconditioning behavior that stems from negative early influences, the skilled hypnotherapist will regress the subject to early memories and use the information for reprogramming.

The most important influence upon a child's early development comes from parents, who set the standards for behavior. Parents' habits register on the minds of the tiniest children. Attitudes and actions are transmitted from the mature to the immature along with assorted information and misinformation. Brooding about what their parents did and didn't do causes many people to spend the best part of their lives on the psychiatrist's couch rehashing and regretting early happenings. Focusing on the past can downgrade the future, and therapy often fails because to dwell on misfortune and mistakes only reinforces their continuance.

One of the outstanding achievements of the therapeutic trance is its ability to wipe out traumatic memories. The subject finds upon awakening that his modes of functioning, both mental and physical, have been altered for the better. With the help of the hypnotherapist, a kind of subtle brainwashing takes place. The troubled person finds that his attitudes have switched from anxiety about the past to enthusiasm for the present and the future. Best of all, this occurs without striving, in a state of serene, positive anticipation.

Hypnosis not only utilizes positive suggestions, but also makes use of a very important aspect of suggestion, *the art of forgetting*. Under hypnotic and posthypnotic suggestion you learn to forget as deliberately and easily as you learn to remember or choose to forget. Without realizing what we are doing, some of us cling to memories as a self-punishing device because we are too guilt-ridden to allow ourselves the pleasure that comes with being guilt-free. Useless memories which limit happiness should be obliterated to make room in the subconscious for useful ones.

In cases of extreme emotional disturbances such as those resulting from rape, child abuse, fires, accidents or torture, a skilled hypnotist can perform techniques of amnesis and wipe out the memory entirely. When used for behavior modification, hypnotherapy erases habitual flashbacks to old images at the same time it lowers the tension level.

HOW THE NERVOUS SYSTEM WORKS

The human nervous system is composed of the brain, the spinal cord, and a network of nerves that branch out through the body. The nerves extend from head to toe, and information about every habit you have follows the route from the brain to the area of the body concerned. All bodily activities are thus controlled. This communication goes on day and night, whether you are awake or asleep. In lower animals, the feedback is instinctual. In human beings, however, emotions enter into the process as well as conscious thoughts. This is why so many people are troubled by problems other animals don't have.

The maze of nerves that forms the network of sensory input decides which information to pass on to the brain, unless there is interference by the intellect. Most people, however, are slaves to automatic nervous reaction. They react like robots to suggestions to chain-smoke, overeat, overdrink, etc.

Anyone can train himself to break the pattern and reverse the process. When conscious intelligence tells the nervous system what to accept and what to reject, we can become masters of our habits. In addition to the involuntary functions of the brain, the area known as the cerebral cortex is largely responsible for decision making. Hypnosis can be used to help the cortex to function better and, thus, to make better decisions. The cortex is taught to desensitize the nerves dependent upon harmful substances such as nicotine, alcohol, or other drugs. Actions and habit responses will reflect negative conditioning until the nervous relay syndrome is deliberately changed on a subconscious level.

IT'S ALL IN YOUR HEAD

Nothing that man's brain has invented can compare with the brain itself. If man were to build a computer to do the work of one human brain, the computer would have to be as enormous as the Empire State Building and a lot more complicated. When we consider the size of the human brain, it is amazing to realize that this one organ accounts for the activity of the voluntary and involuntary systems of the body as well as consciousness, thought, perception, and creativity.

The specialized compartments of the brain each has a particular job to do in servicing the body and the thinking processes of the mind.

They not only govern the involuntary internal organs, such as those that make up the digestive, circulatory, reproductive and respiratory systems; they also direct every single physical motion, down to the flicker of an eyelash. In addition, *every automatic habit and personal idiosyncrasy originates there.*

Since man first developed his ability to question, he has searched in awe for the answers to the mysteries which surround him. Man has used his intelligence to project far out into his environment, to the point where now he can study even faraway galaxies. Yet the greatest of all mysteries is not in outer space but in the inner space of our skulls. Inside the bony cave of the human head lies the real riddle of the universe, where about a trillion brain cells altogether weighing only about 3 to 3½ lbs., control memory, imagination, communication, health, and happiness.

We have discovered that the neurons in the nervous system are the chemical transmitters of messages from brain to body. Everything is controlled, from the heartbeat and motor abilities to sensory perception and emotional responses. Thoughts and emotions are then transmitted to a special area of the brain which sorts it out.

The cerebral cortex is the brain's analyzer, acting as a receiving station for information fed to it by the nervous system. There are billions of interconnecting nerves that act together to produce individual habit patterns. These nerves are dictated to by the cortex, which receives thought in the form of suggestion from sight, sound, or any combination of the senses. The cortex then transforms the idea of feeling into bodily action. Sometimes it's harmful, sometimes helpful, depending upon attitude and the degree of stress associated with the thought. When stress or troubled emotions accompany a thought to the cortex, the resulting tension interferes with the positive functioning of this part of your brain.

TENSION REINFORCES COMPULSIVE HABITS

Most bad habits have one basic thing in common: they grow stronger in the soil of nervous tension.

What causes the vast majority of modern-day people to be so tense? It seems that man's brain has created more than his nervous system can handle. The increased competitive tempo of the machine age is contrary to nature's need for mental recuperation through tranquillity and physical relaxation.

Too many people are caught up in the pursuit of wealth. In their enthusiasm, they lose sight of other values. They find that the part by which happiness enters in has died within them. Having spent their lives heaping up colossal piles of treasure, they suddenly discover they have built their pyramids in a joyless desert.

In their haste to accumulate possessions, they forget "you can't take it with you." There are no pockets on shrouds and I've never seen a Brink's money van following a hearse to the cemetery. Trying too hard to succeed materially not only increases tension, but can lower life expectancy.

Relaxed people, on the other hand, are not only more flexible in their outlook, they are better able to take in stride the stress that upsets tense people. Instead of allowing every event to fill them with anxiety, they relax, shrug off problems and accept challenges as part of life. Pressures can push you up and help you grow if you're looking in the right direction—upward instead of downward.

WHATEVER YOU PROJECT—YOU BECOME

No one is immune to worry, regardless of color, age, sex, or economic status. The poor man worries about where his next meal is coming from. The rich man gets ulcers over his next million. A wealthy industrialist complained, "If only I didn't have so many responsibilities maintaining my fortune!" This man's blood pressure goes up and down with the stock market report.

Once tension takes over the habit pattern, we respond automatically without conscious thinking. More and more miserable, we find ourselves caught in a nervous whirlpool which pulls us down.

Tension starts in the brain as a reaction to stress. The impulses which the brain receives in the form of suggestion (or sensory input) pass through the body by way of the spinal column.

The spine encases the spinal cord, which passes bundles of nerves through the openings in the vertebrae. These nerve bundles separate into countless long, thin fibers that connect the brain to every part of the body.

Your nervous system is as vital to your health as an electrical system is to the proper functioning of an industry. Sensations are flashed to the brain and immediately a reaction takes place in some part of the anatomy. There are more than five hundred muscles attached to the various parts of the body. When a muscle receives a message from the brain, the muscle impulsively shortens and contracts, thereby causing pressure on the nerves that pass through it.

Should there be no release of this contraction, the excess tension remains in the muscles surrounding the nerve fibers. This prolonged contraction is at the base of nervousness. Therapists refer to this condition as "residual tension." Dr. Hans Selye, father of the theory of psychosomatic illness, believes that unresolved areas of tension within the body eventually lead to the breakdown of healthy functioning and thus are the forerunners of disease. However, not all tension is bad. Some is essential to survival. A certain amount of tension supplies the alertness which is essential for an emergency.

The trouble comes when a person is tense most of the time whether he is threatened or not. Instead of tension functioning as an emergency measure, it accumulates from hour to hour and day to day without release. Living under pressure all the time eventually overwhelms the nervous system.

DON'T OVERBURDEN YOURSELF

If you place too many burdens upon yourself, you will surely add tension. Learn to set priorities. Select one project at a time on which to focus your attention.

If you are in a constant state of rushing to meet responsibilities, you will find people very eager to load you with them.

Treating every crisis as a calamity also adds tension. Take care of the most essential problem and don't look for new ones.

If you try to cram too much into any one day, you will add to your tension.

If your boss has been giving you a hard time, talk it out with him, instead of holding it in. Explain how you feel without losing your temper or your job. Chances are he will respect you for it. In general, to end inner tensions, face up to the facts which are upsetting you. Worrying about a problem without taking positive action only prolongs the problem.

Improvement in one's condition must come through accepting reality and exercising the art of the possible. Sometimes that means compromise, adaptiveness and flexibility. This is what it takes to be the kind of easygoing, outgoing, relaxed person who thinks in a creative and productive way.

Without the satisfaction of total living, tension mounts. The resulting physical breakdown from unresolved tension can cause serious damage. When you hear someone say, "My stomach is tied up in knots," this is a simple indication of how tension might lead to a physical problem like an ulcer.

Hypertension and high cholesterol are additional ways in which our body chemistry reacts to excessive stress. Investigators explain that our adaptive mechanism becomes weakened under prolonged nervous anxiety. Doctors who specialize in psychosomatic ailments recognize tension as the great masquerader. Hundreds of physical and mental disorders can be traced back to this source.

How Does Hypnosis Deal with Tension?

From the very first session, subjects report a deep feeling of relaxation throughout their muscles and nerves. This pleasant feeling remains for from three to five days depending upon the depth of the trance and suggestibility of subject.

Can Anyone Be Hypnotized?

Anyone who wishes to be can be, with the possible exception of morons and babies, since they do not know what the hypnotist is attempting to do and can not concentrate upon his voice. Various reports on hypnotizability, based on controlled research, indicate that, of those tested, 95 percent are influenced to some degree. Of these, 20 percent reach a medium trance and 10 percent a deep or somnambulistic trance level. The rest responded with a lighter trance but were able to increase depth after one to three repetitions of hypnotic induction.

Personally, I believe just about anyone can be helped through hypnosis. Who can say that the five percent were not hypnotizable until every hypnotist has given up on them? I have hypnotized many people who were told they could not be hypnotized. Factors such as motivation, personal rapport between therapist and subject, and physical surroundings all contribute to, or detract from, hypnotizability.

How Does the Hypnotist Work?

The art of inducting the hypnotic trance begins with putting the subject at ease. Physical comfort evokes relaxed feelings. The chair or couch is important, the temperature of the room, light, and outside sound must all be taken into account so that distractions can be minimized. The therapist begins by exploring the subject's motivation and expectations. It is important that the hypnotherapist remove misconceptions and fear of the trance by explaining that it is a natural state of mind and body. The first session establishes confidence and rapport. Subsequent sessions reinforce suggestions based on personal programming.

Does the Hypnotist Become Emotionally Involved?

Yes. To this degree: the subject, or troubled person, reacts more positively to genuine interest and concern. I have found that an element of love is the strongest factor in the therapeutic situation. This is a detached kind of love. Personal attachments are avoided because in the final stage of hypnotherapy control is turned over to the subject through the teaching of self-hypnosis.

How Does Hypnotherapy Differ from Stage Hypnosis?

The hypnotherapist shares many of the views of other psychotherapists concerning the dynamics of unconscious processes. An appreciation of the subject's responses and needs are uppermost in the mind of a good hypnotherapist. The hypnotherapist is not a showman. We do not use verbal magic to impose anything alien upon the subject. There is no mysterious manipulation or possession of the subject by the hypnotist. The skilled therapist is involved in helping the subject to use his or her own latent mental powers.

How about Self-Hypnosis? Does it Work Just as Well?

Sometimes even better. An important aspect of self-hypnosis is that the skill is with you twenty-four hours a day and wherever you happen to be. Thousands of people have trained themselves using the simple methods described in this book. Some people with serious problems need an instructor to set up a suitable program for them. Once this is established, self-hypnosis is carried on by the subject in real-life situations on a day-to-day basis. The role of the hypnotist is that of a teacher, activating and developing what is already inside the person rather than imposing foreign suggestions from the outside.

Self-Hypnosis:
The Deepest Meditation

Cicero, the Roman orator said, "A happy life begins with tranquillity of mind." Sounds simple, doesn't it? Yet this quest has confounded sages through the ages. For a special few, meditation has proven to be the answer. Although practiced throughout human history in many remote regions of the world, it still remains an esoteric art. This book is dedicated to exploring the mysteries of your mind and how you can master those mysteries with hypnosis.

There are still witch doctors in the Amazon jungle and Yogis in Indian temples who believe they have a God-given gift that makes them different from other human beings. The truth is, we all possess the ability to perform mental magic, but few know how to put the power to use. Almost anyone can master mind-control techniques and turn himself on to unlimited self-enrichment.

The fundamental difference between meditation and self-hypnosis is that whereas meditation helps one to detach from problems, *hypnosis zeros into the problem, examines its causes, finds a solution, and then eliminates the problem.* The secret of hypnosis is focused concentration excluding all outside interference. Self-hypnosis is more than inner-dwelling. It is also inner-direction and self-protection. Its use of carefully constructed personal programming with regard to specific goals is another aspect of hypnosis that lifts it above mere contemplation or reflection.

Many of the meditative forms used by modern-day practitioners draw their techniques from ancient Eastern religions. The object of Eastern meditation is spiritual detachment from one's environment. Characteristic of meditation is a vague, drifting-away quality that puts the subject out of touch with responsibility. Both traditional meditation and hypnosis relieve unbearable pressures and enhance one's ability to cope. They both feel pleasant, are useful in relieving tension, and provide a temporary escape from reality. However, when reality returns with its pressures and problems, hypnosis has tuned the mind in instead of out.

People who have had some experience with meditation, whether it is TM or yoga, find it easier to attain hypnosis because one level of meditation leads to the other. Meditation takes you from the wide-awake state of mind called *beta* to an altered state called *alpha*. *Alpha* then leads to *theta*, which is hypnosis. When a person becomes proficient at using self-hypnosis he can easily drift into *delta*, otherwise known as sleep.

Self-hypnosis, also called autohypnosis, is a state of heightened suggestibility wherein personal programming can be directed to and accepted by the subconscious mind. The untapped reservoir of intelligence is brought to the surface and almost anything is possible. Well-trained practitioners sometimes can match the success of professionals in alleviating their own behavioral problems. Self-hypnosis also reduces stress and promotes a stronger personality.

Most people learn how to induce self-hypnosis by first being hypnotized by a professional. However, this is not always necessary if the person is willing to practice regularly with the techniques described in this chapter. If you have had some experience with meditation or yoga breathing methods, self-hypnosis will be easy for you to achieve. It is the scientific application of planned positive autosuggestion during the meditative state that brings about the desired results. Without a concise, practical program, meditation remains a method of "spacing-out" instead of "spacing-in" where the power of change resides.

Autohypnosis is the spotlight which brings enlightenment to the darkest corners of despair. You can use it to set fire to old habits and clear the field for better ones. Once you eliminate negative thinking and faulty self-imagery you will find a resurgence of submerged creativity. Each time you reach into the limitless well of your potential you will uncover and discover personal treasure.

HOW DOES HYPNOSIS FEEL?

To begin with, hypnosis is not sleep. When we are asleep, we are largely unconscious, with our conscious minds inactive. During sleep, the subconscious mind as well as the conscious mind is inaccessible to the "input" of suggestion. Hypnosis, rather, feels like suspended animation. The body sleeps while the mind is totally aware and receptive to ideas. There is a profound feeling of relaxation through every nerve and muscle of the body. This physical contentment is combined with a feeling of blissfulness.

The self-hypnotic trance is a planned extension of an everyday experience. Most of us spend a part of our waking lives in trances of varying levels. Everyone slips into an altered state of consciousness at least twice a day: just before fully awakening in the morning and just before falling asleep at night. During these times our senses are detached from outside influence. We may also drift into hypnosis during periods of reflection when our thoughts are concentrated inwardly. It happens to some people when they listen to music or watch television. The difference between haphazard self-induced hypnosis and planned, scientific self-hypnosis is the result. Characteristic of the latter state is a sense of purpose. You allow nothing else to enter the creative, curative space. During accidental hypnosis you remain the same; during planned self-hypnosis remarkable improvements take place.

In exploring the interior world of your mind and its links to your body, you begin to see and feel beauty within yourself and learn how to reach out to the wonders of the world around you. People have said the state of hypnosis has brought with it a new idea of space, a feeling of airiness, and a sense of timelessness. Others have said, "I feel a new freedom, not only physically in a sense of weightlessness, but also emotionally free from feelings of worry or concern. Anything seems possible." Another member of the self-hypnosis class explained her feelings this way: "There is a total disembodiment. I float up and away from the surface of this planet to a new and unexplored dimension." A number of other people have described the experience as one of "birth or rebirth" or "as if I am starting life all over again." For some, the feeling is even spiritual: "My soul feels immortal, eternal. My inner space merges with the vastness of outer space."

Yet none of these expressions may convey what the feeling is like when it happens to you. Like falling in love, it's hard to describe, but you'll know it when it happens. At the beginning, the hypnotic trance may come in brief flashes. Those flashes will last longer as you practice. The novice knows that he has properly locked on when the sensation is one of almost, but not quite, falling asleep—that moment just before drifting into an altered state of consciousness.

Once you learn to recognize the feeling of self-hypnosis, you will train yourself to prolong and deepen the trance. The deeper you go, the stronger your ability to improve will grow. However, even in a very light state of meditation, which we call "hypnoidal," positive suggestion is very effective. What people may lack in depth they can compensate for in the manner in which they apply the principle of positive autosuggestion.

Hypnoidal, or light, self-hypnosis is characterized by some disassociation from tension and negativism. This can sometimes occur without our realizing it, as when we listen to music, watch TV, or are being entertained by a speaker or comedian. Daydreaming is another example of self-hypnosis. When we find ourselves fantasizing while staring off into space, reading a book or watching a movie, there is a tendency toward light autohypnosis. The state develops from concentration of thought and relaxation of body.

The main difference between self-induced hypnosis and that which is induced by a professional practitioner is the depth of trance. While some few people can bring about a deep level of self-hypnosis most need the help of a professional for deep-seated problems such as phobias and psychogenic disturbances.

There are five component parts to self-hypnosis:

1. Motivation   4. Imagination
2. Relaxation   5. Autosuggestion
3. Concentration

Voltaire said, "When I can do what I want to do, there is my liberty for me." There can be no freedom to enjoy life when a person's mind is chained to obsolete behavior. The self-induced trance, properly utilized, is a powerful force which liberates the body, mind, and emotions. Instead of being at the mercy of a controller, you become your own controller.

Self-hypnosis is based on the premise that you can explore formally unexplored areas of thinking and guide yourself away from constricting problems linked to the past. Self-examination leads to re-evaluation and then to eradication. Each of us is equipped with deeper areas of brain-power capable of decision making and profound logic. During hypnosis, you enter into that center of high intelligence and find new awareness which endows your life with deeper meaning.

You will develop an ability to concentrate on a given subject and exclude the troublesome flashbacks. Later, in a waking state, you will find yourself resisting the flow of that old behavior you want to get rid of. You will learn to sort out what mental material is important to you.

One of the wonders of the mind is its faculty to absorb and assimilate information constantly. Events, attitudes, every new happening is tucked away for future reference. This elasticity gives the mind not only an almost unlimited ability to store up impressions, but also the flexibility to alter concepts, thereby expanding personal development.

Problem solving begins with a strong emotional desire for a change. Without motivation, self-hypnosis will not work. One would be better off visiting a professional hypnotist for conventional hypnotherapy. Even in cases where hetero-hypnosis (induction by another person) is used, lack of motivation forms a barrier against the acceptance of positive suggestion. The will to improve is basically essential to the process.

Some people overcome obstacles, others are overcome by obstacles. Which kind of person are you? If you tend to be negative, take heart, for happiness can be learned. Anyone with normal intelligence can unlearn defeating attitudes and learn more winning ones. The process begins when you *make up your mind to change your mind.* Slow starters become self-starters through hypnosis. You can learn to discipline your thoughts and discard emotional lethargy as a tiresome burden.

Directional drive provides a reason for awakening in the morning with enthusiastic exuberance. Instead of being satisfied with mediocrity, we begin to see possibilities for improvement. People with drive don't wait for their ship to come in. They row out to meet it.

SPURS TO MOTIVATE YOURSELF

Do Small Tasks Well

Add enthusiasm to routine chores. Small things become larger in importance when you do a special job. Live by Émile Coué's slogan, "Every day in some small way, I do things better and better." As you develop skill in doing little things you will be strengthening your capabilities. Every positive happening is a link to larger successes.

Seek New Interests

Look for a missing ingredient in your life. Is there something you've always wanted to do but didn't get around to? Seek out and explore new activities. Study new courses. Look into the activity of worthy organizations. Add new interesting people to your circle of friends. Examine your own hidden talents.

Allow Yourself to Feel

Become more involved with all of your senses. Listen to the sounds around you and to what people are really saying to you. Observe the world with the wondering eyes of a child. Stop to breathe in not only the scent of flowers, but the fresh air that accompanies the birth of each new day. Feel the loving sensation of touching and being touched. Enjoy life.

Communicate with Others

Become more involved with other people. Too many people suffer from "spectatoritis." Life's bystanders bore not only others but themselves. Look. Listen. Feel. Touch. And smile frequently. Enrich your personality by exchanging points of view with others. Be assertive as well as attentive to the other person's side of an issue.

List Your Good Qualities

Many people who lack drive underrate their capabilities and talents. If you can see yourself as having possibilities for success in any field of endeavor, your motivation will be increased. The quality of self-worth is basically essential to any achievement, because if we feel worthless, we also feel undeserving.

Live Life with Purposefulness

Everyone needs goals and a plan to achieve those goals. Whether the goals are for improving your inner environment or the outer environment, you have to have a program. PLAN THE WORK AND WORK THE PLAN. Without a guide or a roadmap, how can we ever reach a destination?

YOU CAN'T GO WRONG IF YOUR GOALS ARE RIGHT

The smallest goal achieved is better than the largest unfulfilled dream. Be practical about your goals. Striving for the unattainable is the surest road to failure. Expand to your highest potential while at the same time accept your limitations. For instance, many writers dream of writing the great American novel, but few come close. For every book like

Dostoevsky's *Crime and Punishment*, millions of lesser books are quickly forgotten. However, this doesn't mean people of lesser talent should not create. Rather, success is measured by how closely your abilities are matched by the effort you put forth. Goals should be fitted directly to one's potential. If you develop a passionate interest in something greater than what you are involved in at this moment, you may find that your petty problems diminish, your mind becomes clearer, and your emotions become more stable. The first ground rule in setting a goal is self-confidence. Proceed on the assumption that success will come in stages. It's easier to reach the top of a mountain if you follow the sloping path that circles around it, than it is trying to climb directly up the steep side.

How to Begin Your Changeover?

First, write down the things you believe will make your life happier and healthier. By writing down your thoughts, you will immediately have a clearer idea of the changes that need to be made. Next, give one problem priority. If you attempt too much at one time, the task may seem overwhelming. When the mind is cluttered, it's difficult to get started.

To encourage yourself to get started, select one small immediate task that will help in solving the problem. Taking action triggers energy for the next step. At the end of the day review your achievement. Then ask yourself, "What can I do next?"

Organize. Organize your thoughts. Organize your actions. Indecision and procrastination deter us, keep us dangling in limbo. We make progress by moving in a definite direction, not by debating, arguing, or rolling around in circles. Once you have a plan, the next step is to let the plan have you—your mind, your heart, your energy, and your confidence. Your goal is the rope to hang on to as you move forward. A goal is not only the rope but the hope.

Fears, self-doubts, susceptibility to bad habits all diminish and can vanish when one gets caught up in striving for a good goal. Throughout time, the finest achievements of mankind have been accomplished through good planning. We may not all be world leaders, but for *your* life there is no greater leader than yourself. Aldous Huxley puts it simply, "There's only one corner of this universe you can be sure of improving and that's your own self."

Once you have gained control over some of the negative factors in your behavior, it's important that you use self-hypnosis to "stay clean." Repeat your positive autosuggestions several times a day in addition to periods of meditation. And tell yourself, "I am determined to stay clean of harmful habits and I am building better ones."

Think positively at all times. Never say, "How will I do it?" Instead say, "How about doing it this way?" *See the problem as temporary, the solution as permanent.*

Self-hypnosis acts as the magic lantern of your mind, highlighting buried strengths and ferreting out causes of problems long forgotten. During periods of self-hypnotic meditation you learn to master your mind so that constructive decisions can be reached. In short, self-hypnosis brings awareness.

There are numerous spin-off benefits. Your personality will take on new poise and serenity. Many people become more orderly and organize their personal and professional lives. On a physical plane, psychosomatic symptoms such as headaches, nervous stomach, insomnia, and sexual dysfunction will automatically lessen. This improvement can be directly traced to the relaxed state that follows a session of self-hypnosis. Self-hypnosis will change your life in every way—physically, mentally, and even spiritually. Ordinary living becomes extraordinary.

DEVISE YOUR OWN PERSONAL PROGRAM

Since the time of the caveman, both thinkers and doers have done their thinking first and their doing later. Creative people are only as great as the size of their thinking. Successful ones see beyond petty problems to the larger canvas of life. A personalized plan helps you conquer the obstacle course and leap over the hurdles.

One's own destructive habits are the greatest obstacles to personal success. However, take heart, for much can be done by following the steps described here.

As Mark Twain said, "A habit cannot be tossed out of the window; it must be coaxed down the stairs—a step at a time." While some personality problems can be changed quickly with hypnosis, bad habits must be diligently worked on because they cling tenaciously. The steps from Motivation to Actualization comprise a system that works in many areas, as you will learn. However, self-hypnosis is not an instant formula for perfection. The pursuit of perfection is doomed to failure. Nobody can become perfect, but, with persistence, you can expect to elevate your way of life and make a new world for yourself. That it can be done is attested to by outstanding people throughout the world.

Without a plan for success, we fall prey to all sorts of destructive environmental pressure. Pent-up human potential turns into frustration and morbidity. One of my students bemoaned the fact that he was getting nowhere in his job. A commercial artist, Paul Z. had many creative ideas, but was relegated to tedious work such as setting up lettering on layout ads. He possessed the talent, but not the motivation to push himself forward toward a more rewarding position. Others with less ability but more confidence were giving him orders and receiving almost twice his salary. "I know I'm capable of much more but I don't have the will power to do anything about it." Paul griped as he plodded along. "It's not just the money. It's the idea of not living up to my artistic potential. I just can't make aggressive demands other people do. Maybe I fear rejection, I'm not sure."

Fortunately, something unexpected happened to fire Paul's motivation. He had been living with Dorothy, whom he loved, but had not married with the excuse he could not afford the financial responsibility. One day she revealed that she was pregnant. Paul was delighted and hugged Dorothy as they laughed and cried together. Now Paul had the magical emotion—*motivation*. He knew he'd need a larger income to face his new responsibilities. Money was the carrot dangling before his nose. Paul spoke to his boss, persuading him to look at some ideas on a layout for a newly acquired account.

Before long Paul was working in a private office with his name on the door and a secretary to do his routine work. By the time Junior had arrived, Paul's salary had almost doubled and he was on his way up the ladder. Thus, sometimes circumstances alone can provide the motivation to succeed. Responsibilities to others help many people wipe out fears and apprehension.

While we know that, under the stimulus and spur of intense emotion and desire to please a loved one, one's reserves of will may be tapped, we can also develop motivation by a "self-reward system." The desire to succeed is in direct proportion to the expected reward, whether monetary or emotional. Sometimes the reward is a greater actualization of the self.

List your unused talents on a piece of paper so that you can study yourself. Seeing your capabilities clearly stated will help to inspire you to reach outward and upward.

Arnold F. was an alcoholic who had been fired from a succession of jobs. "What are some of the nice things people have said about you?" I asked him. He couldn't think of one until he was hypnotized. Then he wrote:

"I make friends easily. I have a pleasant voice. They say I have a sense of humor. I'm a neat dresser. I'm a good sport, spend easily. Women say I'm attractive."

Without doubt Arnold was all of the things he described *when he was sober*. However, after a few too many drinks, he became belligerent, his voice raucous, his personality offensive, and his clothes sloppy. And women certainly did not find him attractive then.

It was important for Arnold to examine the underlying reason for his drinking. We were able to discover the origin of his problem by using Regression, and Automatic Writing, techniques described elsewhere in this book. Once armed with this knowledge, he realized that his job was serving as a constant source of temptation. As an executive in a large import firm, he often took buyers to lunchs where social drinking was expected of him. Finally, he asked for a transfer to another branch of the company and has been sticking to a program of non-drinking with the help of self-hypnosis ever since.

An honest appraisal of one's routinized behavior is valuable in order to become aware of why we do things. Negative habits are strengthened by self-deception. We often hear people say:

"Cigarettes steady my nerves." Truth is cigarettes are injurious to the nervous system and to the rest of the body.

"Alcohol helps me unwind." Truth is alcohol can unwind you until you fall apart. For some people one jigger wrecks their equilibrium.

"A little dessert sweetens my stomach." Truth is too many sweets can cause health problems, including diabetes, obesity, and hypoglycemia.

"Marijuana turns me on sexually." Truth is persistent use of pot can not only lower the sex drive, but might also cause hormonal changes.

Failure to look at themselves realistically causes addicted people to remain trapped in limbo, powerless to break the grip of self-defeating habits. The most difficult part of correction lies in identifying the problems and then taking responsibility for them. We tend to blame others for the way we behave. "If my wife didn't bug me, I wouldn't drink so much." That's a classic one. Or: "I don't want to insult the hostess, so I eat the dessert." Only by taking responsibility can we gain control.

RELAXATION AND CONCENTRATION

Meditation and self-hypnosis both require complete physical relaxation. Only then is the mind free to do its magic. With training, it takes five to twenty minutes to reach a tension-free state.

Begin by selecting a place conducive to privacy, one where you will not be disturbed by friends or the ringing of the phone. The process works best when you can return to the same place time after time. Using the same setting repeatedly has a reassuring, comforting effect. Stretch out on a bed, lounging chair, or even the floor—whichever suits you best. The familiarity of the position you relax in also helps your nervous system to let go.

Loosen any restrictive clothing which might limit your deep breathing. Unbotton buttons. Unhook hooks. Unfasten belts, girdles, brassieres. Remove your shoes and socks. Take off glasses, jewelry, and anything else which might interfere with relaxation. Now that you have settled into a comfortable position, empty your mind of any precise thinking. Let it wander. Let problems wait for another time. Luxuriate in the sweet peace of doing nothing. Savor the sense of just being.

If your body is resistant, the following technique will help. It's called *muscle-tensing*. Contract the large muscle groups: in the thighs, buttocks, stomach, and upper arms. Grip them tightly as you think, "Tense up! Tighter!" Then command muscle-release by thinking, "Let go! Completely!" Feel your body go limp and heavy. Next, think of your body as disjointed, like a big, loose rag doll sprawled on a soft pillow.

Now focus your eyes somewhere above eye level. Feel your eyelids grow heavy, but hold off closing until you count backwards from ten to zero. When you reach zero, close your eyelids slowly as you say to yourself, "There is nothing to see on the outside and so much to experience on the inside." Now your resting eyes send a message of restfulness to the mind and the mind transfers the restfulness to the rest of the body.

Focus on Diaphragmatic Breathing

Slowly breathe in to the count of five and breathe out to the count of five. You should be lying or sitting faceup with one hand resting on your diaphragm so that you can monitor your breathing rhythms. The regular vibrations of your respiratory system will lull you into deeper relaxation. When you inhale, your tummy should rise because the diaphragm acts like a bellows opening the chest cavity enabling you to draw in your full capacity of oxygen. One third of the oxygen we breathe goes directly to the brain. This helps us not only to feel relaxed but also to drift closer to a sleeplike state. When you exhale the tummy recedes and all muscles tend to relax even more. Throughout the breathing process you should keep your chest and rib cage still. The only motion is the slow, easy rise and fall of your tummy. The relaxed pulmonary sensations soothe the heart and all of the internal organs of your body. Feel yourself become part of the ebb and flow of energy that moves all life on this earth. Be aware that you share the air with everyone.

Get Ready to Relax Completely

Now that your eyes are closed and you're breathing smoothly and regularly, you will release the tension in your muscles, nerves, and blood vessels. Stress causes muscles to go into spasms that grip the nerves and blood vessels. This reduces circulation of blood to other areas of the body and can lead to pain and disease. *Disease* exists in relation to the absence of *ease*. Fortunately, we are all capable of increasing easiness. Let's begin. Make a suggestion to your body to "let go all over." We start with the scalp and progressively suggest "a heavy, loose, limp feeling into each area of the body."

The following relaxation routine can be recorded on a cassette player and played back for easy memorization. However, if you have experienced meditation, you are probably familiar with feeling relaxed and drifting into "your level."

PROGRESSIVE DIFFERENTIAL RELAXATION

"My scalp feels loose, limp, and relaxed. My forehead is smooth, serene like a newborn baby. My eyelids are very heavy, deeply at rest. All the little nerves and muscles around my eyes are totally relaxed." THINK THE THOUGHT AND YOU WILL FEEL THE FEELING. Proceed down through every muscle of your body.

"My cheeks are soft and smooth. The hinges of my jaw are slightly parted, loose, and limp. Lips barely touching. Teeth are apart. Tongue resting in lower part of my mouth. Tongue feels soft, limp. My neck feels very open and extremely relaxed. Shoulders so heavy. Arms heavy . . . loose, limp. Deeply, completely free of tension. My entire torso is heavy and relaxed. My hips are very heavy, the buttocks seem to melt their heaviness into the surface which is supporting me. A pleasurable feeling flows down through my legs and into my toes."

If an area of your body is especially tense or feels stressful, dwell on that area a little longer. For example, let's consider the back. Many people suffer pain in areas of the back, and if you do not give that spot particular differential relaxation suggestion, the discomfort will interfere with the depth of meditation and decrease the benefit derived from self-therapy. To relax the back thoroughly, try this subliminal patter:

"I am going to count down the vertebrae in my spine from 33 to 0. 33 . . . 32 . . . 31 . . . 29 . . . 28 . . . 27 . . . 26 . . . 25 . . . 24 . . . 23 . . . 22 . . . 21 . . . 20 . . . all the way to 0." As you count backwards, visualize your entire back as twice as wide and twice as long as you would ordinarily. When you finish counting, say: "My back feels so wide and long, so very open. Lots of room for the nerves, the muscles, and the vertebrae to float around aimlessly in the wide open spaces of my back. All tension is gone and will not return." LET YOUR THOUGHTS RETURN TO THE ENTIRE BODY.

"Now my entire body feels pleasantly limp . . . from the inside of my bones to the outside of my skin . . . I feel no tension . . . free of all pressure, just a loose, limp, heavy sense of well-being."

Let your mind surrender to this sublime restfulness as you just hang loose. When your body is completely at ease, your mind begins to clear away its trivia and debris. Within moments, you will be aware of a revitalizing glow which will permeate your entire physical and mental self. When this sensation of super-elation rises to its height, you will drift closer to the ultimate source of your own life-giving energy. This serene state marks the threshold of *alpha*, a mental state particularly receptive to positive suggestion. *Alpha* will lead you into *theta*, a mental state wherein the life forces of your body will be recharged, rejuvenated, and energized. At this time, a glow of exultation will flow through every nerve and fiber of your being and you will experience rebirth, not only in mind and body, but in your spirit as well.

Direct your awareness toward specific areas of your body. You may detect fine vibrations, a tingling sensation, perhaps a feeling of warmth. You can select any area for special attention. Let a healing feeling of well-being penetrate that exact spot. Get in touch with the vibrations of your breathing and imagine an opening about the size of a quarter directly in the center of the problem area. As you exhale, picture a thin, misty stream of air coming out of the opening and say to yourself, "With this breath I release all tension and stress from this area. I will now enter a deeper, healthier state of mind."

If your problem were a headache, for example, you would imagine an opening at either side of your temples and see the headache evaporating as you exhale the stress out of the openings.

CONCENTRATING YOUR MENTAL ENERGY

Before you can concentrate your mind on goals and self-enrichment, you must clear the mind's passageways. Once you are relaxed, suspend conscious thinking. Postpone decisions and judgments to another, more suitable time. Now that your body is making no demands on your mind, be aware of "peace of mind." If an unwanted, undesirable thought tries to push its way in, push it out again. This is your time of tranquillity. Don't allow any intrusions.

To help yourself mentally relax, think of a restful scene: a day in the country or at the beach, or perhaps a time when you were fishing or swinging in a hammock, free of all worries. Here is my favorite patter for mental relaxation: (If possible, record it and listen with eyes closed).

"I see myself walking in the country on a beautiful summer day, just the right temperature. A gentle breeze sways the branches of the trees and somewhere a bird is singing. The look and sound of nature empties my mind of all problems. Old memories float away from my center. I feel free. I picture myself looking younger, healthier. I see before me two tall trees and a hammock hung between the trees. I stretch out in the hammock and watch the clouds in the sky. Puffs and fluffs of clouds drift and shift, changing their shapes and then disappearing. The sky is blue and a little airplane is writing a message.

The message says, 'PEACE OF MIND.'" As you concentrate on the message, see it grow dimmer and dimmer and vanish completely.

At this stage of your induction into self-hypnosis, you will feel an intimate sense of togetherness within yourself. The difference between concentration in a waking state and in the hypnoidal state is as follows: During ordinary concentration, the mind focuses on an object or problem from the outside, whereas, during hypnosis, the mind is inverted and thoroughly thinks through a problem from the inside. There occurs not only transcendence of mind over body, but the deliberate exclusion of any intruding outside influence. Hypnoidal concentration brings into focus untapped intelligence capable of penetrating the reasons and causes of troublesome behavior. Complete absorption digs out the truth of your problems. In order to benefit the most from the power of hypnosis, use this period to sort out your problems, stresses, and worries:

1. Focus your thinking upon the *troubles you cannot control.*
2. *Accept the above conditions* as beyond your influence.
3. Concentrate on the negative factors *over which you have control.*
4. Think of *possible solutions* to those stress factors.

Many people waste their mental energies trying to control conditions which are really out of their control. The advanced illness of a loved one. Accidents. Taxes. The hostility around the world. If you cannot solve a problem, let it go. Narrow down your responsibilities. Set realistic goals, select one, and give it priority. Concentrating your mental and emotional powers on attainable goals will give you the spirit you need to propel yourself to reach your destination.

Inevitably, disturbing thoughts of past conflicts will try to enter into your concentration. There is a resistance factor we must overcome. When unwholesome thoughts rear their ugly heads, dispel them by going even deeper into your concentration on positive solutions. The correct way to conquer negativism is to turn your focus as quickly as possible to the opposite idea. Eventually, *negativism dies through sheer neglect.* And then, problems which once appeared complex and insurmountable dissolve under the concentrated focus of your deeper intelligence.

Concentration clears the muddled mind and opens the door to the infinite creative reservoir that all of us possess and so few of us ever tap.

Concentrated introspection awakens the creative imagination. Hidden talents remain buried unless we focus energy into them. A painter becomes a better painter by shutting out of his thoughts everything except the vision he wants to place on the canvas. A poet or musician can only create when he has channeled his thinking directly to the center of his creation, blocking out all else. Tension is the opposite of concentrated relaxation, and the stressed person cannot reach the deeper areas of his abilities. The mystique of psychic improvement comes from the selective, exclusive direction of the mind's forces.

The pensive mind generates *theta* vibrations of creativity. This flow of energy provides a piercing insight into the heart of the subject concentrated upon and is the secret of creative genius. When hypnotic concentration is used in conjunction with a personal plan for creative improvement, dramatic reversals of behavior are possible. I know of a heroin addict whose whole life was devoted to aimless wanderings about New York City, during which he committed petty robberies to support his habit. After learning how to hypnotize himself and develop his creativity, he discovered he had talent for painting. At the time, he was hospitalized for drug withdrawal and had a lot a time on his hands. I arranged for him to receive art materials and soon he changed from a pathetic, addicted person into a vibrant, confident one. This person, who was previously unable to concentrate for even a few moments, is now painting for long hours and earning a living from it. Upon visiting his studio, I was amused to find him concentrating so deeply on his work that he did not hear while I entered and strolled around for quite some time. He explained, "When I paint I go into such deep concentration, I reach *alpha* even with my eyes open. When I practice self-hypnosis, I only have to close my eyes and I immediately drift into *theta*."

History is filled with stories of great discoveries which occurred during periods of deep concentration. After people had given up on a problem, they found the answer when they least expected it while daydreaming or drifting into slumber. Elusive solutions do not respond to forced concentration in a waking state because we *tend to try too hard*. However, when we concentrate our mental powers during a period of meditation, we open latent mental powers which oftimes surprise us.

Major advances in human progress have taken place when creative geniuses least expected it, while they were catnapping or in a detached state of mind. They variously described their mental condition at times of revelation as, "daytime reverie," "in a world of my own," "withdrawn into my private thoughts," "snoozing," "spaced out." The story goes that Henry Ford once hired an efficiency expert to evaluate his company. After several weeks, the expert reported back to Mr. Ford. His appraisal was extremely favorable except for one flaw.

"It's that man down the hall," complained the efficiency expert. Whenever I go by his office, I see him leaning back with his feet on the desk taking a snooze. He's wasting your money, Mr. Ford."

"Oh, that man," answered Henry Ford. "Once he got an idea that saved us millions of dollars. At the time, his feet were planted right where they are now."

Mavericks and dreamers are sometimes the genuine geniuses of our times. Freedom from the usual limitations of deadlines allows them to innovate during periods of deep concentrated relaxation.

What inventive minds have in common is the ability to withdraw from outside communication into an inner communication. By so doing, they gain insight and a special kind of wisdom that leads to great achievement. The roster of famous people who have changed the course of history by using some form of mental programming, which we now know as self-hypnosis, covers every field of accomplishment.

In world affairs, there was Napoleon Bonaparte, Winston Churchill, Franklin Delano Roosevelt, and Mahatma Gandhi, to mention just a few. Among artists, Leonardo da Vinci and Pablo Picasso described in their writings how they visualized a painting long before they did the actual work. Da Vinci's inventions often came to him while daydreaming. Many of the world's most outstanding musical composers created while in a trancelike reverie. Works by Brahms, Beethoven, Mozart, Puccini, and Wagner have endured for years giving deep pleasure to millions of people. All of these composers used some variation of self-hypnosis. A modern-day composer explained, "I go into my shell and listen to my music before I set it down on paper. Creative work is preconceived."

Inventors tell us their products were preconceived during periods of relaxation and concentration akin to autohypnosis. Thomas A. Edison often mentioned, "My ideas leaped out of my dreams." He was famous for his daily catnaps during which time there was a pad and pencil beside his bed. When an idea came to him, he would immediately jot it down for future development. Sometimes Edison would meditate on unresolved problems while fishing. One day, as he pondered the problems caused by a rubber shortage, he drifted into his subconscious and came up with a solution. In a flash of insight, he thought of crossbreeding the goldenrod, a hybrid rubber-producing plant, with a similar plant. The miracle plant which resulted contained fourteen percent rubber, enabling the United States to produce a synthetic material necessary in winning World War II.

Let's go back a little further into our history. Elias Howe, while working on the first model of the sewing machine, was stumped by the problem of threading a machine-driven needle whose point reached into the shuttle. One evening, as he drifted into a light slumber, he had a vision of a harpoon with a rope threaded near its point. This triggered the invention of an effective machine needle and changed the course of the entire textile industry.

Albert Einstein was among the many other scientists who took time to ponder and sleep on a problem in order to form the essence of a revolutionary new theory. His contribution to our understanding of relativity was made in this manner.

The molecular formula for benzene, which became the foundation of twentieth-century organic chemistry, was also revealed in a dream to the English scientist Michael Faraday. The list goes on and on. What did these successful people have in common?

They possessed strong motivation, a desire to succeed.
They were aware of what they wanted to accomplish.
They used relaxation deliberately and concentrated deeply during periods of meditation.
They also knew how to use their imaginations in a creative manner.
They had to be positive thinkers, applying the principle of autosuggestion to find solutions.

You don't have to be a genius to apply the same principles to your own life and goals. Remember, a well-conceived personal program can turn any course of events from failure to success. The steps described herein were developed over a period of many years of extensive experimenting and experiencing. The system works for others. It can certainly work for you, too.

Expect that for a few sessions you will simply be daydreaming or in a light state of meditation. It takes repetition to drift into the hypnotic, therapeutic trance level. Keep practicing; the results are worth the effort.

Self-hypnosis has been successfully used to correct, prevent, or alleviate a wide range of bad habits as well as to move people's lives in better directions. The steps of self-hypnosis are workable tools. But the best tools cannot be effective without human effort. The more dedicated you are, the more dramatic the benefits you'll derive.

Behind all remission of harmful behavior or illness lies faith in a system. For some people, the system might be the one used by their psychiatrist or surgeon. Believing only in external forces, however, limits improvement. Turning over the responsibility entirely to someone else just makes you part of *their* system. The system that works best is your own inside-yourself-system. That's where the real power is.

Life is made up of the things that happen to you from the outside, called *input,* combined with the way you react to that input, which is called *output.* The inner system that you develop is called *personal programming.* And the best inner system for successful personal programming is self-hypnosis. While there are people who can improve and elevate themselves without consciously being aware of an inner system, they are in the minority and their success is merely accidental.

Through self-hypnosis, you will find that your success is inner-directed, goal-oriented, and cannot fail. In order to discover how an organized plan can work for you, *decide what it is you want.* When you know, then you can write the script to live your life. Tell yourself, "I am author of my own world and only I can change it. It is not always the situation in which I find myself, but rather the perspective that I choose to take that's most important, and that perspective will always be a positive one."

Imagination and Autosuggestion

The basic principle of role-playing from childhood on is that people become what they pretend to be. Imagery exerts its control within the consciousness of each of us, usually without our being aware of it. Mental pictures flash incessantly on a subliminal level of perception. Insidious images can chain you to outmoded habits and emotional reactions which do not serve your best interests.

How do you see yourself? Before you can improve your self-image, you must examine the one you have. Your imagination will help you unsnarl the knots of tension resulting from past role-playing. Instead of being restricted to illusions of a lesser self, you will unravel the cord of past conditioning and build a new identity based on the reality of your full potential. Hypnosis structures the images for you. Once a person is freed from haunting visions of the past, new, self-fulfilling dreams lead to a better life.

Images are the maps which direct us to a new destination. It's more important to see where you're going, because you have already seen where you've been. (That's why your eyes are in the front and not in the back of your head.) Unfortunately, many people cling to hurts and hardships linked to the past. What is *your* view of your earlier life? Do you see it in the far distance . . . or very close? Too many people are unable to live in the present because the past has burdened them with unhappy memories. Instead of assuming responsibility, they blame others for victimizing them. Decide what you want in life and take the responsibility to work toward that goal. Imagination will make the trip a pleasant one.

"You've got to have a dream if you want a dream to come true," goes the lyric from "South Pacific." Your dream must be more than inspiring, it must also be feasible. Fantasy can only become reality when your intelligence believes in the practicability of your vision.

"To accomplish great things, we must not only act but also dream, not only plan but also believe," said Anatole France. An achiever must be a believer—in himself. Underachievers see themselves as less capable than they are. Their concept of self is limited to the meagerness of their dreams. We are limited only by our own reluctance to believe in our own capabilities. Yet, even mediocre people have slumbering aspirations held captive by humdrum thinking. Imagination directs all human actions. Your vision of yourself can make you a star, an also-ran or a never-will-be. Your mind is the engineer and its "imagineering" creates the blueprint for your life.

Once you are able to envision success-oriented goals, your anticipation of the future will become a strong driving force. "Possibility thinking" will eliminate vacillation from your belief system. Positive expectations will produce assertive enthusiasm, which is the spark of success. See your images vividly; the stronger the picture, the stronger your emotions will be stirred. When you are able to conjure up the new image, tell yourself, "I can, I will, and I must achieve my goals." Imagination coupled with self-confidence inevitably brings realization.

SEVEN VISIONS TO A BETTER LIFE

Once you are completely relaxed and have drifted into a concentrated state of meditation, imagine you are watching a preview on a TV or movie screen.

You will play all roles in *The Theatre of Your Mind:* you are the director, the actor, and the audience.

Set the scene; create the situation suitable to your needs. Visualize your future as you wish it to be.

Vision One: Improved Health

Consider this vision as something to do until the doctor comes, or if he has declared, "Nothing can be done. You have to live with it": see yourself standing in front of a full-length three-way mirror. From every angle you look ten to twenty years younger and in perfect health. See the happy expression on your face, confident and free of anxiety. Imagine a blue light which we shall call *the healing energy* focused on the troubled area, a strong searchlight piercing through to the mysterious source of the illness and wiping it out . . . completely and deeply. Look into the mirror and repeat to yourself ten times, "I am healthy and normal. All traces of my old problem have vanished and will not return." The more you know about your ailment, the more effective the visualization will be. If an organ of your body is impaired, learn as much as you can about the physiology of that organ. If your blood chemistry has gone awry, question your doctor about it. Become knowledgeable. The more authentic your image, the more dramatic the results.

Dr. Carl Simonton, known for his work with visual imagery in treating cancer patients, tells of the case of a man with an advanced malignancy in his throat. The patient was taught to enter *alpha* and visualize a war taking place between his white blood cells and the cancer cells. The defending white cells were seen as the conquerers, destroying the cancer cells and freeing the victim. This visualization proved effective in combatting the malignancy.

Vision Two: Ego Building

The person with low self-esteem often got that way by seeing himself as less than real. To compensate, make your fantasy *better* than reality. Picture yourself at an elegant testimonial dinner in which you are the guest of honor. Imagine the music playing as you enter the large spacious dining room. Lots of flowers. Everyone dressed formally. Imagine people on the dias arising and saying great things about you. See yourself receiving an important award. If you were an actor, you'd see an Oscar. A writer or scholar envisions the Pulitzer or Nobel prize. In addition to the prominent people praising you, see members of your family and various people from your past, including anyone who has been less than kind to you. Then see yourself taking over the speaker's platform and delivering a speech about your aims in life. Finally, picture the audience standing up to give you a rousing ovation. As the image fades, see the most important people clustered around you to shake your hand and pat you on the back.

Daryl T. was a struggling musician who worked at a menial job during the day and practiced his guitar evenings and weekends. He often said, "I play for myself. Other people do not want to spend money on my kind of music. Besides, I'm not really that good." After training himself in visualization, he finally boosted his confidence and began to play professionally. He also learned to visualize improvements at each performance. This creative rehearsal improved his skill to such an extent he is now sought after.

Vision Three: To Achieve Goals

To achieve goals, you must first picture in your mind exactly what you want to accomplish in life. Meditate upon your choices. Then select the one that feels the most emotionally gratifying. Decide where you want to be five years from now. Consider the means of reaching your destination. As you visualize the mental screen, list your short-term and long-term goals. Act out the various scenes and options that might present themselves. In your mental picture, confront the different possibilities and consequences of success. Imagine conversations with experts in your field of endeavor. Ask questions and receive meaningful answers. See yourself pursuing your goals. Notice how assertive your attitude is, how well you look, and the affirmative responses of people you come in contact with.

"I'm always rushing around and never seem to get anywhere," a woman complained to me. She was an outstanding actress who spent most of her time going to auditions and being rejected. Through self-hypnosis and positive imagery, she discovered that what was missing from her aspiration was proper training. She planned the work and then worked the plan. Her immediate goal was to improve her appearance, so she lost weight and bought a new wardrobe. Next, she took additional training in voice and stage presence. Visualizing herself as a winner made it happen. She is now appearing in a smash Broadway musical.

Vision Four: Personal Relationships

Improving communication with a spouse or lover sometimes takes more than conscious effort. You can share a relaxing, inspiring fantasy and ease a great deal of stress out of a relationship. Meditate together while holding hands. Picture yourselves sailing away on a cruise ship to faraway corners of the earth. Make love in exotic hideaways. Sail around the Hawaiian Islands. Bask in the sun on some deserted beach. Rehearse a deeper kind of intimacy between you; gain insight into each other.

Very often, failing relationships can be traced to minor misunderstandings. Use periods of contemplation to review conversations that lead to anger or frustration. Preview improved dialogue and notice the difference in response. Envision yourself deeply loved and desired. Flights of fancy have no bounds when it comes to romance. They can make an endearing relationship out of one that was merely endured.

In addition to intimate communication, use your imagination to enhance the manner in which you relate to co-workers and friends. See a closer understanding develop between yourself and others. During your reverie, be completely honest. Air your gripes and grievances. Ventilate buried angers. Explain yourself to this imaginary friend and accept his opinions and suggestions. As tension subsides, express your appreciation and ask to hear his side of the argument. Listen and learn about the other's deeper feelings.

Paul M. complained that his co-workers didn't like him. "I don't know why, but every time I walk into a room, they stop talking as though they had been saying things about me." But there's no need to wonder when you can use your imagination. Paul learned to conjure up the troublesome scene. He imagined he was hidden in a closet and eavesdropped on their conversation. True, they were discussing him. But not in the manner he suspected. Quite the contrary. What they were saying was, "Paul is so unfriendly. He behaves as if he thinks he's better than other people." Paul's imagination brought him closer to reality.

Vision Five: Personality Problems

Select a character trait or personality problem that you would like to improve. If you have several, as most of us do, give the most urgent one top priority and focus your meditation upon it. If it is shyness, for example, you begin by building a situation in which you behave in an assertive, self-confident way. Reverse your responses from acting withdrawn to acting boldly. See yourself behaving dramatically different. Originate a new personality, with magnetic charisma attractive to the most exciting people. Remember that all reality was once a figment of someone's imagination.

Consider the problem of *procrastination*. Most of us are guilty of it at one time or another. Some people procrastinate until they are too old to do anything about their dreams. Don't be guilty of waiting too long. While meditating, picture youself as doing the chore or taking the trip you've been putting off. See yourself enjoying the activity. Involve positive emotional satisfaction in your dreaming. Once you see yourself performing tasks which you have avoided, you will have a sense of having broken the ice. Doing the real job will then be so much easier because you will have eliminated the pitfalls and interferences.

Another personality problem is jealousy. Extreme possessiveness can ruin an otherwise close relationship. Jealous people have an active

imagination in reverse. They imagine their loved one as being unfaith-
ful even when fidelity exists. Instead of confronting the partner and
causing dissention, here's what one woman imagined: "I see my husband, who is a traveling salesman, relaxing and reading in his room.
When I see him having dinner out of town, I picture him with male
friends telling them about his wonderful wife and how he looks forward to coming home." In the past, she had visions of his cavorting
around with women, and when he returned from a trip, instead of
enjoying their time together, they quarreled. With the help of positive
mental imagery, their relationship improved to such an extent that, the
last I heard, he had invited her along on one of his business trips.

Vision Six: Fears and Phobias

Many unfounded fears and anxieties are caused by imagining disas-
ters that never occur. The list is endless. From A for Agoraphobia
(fear of crowds), to Z for Zoophobia (fear of animals), it seems
everybody is afraid of something. Many people have irrational fears
which limit their daily existence. Fear of riding an elevator is a classic
example. Fear of flying is another.

To overcome fear, face it! Confront in your mind whatever
frightens you. Instead of letting your thoughts run away from the
phobia, focus your concentrated energy right into the anxiety. Sup-
pose, for instance, you have a dreaded fear of high places. Begin your
play-acting by seeing yourself climbing up three steps on a short
ladder. Next time you meditate, visualize yourself at the top of a tall
staircase looking down. Each time you confront your fear, act more
boldly, as you take yourself higher and higher. Finally, picture yourself
looking down from a window in the Empire State Building or some
other skyscraper. Add to the vision a close-up of your face, relaxed and
smiling without any sign of discomfort.

Jimmy K. had been frightened by a dog when he was six years old.
At the age of eighteen, Jimmy was still terrified of animals. To cure
himself of this fear, Jimmy was trained to see himself first petting a
very small puppy who was on a leash. In a subsequent session, the dog
grew a little larger. Each time he worked with the image, the dog
matured, until Jimmy pictured himself feeding a large dog and taking
him for a walk on a leash. Finally, he envisioned himself rolling in the
grass with a dog who loved him.

Vision Seven: Bad Habits

Whether the bad habit is nail-biting, heroin, or chocolate cream pie, bad habits often become cruel masters, robbing us of our freedom of choice. To regain your liberty, you must study the prison you have constructed for yourself. What are the bars holding you in? Each individual has a distinctive style of behavior, with qualities both good and bad. Somewhere in that configuration is the need for redesigning the inner diagram. Constructive fantasy alters perception. The dependent person who once saw himself trapped in a prison of habits begins to envision possibilities of escaping from his bonds.

Here's a case of a woman who's biggest problem was her mouth: Katherine M. suffered from a number of compulsive oral habits, one linked to the other. If she wasn't chewing, she was puffing a cigarette or drinking alcohol. Apathy and indulgence had turned her from an attractive young woman weighing 120 pounds to a despondent, rotund matron who weighed 220. In a letter to me, she described herself as "a sloppy pig." When I met her, I knew why. Her clothing was too tight, and the fat bulged in layers around her body. Her once lovely hair was dishevelled and her teeth discolored from smoking.

"I can't help myself," she moaned in self pity. "I have no control." Obviously, she needed control, but more than that Katherine needed a new self-image. After trained to reach her center of control through self-hypnosis, Katherine created a corrective illusion which brought her excellent results. She is now back to 120 pounds and looks just fine.

THE IMPROVED IMAGE

Katherine visualized a movie screen with the title, *The New Katherine M.* She saw herself on the screen slim and well-groomed, she was surrounded by a group of admirers congratulating her on a job well done. While others were behaving like gluttons—overeating, guzzling booze, fouling the air with smoke—Katherine remained serene, aloof. She saw herself smiling with a bright "toothpaste-ad-smile." She scanned her body, noticing the improvements: flat stomach, fingers free of stains. Each time Katherine meditated on her self-image, she added something new. She saw herself with a special man who showed special interest in her. She saw herself succeeding in relationships, something which had been impossible for her before. She began to know and understand the emotions which churned inside of her, the desires and needs which had been unfulfilled. Her improved image was with her at all times, carried over from hypnosis to the waking state.

AUTOSUGGESTION FOR REPROGRAMMING

"We possess within us a force of incalculable power, which if we direct in a wise manner, gives us mastery of ourselves. It permits us not only to escape from physical and mental ills, but also to live in relative happiness."

So wrote Dr. Émile Coué of France over a half century ago in his book *The Coué Method*. Dr. Coué, exponent of the theory of autosuggestion, achieved his successful results long before the theory of psychosomatic medicine became popular. Not only did he cure various illnesses, but converted despondent people into happy, fulfilled ones. Through his method of positive thinking, Dr. Coué transformed the lives of millions of people and started a long trend of books on using the mind for positive improvement. Many modern movements of the mind, like Silva Mind Control and E.S.T. have drawn basic concepts from Dr. Coué's work.

Émile Coué's method is based on two factors:

1. Where willpower and imagination come into conflict, the power of imagination will always win out. This is so because the will comes from the periphery of the mind and imagination reaches into its core.

2. Imagination can be trained and expanded more readily than willpower, which is more elusive. Willpower needs to be forced emotionally and thereby increases stress. Imagination is free-flowing and diminishes stress.

Autosuggestion creates a new kind of reality when it is combined with imagination, a reality that is different and better than before, free of past echoes. Unfortunately, most people are oblivious to the workings of their unconscious minds. What you know consciously represents only about one-tenth of the iceberg. With self-hypnosis, it will be easy for you to probe into the other nine-tenths buried beneath the surface.

Dr. Émile Coué said "When you wish to do something reasonable, or when you have a duty to perform, always think it's easy. *Make the words "difficult," "impossible," and "I cannot" disappear from your vocabulary.* Tell yourself "I can, I will, I must."

By considering anything easy, it becomes easier for you, though the act might seem difficult to others. You perform quickly and well, and without fatigue since no willpower on your part need be applied. Whereas, if you had considered the task difficult, it would have become so because you would have failed to believe in yourself.

When you know how to direct positive thoughts, they work as a benevolent kind of brainwashing.

The conditioned reflex which produced the harmful behavior is removed once a more appropriate idea is accepted by the subconscious. Suggestions need not be verbalized. Silent thoughts are also "self-suggestions," influencing us to move in a determined direction.

Stop and consider: what are the silent suggestions you are now giving yourself? Your mind constantly turns your thoughts into bodily reaction. You will see dramatic evidence of this when you learn to direct your brain power to serve your best interests instead of the other way around. Be prepared to see a phenomenal change for the better. Emphasizing possibilities of success instead of failure starts the change-over. Positive conditioning works the same way that negative conditioning does, except *in reverse*. Patiently hammering away at a bad habit will not only eliminate it, but clear the site for one which will serve you better.

Once you see improvement, however slight, encourage yourself by affirmation. Self-praise helps build self-confidence. Nothing is as powerful as your own voice. Ego-strengthening is needed to compensate for the downgrading most people are subjected to during the growing-up years.

DECONDITION YOUR BEHAVIOR

Habits are projections of the roots that once nurtured us. How about your habits? What sort of soil nourished them? When you become aware that the behavior that suited you in childhood is no longer suitable for you as an adult, you will be on your way to deconditioning yourself.

Awareness clears space in the mind for a new set of habits. It's like cleaning out an old closet that's accumulated junk. During hypnotic meditation, you take a long hard look inside your space, spend enough time to understand, and then proceed to the positive reconstruction.

Once the slate is washed clean, the creative mind has unlimited freedom to plan a new life-style.

RECONDITION YOUR LIFE

Positive programming is implanted through carefully selected suggestions which reverse signals to the reflexes. Suggestions are reconditioning phrases. When they are repeated over and over again, they reroute your actions into a new groove. The degree to which you improve depends on how willing you are to change. Motivation and level of self-esteem influence the rate of success.

ATTITUDE AFFECTS LIFE'S ALTITUDE

How high or low you feel is a reflection of how strong or weak your self-image is. The purpose of self-suggestion is to make the most of the best and the least of the worst of your natural attributes. When you tell yourself *I can't*, chances are *you won't*. On the other hand, if you tell yourself, *I can* and *I will*, you stand a much better chance of reaching your objective, since thoughts predetermine action.

A common stumbling block to self-realization is anticipation of failure. When one secretly expects to lose, confidence takes a back seat. One of my clients, Stanley R., talked to me about his past. "I can still hear the unkind criticism I received from my parents as a boy."

Every time Stanley allowed the past to influence him, he reinforced his problem. "My family said I was clumsy. Badly coordinated. Being the youngest in a large family, their evaluation of me seemed accurate. How could a ten-year-old boy know they were judging me by adult standards?"

With autosuggestion under self-hypnosis, Stanley programmed himself to step away from the past and see himself in the present. He trained himself to play golf, tennis, and the piano. This so-called "clumsy, badly coordinated" child had matured sufficiently and stopped listening to voices from his past. He was able to talk to himself like a winner.

The lesson to be learned from Stanley: *Stop listening* to other voices from faraway rooms. Nobody knows you better than yourself. Take charge, reclaim your mind. This process is called counter-hypnosis because it is a correction of bad hypnosis inflicted upon us by others. We replace outside mental manipulation with mental self-control.

YOU ALWAYS HAVE A CHOICE

We are all bombarded with things other people would like us to do. However, we don't have to say yes. We can also say no or, better, we can use two significant words: *I prefer*. The meaning is obvious. Preferring gives you not only choice, but control and mastery over events. Use these two words to start your program of autosuggestion for behavioral improvement:

> I prefer not to smoke. I prefer to be healthy.
> I prefer not to overeat. I prefer a youthful body.
> I prefer not to be an alcoholic. I prefer to think clearly.
> I prefer to sleep through the night and awaken refreshed.

Exercising your preferences will make you a more assertive person and more highly regarded by all who come in contact with you. If you don't make choices, others less interested in your welfare will make the choices for you.

Words have power. Especially the words you use to describe yourself, to yourself as well as to others. Your choice of vocabulary can not only make or break behavior patterns, but make or break your life. Certain four letter words, for instance, carry with them automatic stigma and hostility, no matter how casual the intent. On the other hand, four letter words like *love*, *life*, *good*, and *fine* can heal and help.

Mark Twain said, "The difference between the right word and the almost right word is the difference between lightning and the lightning bug." In formulating autosuggestions, the right choice of words can accelerate improvement and the wrong choice retard growth. Some words are very special. They can bring about a sense of elation, instill pleasurable feeling, and inspire great confidence.

Using the proper words, it is possible to overcome many major obstacles in your life as well as expand your scope of accomplishment. I have put together a list of ten words with positive power. They pack a strong vibrational wallop on the subconscious mind. If they suit you, use them. If not, create your own.

SERENITY	ECSTASY	SUCCESS
CONFIDENCE	LOVE	GLOWING
ENERGY	POWER	CREATIVE
HEALTH		

POSITIVE THINKING FROM A TO Z

Here is an interesting list of positive words created by a member of my class. Grover T. was a salesman and had excellent results not only in improving his self-image but in increasing his income. He combines the blackboard technique with "alphabet suggestions." In this manner, he not only deepens his trance level but programs himself at the same time. While under hypnosis, imagine yourself writing and erasing the alphabet from A to Z as you focus on each corresponding thought.

A. AWARENESS AND ACTION
B. BETTER BUSINESS
C. CALM, CONFIDENT
D. DISCIPLINE, DRIVE
E. ENTHUSIASM, ENERGY
F. FEELING FINE
G. GREAT GOALS
H. HEALTHY, HAPPY
I. INCREASE INCOME
J. JOG JOYFULLY
K. KEEP KEEN
L. LONGER LIFE
M. MIND MASTERY
N. NO NERVOUSNESS
O. OVERCOME OBSTACLES
P. POSITIVE PROGRESS
Q. QUALITY VS QUANTITY
R. REMARKABLE RESULTS
S. SENSATIONAL SUCCESS
T. TRANQUIL THOUGHTS
U. UNIFY, UNDERSTAND
V. VIM & VIGOR
W. WEALTH WITHOUT WORRY
X. XCITING XPERIENCE
Y. YOUNGER & YOUNGER
Z. ZIP, ZEST, ZENITH

Begin by finding one word that has especially good vibrations for you. Even one uplifting word can do wonders for you. Repeat it again and again as you meditate upon it. Remember, repetition caused the negative traits to become entrenched, so reversing the procedure will help positive traits gain a foothold. Build groups of words and short sentences. Reprogramming requires choosing words and thoughts that have strong emotional conviction. Once you have found them, never let them go. Use them over and over again, while you are day-dreaming, meditating, or using hypnosis.

When awake, sometimes say your positive autosuggestions out loud. Look into a mirror when you awaken in the morning and just before bedtime, look into your own eyes. Tell it to yourself until the words slip off your tongue without effort. Recite them slowly, passively with anticipation of realization.

Most people assume thoughts are involuntary and that they cannot help thinking what they think. Nothing is further from the truth. Even the most obsessive thinking can be restrained and retrained. Do you minimize your capabilities or attributes? Most people do, mistakenly believing that modesty is respected. Unfortunately, many people go to extremes and behave in a humble fashion. By so doing, they fall prey to manipulation by others who think little of them.

Where does self-limiting behavior come from? It draws from an inner source of self-destruction. Self-putdowns are born inside the troubled mind. Even more detrimental than talking to others in this way is the silent conversation people carry on within themselves. Have you ever silently thought, "How could I be so stupid?" or "I look too fat," "too thin," "too tall," "too short," . . . etc . . . etc. Everyone has. When you find yourself resorting to such attitudes, use the *cancel-out* technique. Say to yourself, "Stop! Cancel out!" or "Cease, desist, I've had enough of that!" "Quit that garbage! Get lost!"

The cancel-out technique can be used silently or verbalized. You will find it useful in correcting habits such as overweight, smoking, and insomnia, as well as in behavior modification in personal relationships. Once you have mastered this method, you will find yourself automatically responding to negativism with authoritative positivism. Then you can simplify the command using only one word repeated several times: "Cancel!" or "Stop!"

After giving yourself the command, say to yourself, "You will, instead, accept this positive suggestion. . . ."And then you proceed to feed to yourself your own suggestion, which will contradict the negative thought or activity.

Below are a few autosuggestions which have proved useful to others. You can create more specific ones to deal directly with your own problems:

I am free of fear and feel more confident.
Whatever happens, I will not lose my temper.
I value myself and will behave with pride.
I will stick to the diet and lose weight.
Smoking is for sick people. I quit.
I am master of my fate, captain of my soul.
All pain is going and soon will be gone.

FORMULATE A SURVIVAL SYSTEM

The key to maximizing your way of life is having a method to counteract the destructive forces that face all of us. The method must be based on an overview of yourself and your own attitude toward your mind and body. See yourself as uniquely special, very worthy, with everything you need to survive and overcome all problems. Think in terms of what you can do, not what you cannot do. From a cold to cancer, you've got what it takes to overcome. Others have done so and so can you. From the top of your head to the tip of your toes, be aware constantly of a *healing-feeling* drifting and shifting to every area of concern.

Almost everyone has to give up some bad behavior. Explore your own behavior. Are you addicted to any substance that you should eliminate? Before you can develop a system to elevate yourself, you must understand where you have been. Make a list of your bad habits and unwanted behavior. Become aware of what you do, what you say, and what you think. While under hypnosis, you will discover even more as you probe the subterranean regions of your mind. With concentrated thought, you will see clearly the pattern which triggers repetition of your behavior. Once you recognize the "signal," you are one step closer to removing the triggering device which sets off routine habit. Once you have interfered with the regularity of the habit, you have also weakened its hold on you. Once the cycle of *thought-trigger-reflex* is broken, deconditioning can begin. The habit is now neutralized and ready to be wiped out by *signal reversal*.

Any time you feel the urge to repeat an old action that is detrimental to you, that very urge will be the signal to do the opposite. For example, the urge to smoke becomes retranslated as the signal to fill your lungs with fresh air. Cravings to self-destruct become cravings to self-construct. Here is the basic formula for reversing your signals:

Whenever I Think I am Going to ....
                                                    (Old habit)
That Will Be My Signal to Instead ....
                                                    (New habit)

If, for example, smoking is your bad habit complete the formula this way: "Whenever I think of smoking, that will be my signal to instead take three deep breaths."

If you are overweight, your signal reversal might be: "Whenever I think of eating something I shouldn't, the thought will signal me to pull in my stomach and stick to the diet.

Signal reversal is not only effective for changing bad habits into better ones; it works equally well for personality problems. Over a period of time, students have submitted various examples of signal reversal that have worked well for them. Here are a few. Perhaps one will suit your personality. If not, I am sure you will create a more suitable one.

The Unwanted Behavior: Shyness
The Formula: "Whenever I Feel Shy and Tend to Back Away, I
            Will, Instead, Smile and Extend My Hand in
            Friendship."

The formula can trigger specific action or can be generalized.

The Unwanted Behavior: Worry
The Formula: "Whenever I Begin to Worry Needlessly, I Will,
            Instead, Think of a Solution and Do Something
            about It."

Some of the problems that lend themselves to this technique are jealousy, obsessive guilt, possessiveness, perfectionism, indecision, and phobias. These are but a few. The list is endless and extends to every area of human conflict, mental, emotional, and physical. Try creating a formula for transforming negative personal relationships into positive ones. Are you enjoying a fulfilling love relationship? If so, you can make it better. If not, tap your highest intelligence and find out why you are denying yourself this ultimate pleasure. Then formulate your programming to correct the situation. It might be worded this way:

Whenever I Think of Myself as Lonely and Loveless, That Will Be a Signal for Me to Affirm All My Good Qualities and Project Loving Feelings Toward Others.

Some people alienate others by their introverted personalities. A young woman troubled by increasingly frequent periods of depression used this wording: *"Whenever I Feel Miserable and Low, That Is the Signal for Me to List My Good Qualities and Raise My Spirits Higher and Higher."*

Regular practice of this technique assures you that every negative thought triggers the opposite reaction. Create your formula while meditating in self-hypnosis. Reinforce it while in a waking state as often as possible. Be vigilant. At the first sign of the slightest negative feeling, put your foot down firmly. Let your mind know you are free of the old enslavement and will not be lured back.

The best habit you can cultivate is diligent practice. Set aside at least one half hour for hypnotic meditation each day. Stick with it until you succeed. Thomas A. Edison said, "Our greatest weakness lies in giving up too soon. The most certain way to succeed is to try just one more time." Faithful adherence to the technique will not only change your mind, but your body and the course of your life.

In addition to periods of self-hypnosis with positive autosuggestion, repeat your formula the last thing at night and the first thing in the morning. At these times, your mind is less resistent and reconditioning is most effective. Make a habit of reviewing your accomplishments. Praise yourself for showing improvement. Self-approval is the greatest boost to motivation. Success breeds more success and, once recognized, positive forces within you multiply to complete the total changeover.

From time to time, review your personal program and progress. If you reach some of your short-term goals, set new ones. Persist. Stick to your goals. The ultimate freedom will be well worth the effort. Confucius had something to say about everything and this topic is no exception. "In all things," he said, "success depends upon previous preparation, and without such preparation, there is sure to be failure." Your program is your previous preparation.

HOW TO BRING YOURSELF OUT OF HYPNOSIS

After taking yourself into autohypnosis and repeating your autosuggestions at least ten times, you may be ready to come out of the trance. Keep in mind that you are at no time in danger of staying "under." You would simply drift from hypnosis into sleep and awaken in a few minutes. Whether you are hypnotized by a professional or do it yourself, you are always in control and can awaken at will, just as you have awakened many times from a light nap.

After hypnosis, you will feel refreshed and new. Your mind will be sharp and clear, but your body and emotions will be free of the old troublesome tensions. To wake up feeling just great, count from 1 to 10 using positive reinforcement with each count. As you count up, feel your spirits rising.

One . . . Getting ready to wake up now, feeling fine.

Two . . . My mind is clear and keen, raring to go.

Three . . . I am cheerful and happy, eager to face the day.

Four . . . My body feels rested, refreshed, lots of energy.

Five . . . This was a successful session with positive results.

Six . . . Next time I will go even deeper with better results.

Seven, Eight, Nine, Ten . . . Wide awake, feeling wonderful!!

Remember, all skills require time and effort to acquire. I suggest that you *place the special verbalized material on a tape and memorize the techniques.* This will be equivalent to having a professional train you in the art of self-induction, you will be able to look to yourself for answers and corrections in many areas. However, in no instance should a lay person attempt to use self-hypnosis to try to cure a serious illness without first consulting a qualified physician. Self-hypnosis is primarily an adjunct to the medical profession, not a substitute for medical expertise. Those with a serious mental or emotional problem will require the assistance of a trained psychotherapist or hypnotherapist. There is no danger in using self hypnosis in such cases; it simply will not work for the seriously disturbed, who need to be guided into the areas of mental concentration where improvements originate. Mentally disturbed people tend to wander during meditation, and a skilled therapist knows how to bring them into focus. If you are in need of a professional person, contact your local medical or psychological associations.

Eating, Smoking, Drugs and Insomnia

Too many square meals make people rounder and lonelier. America's number one negative habit is overeating. Too many people use food as a replacement for emotional needs such as love and security. The tragedy of food obsession is that obesity tends to further alienate people from others. A cloak of excess flesh does not shield against emotional hurt. Fat cannot cushion blows to delicate egos.

"I've been humiliated by my husband," explained Florence. "He used to take me to his college reunion and always acted proud of me. But this year, Ronnie said he wouldn't attend because he was ashamed to be seen with me."

She paused, dabbed her eyes and unconsciously popped a sweet into her mouth. "I'm so fat," she moaned. "I've gained at least ten pounds a year since we've been married. From a size twelve, I've gone to size twenty and a half. But, Miss Copelan," Florence appealed to me, "if Ronnie really and truly loved me, wouldn't he accept me fat and all?"

In fact, Ronnie couldn't accept his wife's obesity. He had married an attractive, slender girl and now he was embarrassed for his friends to see the shape she was in.

Needless to say, despite all arguments, they did not attend the college reunion. But, to Ronnie's delight, Florence responded positively to hypnotic suggestion. She was placed on a limit of 1200 calories as post hypnotic suggestion. The following year, they attended the reunion in high style. Florence wore a size twelve dress and Ronnie beamed proudly at her side. She is a fine example of the use of professional hypnosis combined with self-hypnosis which she practices every night when she goes to bed.

However, more than Florence's weight had bothered Ronnie. Slimmed down, she reflected the new happiness and contentment in her marriage. When she was overweight, her appearance indicated her emotional insecurity. Ronnie felt her emotions reflected upon him as a husband. They also worked out problems which related to their sexual relationship. You will read the sexual implications in a future chapter.

HUNGER VERSUS APPETITE

Too many people confuse hunger with appetite. Appetite is a habit. Hunger is a real need. The two are not the same.

Appetite is provoked by suggestion while hunger is the message we receive when we need nourishment. Proper diet is essential to provide the elements necessary for the body to renew tissues and keep the organs functioning as nature intended.

Compulsive eaters strain their will power and by-pass mind power. In other words, they consciously struggle to deny appetite instead of correcting the mental programming which causes them to crave unnecessary calories. The body only does what the mind tells it to do.

In order to help overcome the "stuffing" habit, hypnosis begins by teaching the subconscious how to think about food. Overeaters need a bit of brainwashing to clear away conditioned habits.

An overweight teenager, Elsie, told me, "My family used to call me 'the human garbage can.' I always cleaned up everybody's leftovers. When I was a little kid, they thought it was cute. But after I grew up they began to ridicule me."

Hypnosis helped Elsie change her self-image. She had to learn to respect her body and accept healthier living habits.

If you do not already know about calories, a balanced diet, and the importance of vitamins, take a lesson from Elsie, who is now a happy size seven and strolls down the beach wearing a polka-dot bikini.

Get into the habit of a healthy program of nutrition. As Elsie learned, eating a small amount of food doesn't guarantee weight loss.

CALORIES DO COUNT

To lose one pound of fat, you must burn up approximately 3000 calories through physical activity. If a person eliminates 1000 calories a day, he can lose approximately two pounds a week. Most people require less calories than they are accustomed to eating. Once Elsie discovered the power of her mind, she began losing weight in a most natural way, without conscious effort or struggle.

Fundamentals of Weight Reduction:

1. Take in less energy in the form of food than your body uses. Reduce carbohydrates to the barest minimum. Increase proteins to the maximum.

2. Exercise your body at every opportunity. Never sit when you can stand, never ride when you can walk. Stretch and bend every time you can.

People Who Stay Slim Obey the Following Rules:

1. They postpone eating as often as possible.
2. They are selective about what they eat.
3. They chew slowly before swallowing.

If you obey all of the precepts above, you will not only grow slim, but remain slim. The most desirable weight for anyone is the weight at which a person looks and feels best. Height, bone structure and muscular development must all be taken into account.

FACE UP TO FACTS

What has been your maximum weight?_____

Your minimum weight as an adult?_____

How much weight would you like to lose?_____

You can lose from three to five pounds a week through hypnosis, depending upon your physical structure. How many pounds do you think you would be comfortable losing each week?_____

Now divide that number into your first figure and see how many weeks it will take you to lose the total amount. Set your target date._____

Now you have a goal to reach. Your computerlike mind has picked up the message you have just written and will find a way to make the wishful thinking reality. Autosuggestion will communicate this motivation to your body reflexes.

Remember that a great incentive to losing weight is that favorite dress or suit you have hidden away in the closet because it's too small to wear.

SMOKERS ARE SELF-POLLUTERS

The United States Health Department reports that smokers tend to die five to ten years before nonsmokers. That's a pretty good reason to quit, right? Still, tobacco addicts cling to the self-destructive habit.

I heard a hostess tell her guest recently, "Sit down, John, relax and have a smoke."

She may as well have said, "Sit down, John, and have a stroke."

Smoking can be just as injurious to the heart as to the lungs. Actually, when a person lights up a cigarette, he does not relax. Sitting down is relaxing, not the smoke. Smoking increases tension. If you've ever watched a person puff away on a cigarette as if his life depended on it, you would see he is far from relaxed.

One of the most difficult aspects of breaking the smoking habit is its tendency to accompany another activity that *is* relaxing. For example, during coffee breaks or after dinner, a smoker will often light up a cigarette. Coffee breaks are supposed to be a time for relief from stress. But for many people, they represent time to reinforce bad habits. For the overweight person, the doughnut that goes with the coffee just adds to the surplus poundage.

A good idea during coffee breaks would be to change over to exercise or relaxation breaks. Many large corporations recognize the importance of this need to stimulate employees, and have set aside space and equipment for this purpose.

But those employees not fortunate enough to work in a place where special facilities are available can always just find a chair during their "break" and do self-hypnosis to improve their positive programming.

THE EVIDENCE IS OVERWHELMING

Every day new evidence appears linking smoking to more diseases. The secretary of the U.S. Department of Health recently stated in an A.P. news story, "Cigarette smoking continues to be confirmed as a serious health hazard, one which is unquestionably the cause of much unnecessary disease and death."

Consider this. Even the mildest filter tip cigarette speeds up the heartbeat, upsets circulation and limits oxygen to the lungs.

What happens when you quit smoking?

1. You will breathe easier.
2. Your circulation will improve.
3. You will feel less tired and nervous.
4. Your sense of smell will improve.
5. Your cough will lessen or disappear.
6. Your heart and lungs will strengthen.
7. And because you stop with hypnosis, you will never drift back to it again. How is this possible? Because negative suggestion is removed and positive suggestion takes over.

HOW MUCH SMOKING IS HARMFUL?

How many times should a man strike his wife?

How many times should a boy kick a dog?

Even one cigarette is one too many for most people. Remember the first time you tried a cigarette, how sick it made you feel? That was the time to quit.

A good rule about what is healthy and what is unhealthy is to ask yourself, would I offer this to a child? If your answer is no, it is also unhealthy for you, at any age.

A 35-year-old movie director, Frank, R., came to see me to help him stop smoking. He confessed that he smoked from three to four packs a day.

"It's my job," Frank alibied. "I'm under constant tension. Everyone bugs me for something all day long. A cigarette calms my nerves."

I noticed Frank's hands. They were trembling. His nerves were far from calm. He looked down at his quivering fingers, sheepishly embarrassed.

"This is nothing. You should see how I shake when I'm not smoking," he quipped.

"Are you trying to tell me that smoking four packs of cigarettes a day helps your nervous system?" I asked.

"Guess I'm trying to cop out," he answered. "The fact is, I came to see you hoping to be helped through hypnosis. I can't go on this way much longer. Honestly, it's become serious. I wake up at night coughing up black phlegm. I've had to give up playing tennis because I get too winded. I'm constantly tired and know I must be a perfect target for cancer. My brother already has it. I've tried everything and so far nothing works."

Frank took time out to cough. Then he continued. "I've thrown away six cartons of cigarettes; six times I've quit—but I always drift back."

Frank did quit smoking with hypnotherapy six years ago and has not drifted back. He is just one of millions of smokers who have been permanently reconditioned through hypnotic techniques.

CAN THE SMOKER REGAIN HIS HEALTH?

Smoking destroys living tissue. When a person coughs, struggling to breathe, the lining of his respiratory system becomes sticky, coated with an ugly, grey chemical substance. This sludge blocks the passages, eventually resulting in lung infection and sometimes even a collapsed lung. After a person has given up smoking for several years, this sludge is eliminated by the natural processes of the body. After ten years, his life expectancy can even match that of abstainers. These statistics are based on reports from the American Cancer Society's massive survey of a million men and women.

One way to cut down on smoking is to learn how to breathe correctly. Some people lose their desire to smoke once they learn how to breathe the way nature intended, with full lung capacity. The average person is a shallow breather using only about 20% of his lungs for breathing. On the other hand, smokers who inhale bring the fumes down to the unused 80 percent of their lungs. This action momentarily provides them with a contented feeling. However, once they finish their cigarettes, their breathing becomes shallow once again.

When people breathe with 100 percent of their lungs, they not only get a satisfied feeling; they also get sufficient oxygen to rejuvenate body cells and to sustain perfect health.

Practice the following self-hypnosis exercise several times a day for five to ten minutes.

1. Sit upright without having your spine touch the back of the chair.

2. Place your hands loosely on top of your thighs. Space your feet about 10 inches apart.

3. Close your eyes and focus on the rhythms of your breathing.

4. Breathe in and out quickly and rhythmically through your nose. Do this a dozen times. You may cough and spit up phlegm. This is helpful for cleaning the trachia.

5. Place your right hand on your lower diaphragm. Monitor the movement of your lungs as they fill with oxygen.

6. Breathe in and out in twelve slow, deep rhythmic breaths. Inhale to the count of five, then pause and exhale to the count of five. This will cleanse the lower areas of your lungs.

FACE THE FACTS

Ask Yourself:

1. How much do I smoke? _____
2. When do I reach for a cigarette? _____
3. Does tension make me smoke more? _____
4. Do I smoke during the night? _____
5. Do I smoke with my meals? _____

After you answer the above questions and have conscious awareness, be assured that you can cut down on your smoking or quit entirely, if you really choose to do it. Once you face facts, use the following autosuggestion to enforce your determination to quit.

Repeat the following five times each:

1. I have quit smoking forever.
2. No one can coax me into taking a cigarette.
3. When someone offers me one, I will answer, "Thanks, but I do not smoke anymore."

Here are some additional tips on cutting down.

1. Smoke half of a cigarette. The tobacco itself acts as a partial filter. The last half is the worst, loaded with tar and nicotine.

2. Limit yourself. No more than eight cigarettes a day.

3. Use the low tar variety with a filter tip since king-size contains more nicotine and tar.

4. Reduce inhaling. Smoke irritates the bronchial membranes.

5. Keep a record. Mark down each time you have an urge to smoke. When you resist giving in, give yourself a star. Experiments show people who keep track of what they are doing decrease negative habits.

DRUGS, ALCOHOL, AND HYPNOSIS

Alice H., 37 years of age, was an alcoholic. She had tried psychoanaly-sis for about five years without success. While she was under the care of several physicians, medications of every sort were tested and dis-carded. Alice was divorced and the mother of three small children who had been taken from her by the court and placed with the father. The children's father, Mark, was also alcoholic. Mark had, in fact, taught Alice to drink and then accused her of being an unfit mother. Since Mark held the purse strings and had political connections, he managed to keep the children, allowing the mother only occasional visitation rights.

Alice then drank even more heavily. Depressed and dazed about the entire situation, she finally met an understanding young man, Jonathan, who sympathized and went to great lengths to help her. Jonathan stood by her during her worst bouts with the bottle. He supplied funds enabling Alice to undergo analysis and receive all known medical treatment. Finally, when everything else failed (as is so often the case) hypnosis was used.

Alice was serious about overcoming her problem, "the quicker the better." The time wasted and the trouble created by her problem drinking finally got to her. "My children are growing up without knowing their mother," she said unhappily. The love of Jonathan was also an incentive to pull herself together. She didn't just want to cut down or be a social drinker; she wanted to stop drinking completely.

Alice became a willing and eager subject, anxious to lick her problem. With strong motivation and determination, she was able to overcome the habit and become a sensible person again. The reasons which caused her to drink came to the surface and were noted by the hypnotherapist.

Alice had read a book on hypnosis which described the various techniques and presented case histories of the subjects. Her parents were arrogant, which caused her to dislike and resent an authoritative hypnotic approach. She preferred to be corrected and reasoned with in a soft, permissive manner. The hypnotist asked Alice to help in pro-gramming her feelings of aversion to alcohol. Alice made a list, and restructured her thoughts. She then entered into a medium trance during the very first session and was given autosuggestions for aversion to alcoholic beverages. During this state of relaxed receptivity, the suggestions of complete and lasting aversion to alcohol were allowed to penetrate. Because the suggestions increased the depth of her concentration, she demonstrated to the therapist the sincerity of her motivations. *The resistant subject who is not properly motivated will tend to lose depth the moment therapeutic suggestions are applied.*

Alice did not take another drink after her first session. Instead, she was encouraged to find new interests. She went back to work and was able to keep a job for the first time. Jonathan was still supportive. He encouraged her and kept her away from "bad company." Soon Alice herself was able to take charge of their social engagements. She discovered that she could even sit with an occasional drinking group and sip ginger ale or water and it didn't bother her.

One month later, Alice visited my office to report her aversion for alcohol had become so deep and complete that when she went for a massage, the alcohol used for the rub made her nauseous.

WHEN DOES A DRINKER BECOME AN ALCOHOLIC?

The social drinker can stop drinking anytime he or she wants to, or whenever circumstances compel them to, but the compulsive alcoholic cannot control his urge. He continues to drink until he loses self-control and self-respect.

Not every drinker becomes an alcoholic. Some people learn to hold their liquor. They can stop whenever they want to stop. Others go to the other extreme and lose total control of their intake.

George S. was such a man. He consumed at least half a quart of alcoholic beverages every day. Cocktails before dinner, beer or wine with his meal, and the familiar nightcap before bedtime. He was brought to see me by his teenage son, Michael.

"We never realized my father drank until one night when he came home sober and we noticed the difference," Michael said.

George S. interrupted, "I wouldn't be here now if it weren't for my liver. The doctor warned me I'll have to go to the hospital unless I quit drinking right away."

A twenty year old habit is not easy to give up. George was a chronic alcoholic, who lacked discipline and energy. His eating habits were poor and his sex life, nil. For George, it was a case of developing an entirely new kind of program for living. With the help of an audio cassette tape which he played several times a day, and ten sessions of hypnosis, George S. finally learned to control his weakness.

DRUG ADDICTION

The habit monster has many claws. In addition to the widespread problems of overeating, smoking, and drinking, millions are plagued by the drug habit.

The World Health Organization states: "Drug addiction is a state of periodic and chronic intoxication detrimental to the individual and to society, produced by the repeated consumption of a drug (natural or synthetic). Characteristics of addiction include:

1. An overpowering desire to continue use.
2. An emotional drive to obtain it by any means.
3. A tendency to increase the dose as the drug lessens its powers.
4. A psychological and sometimes physical dependence."

This definition includes all three types of drugs: those prescribed by doctors, those sold over the counter legally, and those pushed on the street illegally.

Drugs more popularly addictive are the opiates such as heroin, opium, cocaine, and marijuana. The barbituates and amphetamines, which are often medically prescribed, may be added to this list.

A person who is aware of his habits and honestly wishes to get rid of them can learn how to get high on life. We have all the natural resources, providing we learn how to use them.

To begin with, an optimistic approach is needed in order to cope with the ordinary and extraordinary problems which confront us. This means learning to take life as it comes, and learning to accept the consequences.

Through hypnosis, mental attitudes become more optimistic. We discover within ourselves the "makings" of a better way of life. Hypnosis holds the key to many a seemingly locked door. The greatest treasure in the world is the inner peace and tranquillity which comes from knowing that normal health, both emotional and physical, is within the mind's reach. Naturally induced hypnotic "high" feeling never wears off, but remains with you through all adversity.

SPECIAL BONUS—A GOOD NIGHT'S SLEEP

If you are like most people, there have been nights when you toss and turn, restless and exhausted. The harder you strive and strain for sleep, the more wide awake you become. One of the great bonuses of practicing self-hypnosis is that you will never be troubled by insomnia again. Self-hypnosis is the gateway to regular nighttime slumber, and once you train yourself to relax deeply, you will be able to simply slip over the boundary into a restful night's sleep.

Everyone needs a good night's sleep. Our century's pace of living has become so intense, the human mind is overstimulated by the time evening arrives. People in perpetual motion have problems unwinding the tautness of their mental and physical springs. Falling asleep has become a lost art for man and sends millions of people to doctors for relief. Often relief is elusive because medication does not erase the root cause of insomnia. Only a relaxed body and a tranquil mind can do that.

Doctors, as well as the patients themselves, are sometimes guilty of the overuse of sleeping pills, many of which are sold over the counter without a doctor's prescription. These are called "sedative or medicative hypnotics." Isn't it strange that we use drugs to create a hypnotic effect when hypnosis itself is so simple to learn and so harmless to use? This is another example of how we have been brainwashed to behave contrary to our natural instincts. You are equipped with everything you need to decelerate rapid daytime tempos and slow down the pulses of your body. Your best sleep medicine is always prevention. It is possible to stop insomnia before it starts through the manner in which you handle your daily routine of living. It is important not to overreact to routine pressures.

HOW MUCH SLEEP DO WE NEED?

Everybody needs regular sleep, but not everybody needs the same amount of regular sleep. What constitutes a full night's sleep for one may equal a catnap for another. There are many myths and fallacies about sleep. One is that we all require eight hours per night. A short sleep differs from insomnia. Some people awaken fully rested with as little as four or five hours of profound slumber. Others wake up tired unless they have nine or ten.

The long accepted dictum that everybody needs eight hours falls flat by the wayside when you consider Thomas Edison and Albert Einstein, who slept only four or five hours a night and accomplished so much. Yet everyone needs a certain amount of sleep. When they don't get their required amount, panic may set in. Headaches, backaches, or a dragged-out feeling may result the next day. A pall of anxiety hangs over the insomniac when he keeps trying and fails to sleep.

If a person lives to age 75, for example, chances are he'll spend one third of his life sleeping. Whether that third will make the other two thirds meaningful, depends upon how well he revitalizes himself during sleeping hours. As one grows older, he requires less sleep. A baby sleeps on and off around the clock; an adult usually sleeps between six and eight hours. There is evidence that men sleep longer than women, extroverts longer than introverts, fat people longer than thin people, and worriers longer than relaxers.

HINTS FOR A GOOD NIGHT'S SLEEP

Prepare yourself for sleep before retiring. Don't take worries to bed with you. Tell yourself that you can't do anything about them till morning, anyway.

Instead of ignoring disturbing noises such as rattling windows and creaking doors, get up and eliminate them.

Avoid late night television, arguments, eating, and drinking, because all these stimulate the body and mind.

Relax your muscles completely by stretching your legs and arms fully. Tense, then relax. Repeat a few times.

Give your bed your full weight. Yield into the surface supporting you. Let tension melt away.

Breathe deeply and regularly, allowing each breath to drift you deeper into drowsiness. Then close your eyes slowly. You are now entering the state of *alpha* which is the threshold for self-hypnosis. Stop worrying. Self-hypnosis automatically leads into sleep unless you deliberately wake yourself up.

Visualize yourself stretched out on a hammock, swaying in the breeze from side to side. Or floating in a boat on a serene lake. Counting is also helpful. Instead of counting sheep in the usual way, count backwards from one hundred to zero. You may fall asleep before you have finished counting.

If not, visualize a blackboard. You are holding chalk in one hand and an eraser in the other. Mentally draw a large circle on the blackboard.

Fill the circle with a large X.

Erase the X with your free hand, starting at the center. Erase carefully so as not to erase the circle.

Now write the word SLEEP inside the circle. Write it slowly and deliberately. Erase it and go deeper.

Repeat this until you feel yourself drifting off.

ANOTHER SLEEP INDUCER

Write the number 100 within a circle.

Erase it and take a deep breath, then exhale.

Next, write number 99. Erase it mentally. Breathe and exhale.

Continue down from 100 to 0 on a descending scale.

Feel yourself going deeper and deeper into a state of drowsiness until you drift into sleep.

When you awaken in the morning, the first thought to come into your mind will be: "Every day in every way I feel better and better. When I go to sleep tonight, I will sleep all night and awaken feeling fresh and relaxed."

In seventeen years as an active hypnotherapist, I have never failed to cure sleeplessness, whether the condition was acute or chronic or both. This is because hypnosis itself is the threshold of sleep. It guides the brain from *beta* to *alpha*—then to *theta* and, finally, *delta*, which is sleep.

Acute insomniacs are helped a great deal by using a pretapped hypnosis session which they listen to just prior to falling asleep. The subject is instructed to place the recorder next to the bed and turn the volume down low. After several nights, slumber is inevitable.

Self-hypnosis works for those who are mildly stressed and have occasional problems with insomnia. However, for more deeply rooted sleep disorders that have existed over a long period, the help of a professional may be necessary for one or two sessions.

Part Two
Advanced Techniques

Hypnosis in Professional Practice

After a two-hundred-year struggle for recognition, hypnosis has evolved into a valuable, respectable adjunct to medicine and psychology. Its therapeutic values are applauded by serious-minded scientists. Clinical and experimental research into hypnotic phenomena is now going on in every civilized country. Courses in the subject are being offered by professionals in leading universities, not only in the United States but in many countries behind the Iron Curtain. In the Soviet Union, hypnosis is used routinely for presurgery and postsurgery to eliminate complications and to accelerate the healing process.

Although hypnosis has been only slowly gaining acceptance in the United States among the more conservative physicians, on September 18, 1958, the Council on Mental Health of the American Medical Association recommended instruction in hypnosis be included in the curriculum of medical schools. Since then, many physicians have familiarized themselves with its therapeutic uses. Thousands either practice hypnosis themselves or employ the services of a lay hypnotist. Physicians of all kinds, from plastic surgeons to podiatrists, find it useful both in clinical work and diagnostic analysis. Those with the necessary acumen can use hypnotic methodologies to further the art of healing in hundreds of ways. You owe it to yourself to add this valuable modality to your professional armamentarium.

What makes hypnosis work? To understand the nature of hypnosis, you must realize the patient is not treated by hypnosis, itself. Rather, *he is treated while in the hypnotic state*. Hypnosis catalyzes the curative process. The therapeutic trance is a combination of physical relaxation and mental concentration conducive to the acceptance of suggestion. When positive suggestions for healing are verbalized by the physician or therapist, they register on the subconscious mind and result in an improved condition.

The degree of success is based upon how much *faith* the subject has, not only in his own ability to heal himself, but more important, in the ability of his physician to help him do so. The physician, even before he begins to hypnotize, has an enormous power as a figure of authority. This is equally true of the law enforcement officer, the clergyman, and the politician, all of whom use some form of hypnosis in their work. Authoritative suggestion is easily translated into absolute commands by the subject's receptive mind.

One of the most important aspects of hypnosis for the professional is the added cooperation one receives from the subject because of the removal of resistance. In areas where pain and discomfort are factors that interfere with treatment, hypnosis is especially useful. Dentists have been using it for years. One that I know uses these words: "As soon as you hear the sound of the drill, it will be a signal for you to relax and feel no pain." This is basically the technique of signal reversal and can be used in every field of healing.

Researchers at the Menninger Foundation also reported remarkable results in eliminating the distress of headache pain. Through hypnosis, some patients were trained to tell their hearts to pump less blood into their heads, thus reducing the agony of migraine headaches. The patients were told while in trance to visualize their hands, then to concentrate on their hands becoming warmer and warmer. They were told that as their hands grew warmer, the blood was draining from their heads into their hands, thus relieving the pain and pressure of the headache. A wide variety of experiments has proven the merit of hypnotherapy. At the University of Colorado Medical Center, psychologists report that mind-body therapy cured chronic pain in patients who had suffered for many years, tried everything else, and failed to find anything that worked. The list of such positive results grows longer every day.

Dr. Neal E. Miller of Rockefeller University, working with a team of medical researchers, has demonstrated that involuntary bodily functions such as blood pressure maintenance, heartbeat and even the control of cholesterol levels can be beneficially affected in some patients through mental persuasion. In my own personal experience as a clinical hypnotist engaged in experiments on cholesterol, I was finally able, after one hour of self-hypnosis to lower my cholesterol level almost 100 points. This test was verified with blood specimens taken every hour for 9 hours. When stress was applied, the cholesterol level went up, and when hypnosis was induced the cholesterol level went down. The next day, the test showed that my cholesterol level was about 40 points lower than the highest reading, but not as low as during the trance state.

This experience convinced me of the efficacy of hypnotherapy as a means of stress-management. It also reaffirmed my belief in the need for expanding research in this area. While work is going on in some university medical schools, including Columbia, Harvard, and the University of Pennsylvania, much still remains to be done. A great deal of the current work involves theory and technique. However, theory without sufficient application is as powerless as practice uninformed by theory is blind. This book has been written as a pragmatic guide to help fuse theory with practical application.

When professionals have applied hypnosis, the results have delighted them. Both orthodontists and opticians (particularly in the fitting of contact lenses) have successfully used hypnotic suggestion. And in psychotherapy, the use of hypnosis has increased 100 percent in the last decade. Hypnoanalysis releases subconscious material through dream interpretation and word association as well as the standard methods do. The therapist guides the subject into *alpha*, which is meditation, and then deeper into *theta*, which is hypnosis.

HYPNOSIS AND BRAINWAVES

In the last few years there have been a number of newspaper articles written extolling the wonders of "brain-wave therapy." Feature articles in the New York Times, the Wall Street Journal and scores of medical papers and periodicals inform us of the amazing discovery that the brain has the ability to change its vibrations and affect not only behavior, but even the involuntary workings of our internal organs. Traditionally, science has categorically divided bodily function into two types: voluntary or involuntary—controlled or automatic. This rigid dichotomy appears to be dissolving in the light of new knowledge.

HOW BRAIN WAVES ARE CLASSIFIED

1. Beta Waves

The *beta* state is one of physical alertness, with mind and emotions responsive to the senses. Most of our waking time is spent in this state, which is associated with tension and striving. While in *beta*, one experiences a sense of being controlled by time and space.

2. Alpha Waves

This is the area of mind which brings increased creativity and physical relaxation. Not only is the level of stress reduced but many people enter a light or hypnoidal trance called meditation. At this level, there is a slowing down of brain and body pulsation.

3. Theta Waves

Theta is the portal for entering nighttime sleep. We all pass through *theta* twice a day: when we fall asleep and when we awaken in the morning. With hypnosis, we maintain *theta* for as long as the session lasts. At this level, behavior can be modified.

4. Delta Waves

Delta is profound sleep. There is a further slowing down of mental vibrations. While in *delta*, we dream and sort out our mental and physical machinery. This is a period of regeneration and cell renewal, and, without sufficient *delta* sleep, one can suffer from sleep deprivation. More study of this state is needed.

STAGES OF HYPNOSIS

There are six levels of hypnosis. Some people drift from one level to another during a single session. Others may reach one stage and never allow themselves to go any deeper. In most cases, the subject will reach a medium level of hypnosis after two or three sessions and return to that depth during all future therapy. As long as the results are favorable, the depth reached is unimportant.

Stage 1: Hypnoidal

A feeling of physical lethargy. Heavy muscles and relaxed nerves. Thoughts tend to wander. Drowsiness.

Stage 2: Light Hypnosis

Muscular response to suggestion. Eyes roll back. Subject reacts to suggestion of arm rigidity ("stiff and rigid as a bar of steel"). Mind is concentrated on suggestions.

Stage 3: Medium Hypnosis

Subject deeply relaxed, cannot rise from chair or bed unless told to do so. Subject will not speak except by suggestion.

Stage 4: Deep Hypnosis

There may be partial amnesia upon awakening. Analgesia can be suggested as well as increased sensory awareness. Posthypnotic suggestion works well.

Stage 5: Somnambulism

Complete amnesia and anesthesia is possible. Positive hallucinations. Regression to childhood. Progression to future events.

Stage 6: Profound Somnambulism

In addition to the above, subject is capable of negative hallucinations, i.e., removal of recorded information such as previous brainwashing. Posthypnotic suggestions are carried out as commands.

The first three stages, from hypnoidal through medium trance, are called *mensic*. During these levels, the subject will remember everything the hypnotist has said. Many will doubt they were hypnotized. Through the first three stages, habit correction and behavior modification takes place. With the last three stages, from deep hypnosis to profound somnambulism, the subject will not remember what was said while under hypnosis. These deeper stages are useful in areas such as surgery, childbirth, dentistry, and the correction of criminal behavior such as rape. However, about 80% of the time, hypnosis is used for modifying behavior such as smoking, obesity, and insomnia, or the lowering of pain thresholds—all of which may be done using the first three stages of hypnosis. Deep hypnosis is not necessary in these cases.

PREPARING THE SUBJECT

After a brief conversation to prepare the subject for induction procedure, a series of tests will be applied to determine the degree of response to be expected from a particular subject. Here's one way to prepare and relax the patient in order to eliminate anxiety.

> HYPNOTIST: "Tell me what you think hypnosis is like. What do you expect to feel when you are hypnotized?"
>
> PATIENT: "I guess it's like falling asleep even if you don't want to. Maybe like losing consciousness . . . I'm a little afraid of someone else controlling me."
>
> HYPNOTIST: "Well, it's not exactly like falling asleep. Hypnosis isn't sleep. It's physical relaxation and mental concentration. You will never be unconscious. Just the opposite. You will be aware of everything that goes on. All you have to do is cooperate and concentrate on the things you want to have happen. It's simply a matter of the hypnotist and the subject working together so this very pleasant state of awareness can be brought about to help you. Hypnosis is deep meditation and is very natural. I will show you how it works and soon you will enjoy the feeling very much."

TESTING FOR SUSCEPTIBILITY

Tests reveal to the hypnosis operator whether the person he will be working with is *passive-submissive* or *challenging-dominant*. This determines his choice of techniques and the emotional quality of voice in verbalizing suggestions. Testing is also the beginning of establishing rapport and places the operator in control of the therapeutic relationship. There are two methods of hypnotizing which you adapt to suit the personality of the subject.

1. Authoritarian

The hypnotist makes direct suggestions indicating that something will occur. Speak slowly and distinctly as to a child. Use this approach for the passive type.

2. Permissive

Use a softer tone of voice. Tell the subject to imagine, think, picture, and visualize. Use this approach for the dominant type.

The dominant type is less able to accept orders. Therefore, he must be won over to trust you, so don't come on too strong. The submissive type is used to take orders so you might get right to the subject at hand. Be direct. Say, "I want you to do exactly as I say, for your own good." Be strong and assertive in your choice of words and your gestures as well as in your tone of voice when dealing with the submissive individual.

Proper utilization of the trance state hangs on the delicate thread of a trusting interpersonal relationship between the subject and the practitioner. This is gradually established during the process of hypnotic conditioning and will improve with time. Developing this empathetic relationship is difficult for some therapists whose background has trained them in a cool clinical approach. If so, they will be limited in being able to help the person in need. Oriental hypnotists overcome this difficulty by meditating along *with* their subject. The Master regards the power of hypnosis to be greatly influenced by his own mental attitudes. After viewing some of the remarkable results produced by yogi hypnotists, it might prove interesting to test some of their methods.

The big difference between Oriental methods of hypnotism and the Western methods is that the latter make the use of verbal suggestion primary, whereas Eastern Masters project their own inner images upon the subject. Oriental hypnosis employs only authoritiarian techniques that are shrouded with a great deal of mysticism and religious belief.

CHEVREUL'S PENDULUM TEST

The Chevreul Pendulum, named after a French doctor, is constructed from an object like a small crystal ball tied to the end of a chain or string. The subject is told to hold the string while the weight hangs at eye level. The pendulum is used both for testing and for induction. It also has a fascination for most people, because they are completely in control of its action. In view of this factor, the technique differs radically from other aids to exterior concentration and stimulation.

There is a biofeedback reaction from the central nervous system into the fingers which hold the string. Impress upon the subject that his inner mind is in complete control of its outer motion. He is influencing the swing through internal energy. On the other hand, a rotating hypnosis disc or a flashing light has an entirely exterior influence upon the subject.

Have the subject sit in a comfortable chair. Suggest relaxation. Now place the string in his hand so that raising the center of the pendant is slightly above his eye level. Steady the ball with your hand.

Begin by saying, "Hold this pendulum so that the light strikes it. Keep staring at it and listen to my voice. I want you to think of it as going around and around in a circle. Just think of it going around clockwise . . . around and around . . . going faster and faster . . . around and around . . . and now, think of it stopping. When it stops, think of it going in the opposite direction, counter-clockwise . . . around and around, that's it . . . faster now, around and around. Stop the pendulum with your thoughts. Now think of it going from left to right, back and forth . . . back and forth . . . right to left and left to right. That's wonderful. You've got the idea.

"Now, direct the pendulum to swing in the other direction from me to you, you to me . . . now, in this direction, it's going back and forth, moving faster now . . . swinging wider and wider . . . back and forth. Keep concentrating in any direction you choose, all by yourself, by your own thoughts . . . moving, faster and faster. . . ."

The receptive subject will indicate by the movement of the pendulum just how responsive he is to suggestion. If the pendulum does not swing freely in the directions of suggestions, the test will indicate some degree of resistance.

THE FALL-BACK TEST

HYPNOTIST: "Stand over here, your toes and heels together and relax. That's it." Run your hands down the arms lightly and continue. "Look up at that spot and listen to my voice. Now, as I place my hands beside your face and begin to draw them back, you will feel yourself falling back; you will fall back and I will catch you." Begin pulling your hands back. You may flutter your fingers at the sides of the head where they can be seen out of the corners of the eyes. "Continue falling back, falling, falling back." As the subject falls backward, catch him or her by the shoulders and say, "Good, you see, you concentrate very well." If the subject does not respond, don't indicate your disappointment, but act as though the response was just what you expected. Proceed with the next susceptibility test or waking suggestion. Remember, even with these beginning suggestions, you are actually applying hypnotic persuasion.

HAND CLASP

"Clasp your hands together and gaze at this knuckle (indicate), now listen to me. I want you to picture your hands as gripping together like steel bands . . . tighter and tighter . . . think tight and now visualize your hands as sticking together like glue . . . sticking like glue and now they are stuck, stuck together so tight you cannot pull them apart . . . when I count to 3, I want you to try to pull them apart but you can't, they are stuck . . . 1, 2, 3 . . . try but you cannot . . . stop trying and they will come apart easily."

VARIATION—HAND CLASP

Say, "Stand over there and relax. Put your hands out before you like this." Demonstrate by extending your own arms straight from the shoulders, clasping your hands together. Then instruct, "Clasp your hands together as I am doing. Now turn your palms outward toward me like this (demonstrate). Close your eyes and listen carefully. Raise your arms up, up straight over your head. That's right, until your palms are facing the ceiling. And now, with your hands in this position, they are stuck together like bands of steel . . . now they are stuck tight . . . stuck tight together . . . so very tight you cannot pull them apart . . . stuck tight . . . when I count to 3, I want you to try to separate them, *but you cannot* . . . 1, 2, 3 . . . try, but *you cannot* separate them . . . stuck tight. Now stop trying. Lower your arms and your hands will come apart easily. Open your hands and relax."

Explain to the subject that it is impossible to think two things at the same time. Illustrate this fact by the following exercise.

Have the subject either stand or sit. Say, "Extend one arm and clench your fist. Now think, 'my fist is clenched tight . . . clenched tight, very tight . . . so very tight.' Think 'it's clenched so tight I cannot open it.' When I count to 3, you will try, but you will be unable to open it . . . it's stuck tight . . . very tight . . . 1, 2, 3. Try, but you cannot." If he opens his hand, explain that he simply could not think 'I can' and 'I cannot' at the same time. I often use this test as an explanation of how to cooperate by concentrating on the idea hypnosis will work. Point out that he must think one thing or the other, he *cannot* think both that it's stuck and *not* stuck at the same time. This puts him on the spot.

ARMS RISING AND FALLING TEST

As in the application of the other exercises, have the subject stand in a relaxed position. Say, "Stand over there facing me and relax. Raise your arms straight out, like this, palms facing each other (demonstrate). Turn your right palm up toward the ceiling. Make a fist of your left hand, thumb extended, arm extended toward the ceiling. Good. Now close your eyes and make a mental image of your hands in this position. Listen to my voice as I instruct you. Imagine I am placing a very heavy book on your right palm that is weighing your hand down, and getting heavier and heavier. And now I want you to imagine I am tying a balloon to the thumb of your left hand. Feel your hand becoming lighter and lighter as the balloon pulls your left hand up . . . up . . . higher and higher, feeling lighter and lighter.

"Now your left arm is rising while the right hand is falling. Now imagine I'm placing another very heavy book on your right hand. Think of it as getting heavier and heavier, dropping down, so heavy. And feel the left hand rising higher and higher. Now open your eyes and look at your hands."

If there is no reaction, you can assume at this point that the subject is not suggestible. If the hands do separate about one third of the way, it indicates a *light* trance subject. Half way up, a *medium* trance subject. When the hands separate all of the way, with the left hand overhead and the right hand pointed down, this indicates a *deep* trance subject.

This is often referred to as *the yardstick test*. The subject is usually amazed when the hands separate markedly, since he is not really conscious of where his hands are moment by moment. If he responds very well, compliment him on his concentration and vivid imagination.

If the response is disappointing, pass it off until further testing is done. Don't ever tell a subject you are disappointed. Let him think he did what was expected.

You might give the subject a choice of word pictures, like a very heavy book, a heavy weight, a stone, an extra balloon tied to the wrist, a puff of wind pushing it up, or a string tied to the ceiling and pulling it up. This test is frequently applied at the beginning. If the response to any test isn't promising, consider your subject might feel shy at the start of his therapy and try the test again next time he visits.

The Induction Process

Induction is composed of two parts:

External Focus. The subject is told to look at a stationary object, such as a pen, pencil, glass ball, candle, or spot on the wall. Or a moving object, such as a flashing light, whirling disc, etc. After suggestions for heaviness of the eyelids, the subject is told to close his eyes at the count of 5 or 10 (or any number).

Once the eyes are closed, the subject enters into the second phase of the induction procedure.

Internal Focus. The subject is told to concentrate on inner body awareness, relaxation and deep breathing. The process can be varied by the use of sounds such as music, bell, gong, or metronome.

Hypnotist says, "When you hear the sound of the bell, you will close your eyes and go into hypnosis with the sound of my voice. Your legs are growing heavy, very heavy. Your arms are growing heavy, very heavy. Your entire body is growing heavy, very heavy. You are going deep, deep asleep." (Repeat)

INDUCTION WITH FINGER METHOD

This is suitable for the person who reacts favorably to previous testing. "With your eyes closed, I place my finger on your forehead. Now turn your eyes inward and upward, as I run my finger to the top of your head. Follow my finger with your eyes. Now with my finger up here, continue to look at it and try to open your eyes. You will be amazed to find that you cannot. (Do not let him try too long. Now begin to slowly rotate his head and you will induce the trance.) Your legs are heavy, your arms are heavy, your entire body is heavy, you are deep, deep asleep and you cannot open your eyes. You are deep, deep asleep, legs heavy, arms heavy, body heavy, deep asleep, can't open your eyes; try, you cannot, try hard, you cannot open them . . . stop trying, stop trying, deep, deep asleep. (Stop rotating his head and proceed with the session.)

INDUCTION BY FIXATING ON SPOT

The hypnotist says, "Pick a spot on the ceiling and gaze at it. Keep on looking at the spot and listen to my voice. Relax as you stare at the spot. Feel yourself relaxing all over . . . deeper and deeper. As you keep staring at the spot, your eyes will become very heavy and drowsy. Your entire body is becoming heavier and heavier . . . your arms, heavy . . . limp and relaxed . . . legs limp and heavy and relaxed . . . feet are becoming relaxed . . . relaxed all over.

"As you keep staring at the spot, your eyes may begin to tear, to blink . . you are getting drowsy . . . heavy . . . sleepy . . . a wonderful feeling, warmth and relaxation flowing all through your body as you relax more deeply than ever before . . . your eyes blinking . . . tearing . . . they feel like closing . . . closing soon. When they close, you will fall into a deep, restful sleep . . . deep . . . sound asleep . . . the sound of my voice makes you sleepier and sleepier . . . you are going to fall into a pleasant state of relaxation . . . eyes will close soon . . . think of sleep . . . it is getting harder and harder . . . for you to focus your eyes . . . they are closing. . . ."

Once you have completed the external focus, you tell the subject to internalize. "Keep on going deeper . . . as I count backward from 5 to 0, you will keep going deeper and deeper . . . asleep . . . hear my voice as you let go and allow yourself to drift deeper and deeper. You will not awaken till I tell you to . . . the sound of my voice will send you deeper . . . you want to go deeper. Let go all over . . . feeling wonderfully relaxed as you go deep inside of yourself."

At this point, you may place your hands over the subject's eyes or raise one of his arms and let it drop. Continue to deepen hypnosis through pyramiding suggestions and repetition of hypnotic phrases.

BLINKER METHOD FOR EYE CLOSURE

This is an alternative method for closing the eyes to begin hypnotic induction. Eye closure is produced by steadily gazing at some point or object of fixation while the hypnotist suggests: "Eyelids growing heavier." The hypnotist then counts, having the subject open and close his eyelids on alternate counts as follows: "I am now going to begin counting. I want you to open and close your eyes with the count. I will count from 1 to 20. By the time I reach 20, or before, your eyes will be so heavy, they will stay closed and you will fall into sound sleep. One, your eyes are open, 2, close your eyes, 3, open, 4, close. Your eyes are becoming heavier with each closing. Five, open, 6, close, getting drowsy, sleepy. Very heavy. Seven, 8 . . . getting heavier . . . your eyelids are so heavy . . . you are trying but they do not want to open . . . soon you will be able to keep them closed . . . 9, 10. Eyes heavy, drowsy, sleepy. Eleven, 12. Heavier and heavier, very heavy now. Thirteen, 14, eyes so heavy, so sleepy, pleasantly drowsy. Fifteen, 16. Eyelids so sleepy going into a deep, pleasant sleep soon. Seventeen, 18. Eyelids so heavy and drowsy. Nineteen, barely opening. Twenty. Deep asleep. Now you can let them stay closed."

Eye catalepsy can be produced at this point in many cases, followed by rapid deepening and further challenges for testing of hypnotic depth. This is advisable only with subjects who have shown remarkable suggestibility in the waking suggestion stage.

RAPID INDUCTION TECHNIQUES

Standing Induction. Apply this technique for quick induction of very susceptible subjects—those who have responded well to testing or have been previously hypnotized. Place your hands on his shoulders, look into his eyes and, as you gently sway his shoulders from side to side, say something like this:

"Look into my eyes and relax . . . you are going into deep sleep . . . deep sleep . . . your eyes are closing now . . . you are going deep asleep . . . deep asleep . . . your eyes are closed now . . . *deep asleep* . . . deeper and deeper asleep as I guide you into this chair, you will go still deeper . . . everything will take you deeper. Now you are seated comfortably. Listen to my voice and you will feel yourself letting go and going much . . . much deeper asleep."

This can make a very dramatic presentation in front of a group of people when you have been careful to select the right subject. If a particular technique does not seem to be working, switch to another method. Calmly continue to deepen the trance. Once eye closure is accomplished, keep your composure and keep your voice steady.

ARM CATALEPSY

Demonstrate with a suggestible subject in the way explained above. Then, with an air of complete confidence, raise his arm, extend it straight out and say, "As I raise your arm, it will become stiff and rigid . . . as stiff and rigid as a bar of steel, so rigid . . . you cannot lower it, no matter how hard you try . . . try . . . you try . . . hard . . . you cannot . . . stop trying . . . and now go deep asleep . . . deep asleep . . . now you can lower your arm, and as you do so, you fall deeper asleep . . . much deeper . . . my voice takes you deeper . . . going much deeper now . . . take a deep breath and go deeper . . . inhale . . . that's good . . . exhale now and go deeper." Continue induction with the usual methods. Any of the susceptibility tests can be transferred into induction techniques. This takes advantage of the surprise element. Quick methods are excellent for demonstration purposes. They help to increase susceptibility in prospective subjects who are watching the presentation.

TRANSFERRING A TEST INTO HYPNOSIS

After the Hand Clasp Test which we described previously, say, "Now your hands are stuck tight . . . tight together . . . you cannot pull them apart . . . try, but you cannot . . . stop trying! Go deep asleep . . . deep, sound sleep. Going deeper and deeper. Now, when I try to pull your hands apart, they will loosen up and come apart easily. As they do, I want you to fall into an even deeper sleep. The deeper you go, the stronger your improvements will show."

Some people are so hypnotizable you will be able to achieve instantaneous hypnosis. Experience will help you recognize such easy subjects. Those who are eager to respond to such commands as, "your hands are stuck together," etc., without analyzing them, can be inducted rapidly and it would be a waste of your professional time to use prolonged methodology.

Transferring a test into a trance within a few minutes is feasible with about 20 percent of your patients. You will be able to recognize such a subject not only by strong responses to testing, but he may also appear a bit dazed, with a confused facial expression. The subject may also speak in a muted voice and be somewhat unstable on his feet. If so, all that may be necessary for induction is to: (1) gaze at the subject, (2) point to his eyes, and (3) command, "sleep!" This works especially well where there is a particular readiness to be helped, such as in a patient being prepared for surgery.

HEAD ROTATION METHOD

First say, "Close your eyes as I count to three and snap my fingers." After snapping your fingers, place one hand on his forehead, the other at the back of his head. Slowly rotate his head as you say: "Deep asleep now. Arms heavy, legs heavy. Deep, sound asleep quickly." Then roll the head in the opposite direction and say, "As I rotate your head the other way, I want you to go twice as deep, twice as deep . . . to do yourself twice as much good." Withdraw your hands. As the head falls forward onto his chest, continue to pyramid suggestions to go deeper and deeper. Keep in mind that the responsive subject is eager to be helped quickly. The very fact that you are an authoratative figure speeds induction.

But if such methods are used while the person is resistant, then only failure will result. Once the subject fails to be hypnotized, he becomes increasingly difficult. All techniques, therefore, for inducing "instantaneous or rapid induction" must be applied logically, taking into account all factors. The apparent suggestibility of the subject, the prestige of the operator, whether or not the person has been previously hypnotized, and other factors may influence success.

Direct Gaze

"As you gaze into my eyes, you will feel very sleepy, your eyes will close . . . close your eyes now and go deep asleep." Passes of the hand can be made around the eyes, the fingers can touch the eyelids. You may also cup your hands over the subject's eyes to suggest deepening the trance. Remember to keep your gaze fixated.

Two Pointed Fingers

Close the thumb, ring and little finger, pointing the middle and first finger directly at the eyes, separated like a V. Say, "Your eyes will close as I bring my fingers closer and closer to your eyes . . . let your eyes close now and go deep asleep."

Finger Pressures On Nerve Points

Gaze directly at subject's eyes as you place the thumb of one hand on his forehead and the thumb of the other at the back of the head. Press and say, "As I press these two areas, you will feel yourself falling into a deep . . . deep sleep. Your eyes are closing now . . . deep asleep." The head may be moved forward or downward covering the eyes.

Spiral Hypno-Disk

When using a hypno-disk as a fixation point, give the following suggestions for eye closures: "Keep your eyes fastened on the center of the wheel . . . as you watch it . . . notice that it vibrates . . . the white circles become more prominent, then the black circles become prominent. The circles seem to fade into the distance and you begin to feel as if you are being drawn into the circle . . . your breathing is deep and regular . . . you are getting drowsy, very drowsy . . . soon you will be asleep, very deep asleep. . . ."

Counting backward, say, "As I count backward from 5 to 1, your eyes will close and you will fall into a deep hypnotic sleep . . . 5, 4, 3, 2, 1 . . . deep asleep." You may also have a longer countdown if the individual seems a little tense.

Arm Catalepsy

Approach the subject confidently as you raise his arm up and extend it straight out from the shoulder, saying, "Your arm is stiff and rigid . . . as rigid as a bar of steel. You can't bend it . . . try, but you can't . . . as you try, your eyes will close . . . closed . . . deep asleep. Now your arm will relax and, as it falls down, you will go even deeper asleep."

Touch, Sight, Sound

Hand the subject an object to hold. It might be a coin, a glass ball, or a pen. Say, "As you hold this object, your hand will close over it tightly . . . the feel of the object in your hand is making you very sleepy and, as you look at it and listen to my voice, you are getting very sleepy . . . eyes closing now, deep asleep . . . your hand is closed tight on the object . . . you cannot open your hand . . . try, but you cannot . . . stop trying and go deeper asleep."

Placebo

Hold a bottle of water with a spray attached. Direct subject's gaze toward fixation point and as you begin to spray the harmless liquid on the back of his neck, say, "As I spray this liquid on your neck, it will relax you so you will fall into a deep sleep . . . your eyes are sleepy . . . very sleepy . . . the liquid is relaxing you . . . eyes closed now . . . deeper and deeper asleep." The liquid spray can be used as a deepening technique and also for the removal of psychosomatic pain.

SHORT INDUCTIONS FOR BUSY PROFESSIONALS

Transferring tests into hypnotic induction is sometimes referred to as *"The Surprise Technique."* You say, "Close your eyes and sleep!" The subject is startled by a direct command, and the mind tends to become passive, momentarily, and when suggested, "Arms heavy, legs heavy," the subject obeys because he doesn't have time to think. He is caught unawares. The critical faculties of the mind are bypassed in a moment of passivity. This will be discussed further in the section dealing with overcoming resistance.

Focus On Light. After seating the patient comfortably, suggest relaxation. Have patient look at any light used in medical examination and suggest: "Relax, look at this light. Relax all over. Listen to my voice and let yourself go. Very loose, comfortable. As you gaze at the light, your eyes are growing pleasantly drowsy and heavy. Let go of all tension, relax more and more. Eyes growing heavier and heavier, drowsy and heavy. Closing now, you are going into a deep, deep state of relaxation. Deeper and deeper into relaxation. Listen to my voice and go deeper. Nothing bothering you, feeling very well, so relaxed. Your eyes so heavy, arms heavy, relaxed all over. Deep asleep now." Proceed in the usual manner to deepen hypnosis and utilize the therapeutic state for necessary purposes. Medical examination in which instruments, i.e., eye charts, etc., are used can employ this technique. The patient is taken off-guard so that he does not have time to think or analyze suggestions of the doctor to the effect that changes are taking place. Nothing is said about what is going to take place, as customary in standard induction techniques. The patient is caught off-guard and goes along with the suggestions.

USING SOUND

Metronomes. A metronome with a slow beat can be a great assist to the hypnotist. You may produce eye closure by saying, "Listen to my voice and let my voice relax you completely. Listen and you will hear a gentle ticking, a beat of the metronome. As you listen to the beat of the metronome, the sound will take you deeper . . . deeper and deeper . . . the beat of the metronome is sending you into hypnosis . . . every beat sends you deeper into sleep . . . it says to you . . . deep . . . asleep . . . deep . . . asleep . . . each beat is lulling you deeper and deeper."

Air Conditioners or Fans. "With your eyes closed, listen to my voice and follow what I say . . . begin to concentrate on the soft, whirring sound of the air conditioner . . . the monotonous drone will lull you deeper and deeper asleep . . . the purring sound of the motor sends you deeper . . . much deeper now . . . ever deeper asleep."

Music or Music Boxes. Music can be helpful. It should be soft, slow preferably, with strings. Organs are also effective. Music should be muted in the background, never loud or close by. Say, "As you listen to the soft music, it will keep on helping you go deeper. The music is soothing, very smoothing to the nerves, lulling you deeper and deeper asleep."

Tape Recordings or Records. This is another means of relaxing anxious patients who are in the waiting room, especially at the dentist's office. Such a devise can come in handy during group hypnosis while the operator moves around and speaks softly to individual subjects. Tape recorders are also useful for developing both autohypnosis and general state of relaxation. This gives the overworked operant a rest.

Listening to Breathing. Another way to use sound for induction and also as a deepening technique is to say, "Listen to the sound of your breathing. Breathe more deeply and slowly. As the air comes in, think of it as cool and refreshing, and as you hear the sound of the air being exhaled, let that sound signal you to go into hypnosis. Each breath that you breathe will take you deeper. Listen to your breathing and go deeper."

DEEPENING TECHNIQUES

There are numerous methods for deepening hypnosis, once the subject is relaxed and cooperating. The most effective techniques create an inner change in the state of one's mind, an awareness of the altered consciousness. This is referred to as "deepening through realization." Basic techniques for deepening are:

1. Realization through awareness.
2. Pyramiding of suggestions.
3. Reinduction within the same trance.
4. Endogenic hypnosis suggesting mind/body contact.
5. Picture visualization. Use of blackboard, mirror, etc.
6. Sensorimotor reactions. Hand levitation, rigid catalepsy.
7. Pressures, passes, and stroking.
8. The Hammock, Tunnel, and Canoe techniques.
9. Shock or confusion techniques.
10. Drugs, such as Sodium Amytal, Sodium Pentothal, and Trilene.

DEEPENING THROUGH REALIZATION AND PYRAMIDING HYPNOSIS

Deepening hypnosis must be approached from a very different point of view than *overcoming resistance*. True, in overcoming resistance most of the deepening techniques are employed, but the psychology involved is radically different. During the routine procedure of hypnotic conditioning, the average subject who wants to be hypnotized will follow the suggestions of the operator. When he is told, "Everything takes you deeper . . . go . . . deeper," *he accepts the idea that the things the hypnotist says are true*. The refractory subject, however, will analyze everything, argue with himself as to why it isn't working, and not even realize he is doing it. When the subject fails to respond to the usual deepening techniques, he then becomes a refractory subject, and the approach must be adjusted to the individual situation.

After the initial induction technique, the subject fixates his eyes and soon eye closure takes place. Begin pyramiding hypnosis in the following manner: "Deep . . . deep asleep . . . going deeper. Now count backward from 100 to 0. And with every count, go deeper, counting and going deeper with every count . . . if you lose count, just pick up wherever you think you left off, it doesn't matter. Just keep on counting and going deeper. When you reach 0, raise the index finger of your right hand to indicate you have reached 0 and have taken yourself down deeper." When finger rises, proceed:

"Good, now I want you to picture yourself strolling in the park on a lovely summer day. As you walk along, feeling so peaceful, so relaxed, you see two large trees and a hammock swinging between them. Go to the hammock, let your body sink into it, relaxing more and more . . . the sun is shining down, warm and pleasant. The hammock is swinging back and forth, back and forth, taking you deeper, and deeper asleep. As you lie here, relaxing, going deeper and deeper, you visualize a blackboard before you . . . you take a piece of chalk and draw a large square on the blackboard and trace it around clockwise three times, around and around, and this takes you deeper. And now, in the other direction, around and around, and this takes you much deeper.

"Now you erase the square and begin writing and erasing the alphabet all the way from A to Z and each letter you write and erase takes you deeper. Now you write A. See it vividly in your mind's eye and as you erase the letter A, go deeper. Now write B . . . and erase it . . . keep on writing and erasing, writing and erasing. Each letter takes you deeper. If you lose your place, just pick up wherever you think you left off. It doesn't matter. Keep on writing and erasing and going deeper with each letter. Raise the index finger of your right hand when you reach Z . . . good . . . and now, as I count back from 5 to 0, you will go deeper . . . everything I say takes you deeper . . . 5, 4, 3, 2, 1, 0 . . . deeper and deeper asleep to do yourself the most good."

HAND LEVITATION

"Concentrate on your right hand . . . soon, you will feel your right hand becoming light, as light as a feather. Your fingers begin to twitch. Your hand will begin to rise, getting lighter and lighter . . . so very light as though you had a balloon tied to the wrist, pulling it upward, up, up . . . your hand is growing lighter and lighter rising up, higher and higher . . . higher . . . so very light, always lighter . . . soon it will float up and touch your face. When it does, you will fall into a deeper state of hypnosis. Deeper and deeper now . . . very deep . . . touching soon . . . and when your hand touches your face, you will feel yourself falling into a deep, deep sleep.

"Touching now and going deeper . . . much deeper . . . as I press your shoulders, you will go deeper . . . deeper . . . as I stroke your forehead, go deeper. And now, visualize yourself walking in the country again, beside a lovely lake . . . clear and beautiful. There's a boat drawn up beside the shore, the boatman beckons you to get in and take a ride. You climb in, sink down into the soft cushions, trailing your fingers in the water. The sun is shining down, warm and pleasant . . . the water is warm on your fingers. As the boat glides along, you are trailing your fingers in the water, so relaxing, while going more deeply asleep . . . deeper and deeper . . . and now, the boat has drifted into the shade, and here as you trail your fingers in the water, it is icy cold . . . very cold . . . you can hardly hold your hand in the water . . . you will be glad when the boat goes into the sun again.

"Now it has, and the water is warm in the sun. As the boat glides along, you are going more deeply and deeply asleep. . . ."

TUNNEL TECHNIQUE

" . . . the boat is drifting into a tunnel . . . a lovely grotto, like the Blue Grotto in Capri . . . there's a soft blue light here and you are relaxing more and more. You see beautiful paintings on the wall . . . lovely paintings in soft colors and you hear soft music in the background, your favorite melody. Beautiful soft music like a lullaby, lulling you more and more deeply asleep. And now the boat comes out into the bright sunshine again and as the boat drifts along the shore, you see lovely flowers . . . fragrant, lovely flowers smelling sweet. And now you come back to shore where you climb out and walk up a grassy hill and there's an apple tree . . . you see some lovely red apples and pick one, take a bite of the apple . . . it's sweet and tasty, very good."

Picture visualization routines such as the blackboard, canoe, and tunnel techniques include images incorporating the five senses. The subject "sees" the boat and pictures on the walls, "feels" the temperature of the water—hot and cold, hears music, smells flowers, and tastes fruit.

ANOTHER SENSORIMOTOR METHOD

Hand levitation deepens through sensorimotor reaction. There are several other similar exercises. Another is *the revolving hands method.* Take the subject's hands and set them in motion. Revolve them around each other as you say, "Now your hands are revolving round and round, going round and round, making circles. And it has become automatic . . . they keep revolving . . . around and around . . . automatically, they keep going, round and round, faster and faster. It's impossible for you to stop them. They keep going around and around as you go deeper and deeper. Try, but you cannot stop. Your hands keep on turning, and you keep on going deeper . . . deeper and deeper. Now your hands start turning in the opposite direction, going round and round . . . faster . . . round and round. And you keep going deeper, still deeper as your hands keep on going round. Now, you can't stop them. They are turning round automatically. Try to stop them but you cannot . . . stop trying and go deeper.

"Relax your hands now and as they drop back in your lap, you go much deeper . . . deeper and deeper . . . everything takes you deeper."

The induction employs counting, picture visualization, sensorimotor reactions, hand levitation, and revolving hands, as well as the tunnel and canoe techniques. Realization of hypnosis is increased by hand levitation and the revolving hands with challenge to stop. Through the subject's awareness of a change in consciousness, deepening takes place. *The challenges are important for establishing the awareness of hypnosis in the subject.*

PRESSURE AND PASSES

The passing of hands over the subject without actually touching him was widely used in ancient times, but has gone out of vogue with modern scientific hypnosis methods such as biofeedback. However, if the subject believes passes or other contacts will deepen his hypnotic state, he will tend to respond in the manner suggested by the operator. Passes are made down the arms, chest, and shoulders, while suggestions are made to go into a deep sleep. When the subject's eyes are closed, the passes should be made between the subject's eyes and the source of light in the room. Downward passes are generally used when putting the subject under hypnosis and upward passes when awakening him. A countdown while making downward passes will strengthen the induction and a count upward while awakening also works well.

Pressures are made on the subject's shoulders with accompanying suggestions for cooperation in inducing hypnosis as well as going deeper on command. The operator simply places his hands on both shoulders, or only on one shoulder and then bears down lightly, while whispering in the subject's ear, "Deep asleep!" Repeat several times to reinforce.

Passes over the forehead are executed by using the two forefingers which move from the bridge of the subject's nose out to the temples. When you reach the temples, exert a slight pressure, and then release your fingers. Repeat several times. This has a soothing and relaxing effect on the subject and is recommended for patients with eye problems or headaches.

It is very important to let the subject know in advance when you are going to make physical contact, no matter how slight. Say, "In a moment I will make passes over your forehead and this will take you deeper," or "I am going to press your fingernails and when you feel my touch, this will be a signal to go deeper and never bite your nails again." Pressing the fingernails is also used to reinforce any kind of suggestion. It has a double purpose, to deepen and also to implant suggestions.

CONFUSION AND SHOCK TECHNIQUE

Take advantage of the surprise element by making suggestions which confuse the subject. An example is to have the subject concentrate on the finger method and then transfer it into an induction. "As I place my finger between your eyes, roll your eyes up, following my finger. As your eyes roll up, close your lids and relax. With your eyes in this position, your eyes are stuck tight . . . try to open them, but you can't."

The operator places one hand across the subject's forehead, the other at the back of the neck. Rotate the head as you say, "Arms heavy, legs heavy, deep asleep . . . deeper and deeper asleep. Begin counting backwards from 20 to 0, each count taking you deeper and deeper."

DEEPENING BY COUNTING

Have the subject count to himself silently backward from 20 to 0 while you count aloud from 0 to 20. Have him concentrate first on one part of his body, then another—right hand, left shoulder, left hand, the top of his head, take a deep breath, hold his breath while he counts backward from 5 to 0 and you count aloud from 0 to 5. Awaken him quickly without warning and then immediately put him under again.

Reinduction during the same session catches the resistant subject by surprise and often proves the solution to his inner fears of hypnosis. Repeat several times that each time he drifts into the hypnotic state, he will go deeper than before. When you awaken him between inductions say, "Deep asleep—again . . . much deeper than before." Reinduct swiftly, allowing him only enough time to open his eyes and make some slight movement. Do not arouse him completely.

Stress in an authoritative voice that he "must go deeper than before" as you repeat the counting technique. An interesting variation on traditional counting methods is the following. "I am going to begin counting in a different way. As I count backwards you will go more deeply asleep and when I count forward, you will awaken a little with each count. Now go deeper as I count from 10 to 0 . . . 10 deeper . . . 9 deeper . . . 8 deeper . . . etc." When you get to 0, reverse the counting this way: "Now you will awaken just a little . . . 1 . . . 2 . . . 3 . . . now deeper again . . . much deeper than the last time . . . 10 deeper . . . 9 deeper . . . 8 deeper . . . etc." Repeat this routine several times. And then switch the signals. "When I count forward you will go deeper and when I count backward you will awaken. . . ."

Because you reverse the signals, the subject becomes confused and finds himself concentrating more than he would ordinarily. This switch also makes him feel the contrast in state of consciousness from going deeper to awakening. This produces a greater realization of the part he is playing in his own therapy.

Counting techniques can be varied in many ways. You can involve the subject by having him count silently to himself as you count out loud. Tell him to count by fives or twos as an alternate to simple counting. The length of the countdown can be from 1,000 to 0 or from 5 to 0. This depends on the length of the hypnosis session and the need of the particular individual.

Combining counting with breathing for deepening is also very effective. Say, "Count off ten deep breaths and take yourself deeper with each breath." You can also combine counting, breathing, and giving suggestion, "As you count off ten breaths, tell yourself 'I feel full and satisfied with the minimum of food.'"

POSTHYPNOTIC SUGGESTION

A good reaction carried out after the conclusion of the hypnotic session is referred to as a posthypnotic phenomenon. Stimulus for the improved activity comes from the suggestion which the hypnotherapist gave to the subject. The phrasing of the posthypnotic suggestion should be carefully worked out with the subject before induction. In this way the subject is taught to accept responsibility for the degree of his response to therapy.

Bizarre suggestions that challenge rational thinking should be avoided. Here is an example. Albert T., 54 years of age, complained of impotence which had troubled him for six years. I asked what sort of suggestions he would like to receive once he was hypnotized.

"Tell me I will be able to perform like a superstud. Like I did when I was nineteen," he insisted.

I offered the wording used by people with similar problems: "healthy and normal sexual function."

"Oh, no. That's too mild," he persisted. Suggest that I perform like a superstud. Make it real strong." I followed his instructions, word for word.

That night, when the moment of truth arrived, poor Albert was embarrassed. He couldn't believe his own suggestions because the idea seemed too ridiculous to him. Fortunately, at his second session, he worked out believable suggestions. "Each time I have sexual intercourse, I will show improvement. I am healthy and normal and soon will function with full power and vigor."

During the next visit, he reported a definite change for the better. After eight sessions of hypnotherapy, Albert felt he could carry on with just self-hypnosis and an occasional booster session.

Accepting suggestion involves a personal belief system. Therefore, directives to the subconscious must be realistic and thoroughly understood. Only then will posthypnotic activity replace unwanted behavior. Suggestions must be keyed to the real needs and desires of the subject so that his emotional drive will be stirred. With proper motivation, a posthypnotic suggestion may last days or even years. Sometimes it lasts forever, like the posthypnotic suggestion, "Never touch a cigarette for the rest of your life," or "You will never gain back a single pound that you lost."

Posthypnotic suggestion in such cases is reinforced during periods of meditation or keen awareness.

For people who have special difficulty in managing stress, weekly hypnotherapy sessions are encouraged as a preventive measure against the build-up of tension. Posthypnotic suggestions are worded to help them remain relaxed under trying conditions. "No matter what happens in the family or on the job, you will stay calm and think of positive solutions."

Many professionals feel that the depth of trance at the time of administering posthypnotic suggestion is critical. This is not necessarily so. While a deep level of trance is always helpful in establishing response to hypnotic suggestion, a light trance can also work if the posthypnotic suggestions are repeated many times. Keep in mind that the light trance subject can become a deeper subject the next time. Therefore, give him a posthypnotic suggestion as follows. "The next time you go into hypnosis you will go twice as deep, to do yourself twice as much good."

Posthypnotic suggestion is most effective when tied in with an everyday activity, especially when the activity is as natural as breathing. "Each time you take a breath you will feel full and satisfied and will postpone eating until the proper time. Each breath will satisfy you as if you have just eaten."

For the person working on an improved figure, try this, "Each time you pass a mirror, you will remember to stand up straight, pull in your stomach and hold your head up proudly."

For the alcoholic, it might be, "Anytime you see another person drinking you will remember that you cannot handle alcohol and that you prefer to remain sober. You will have a nonalcoholic beverage, instead."

Posthypnotic behavior modification sometimes works well with aversion techniques. For example, a subject who wants to stop smoking might be told, "If you *buy* a pack of cigarettes, you will have an uneasy feeling in your stomach. If you *light* one, a sense of nausea. If you *inhale*, the nausea will become increasingly worse. You will have to put it out, or it will cause you to throw up." Before employing aversion techniques, discuss it with your subject. He may decide to cooperate rather than anticipate a unpleasant reaction.

Some people are very happy with aversion suggestions. I remember a woman who was strongly allergic to chocolate. "Please tell me it will smell and taste like feces . . . like dog poo." She was adamant and I complied and the results were outstanding. She lost the urge for chocolate after just one session.

Take the time to talk it over. Get to know the subject. What is just right for one individual may be just terrible for the next one.

Another important application of posthypnotic suggestion is in transferring control to the subject. This is done toward the end of each session, before wake-up and at the termination of the therapy. The object of transference is to enable him to provoke the phenomenon in himself by himself. In a case of insomnia you might say, "Each night when you go to bed, tell yourself, "Sleep through the night. Wake up rested in the morning! Giving yourself suggestions will work just as forcefully as when I give them to you."

AWAKENING THE HYPNOTIZED SUBJECT

No one has ever failed to awaken from hypnosis, even when the operator has performed inexpertly. The problem for the beginner is to induce hypnosis. Awakening is the easiest part. If the operator should drop dead, which is highly unlikely, or leave the room without instructing the subject when to awaken, the subject would simply wake up. This would happen naturally, of his own free will, without a suggestion to do so.

Some subjects will awaken by themselves the moment the hypnotist stops talking. These are the light subjects. There are also some somnambulist subjects who will take a short nap, if you let them. This could last from five minutes to a half hour, depending on how deep they have drifted and how tired they were when they arrived.

Inform the subject when it is almost time to awaken. Say, "In a little while it will be time to wake up. You will feel as if you have slept for several nighttime hours. Rested and refreshed. However, this session will not interfere with your sleep tonight. You will sleep especially well." Most hypnotists are counting to arouse the subject. It is wise to combine the wake-up with positive suggestions of well-being.

"When you hear the number 10 (or 5 or 3), you will wake up feeling better than you have ever felt before.

One. "Get ready to wake up now, feeling just fine."
Two. "Your mind is clear and keen. Memory perfect."
Three. "Looking forward to a pleasant evening (day, week)."
Four. "Cheerful, happy, confident with positive outlook."
Five. "You will follow through on all of your suggestions."

Six. Give Him His Top Priority Posthypnotic Suggestion.
Seven. "Repeat . . . Eight . . . Repeat . . . Nine . . . Repeat."
Ten. "Wide awake now! Feeling great!"

For the person who has reached only a light state of hypnosis, a count of 3 is usually sufficient. "When I count to 3 you will awaken feeling fine. *One.* "You are ready to awaken."

Two. "You are beginning to awaken."

Three. "You are wide awake now."

If the eyes are slow to open you may snap your fingers or clap your hands for emphasis, but this is usually unnecessary. If you are doing a demonstration it might add a bit of pizzazz to clap your hands. This is also one way to gain the attention of an audience that may have become drowsy.

There are some subjects who are reluctant to give up the pleasant euphoric feeling of the trance. When a subject regularly drifts into *delta*-deep sleep, he may be doing so to avoid the acceptance of posthypnotic suggestion. In such rare cases, tap his fingertips as you give the wake-up suggestions and raise the volume of your voice. When you speak faster and more loudly, you spur the brainwaves back to the *beta* rhythm.

How to Overcome Resistance

Occasionally a person may seem willing to cooperate and yet unconsciously resist the process. Usually, this is due to two causes. On one hand, some fear may stem from misconceptions about hypnosis, resulting in a high level of nervous tension. Begin by overcoming obstacles to relaxation. Is the light in the room soft enough? Is the temperature comfortable? Is there a chair or couch suitable for reclining? Is a visit to the bathroom necessary? Are there any unpleasant noises such as the ringing telephones? And—most important—does the subject have subconscious fears that must be eliminated?

On the other hand, a latent fear of losing control and revealing hidden secrets may exist. This may surface in the form of trying too hard instead of relaxing and letting the hypnotic feeling happen. A tense, overanxious person often makes this mistake and the hypnotist must find a way to overcome any interference.

During the initial interview, ask your subject what experience he has had with hypnosis. Often people have seen stage hypnotists demonstrate with highly suggestible subjects who are commanded to perform embarrassing acts. They may expect magic or, conversely, believe they are bad subjects because once they did not go "under the spell" of the stage hypnotist.

"I'm too strong-willed to be hypnotized," said one prospective subject.

Others, having witnessed stage hypnosis, will expect one session to correct a lifetime of problems. Anticipation of results, whether negative or positive, has a great deal to do, not only with the initial induction, but with future results from continued therapy for habit correction.

REEVALUATE YOUR METHODS

One approach to helping the refractory subject is to observe how he reacts to different testing techniques—permissive or authoritarian. Test him again, executing several permissive and then several authoritarian techniques. Notice the difference in response. A classic example of improper application of technique follows:

The subject is passive, eager with eyes wide, dazed and trusting. This subject is already partially under self-hypnosis, is already motivated and expecting to be put under. Here the operator should work quickly. In such a case, there is no need for long, drawn-out, progressive relaxation methods. If you use slow, permissive, lullaby-type of voice, he will not respond favorably because he expected to go deep asleep immediately. The subject's expectations should be fulfilled by the therapist. That is why it is important to interview the patient and ask what his previous experience has been in this area. Ask him, "What do you expect will happen?" Based on the answer you receive, plus the results from the testing, you will have your answer about whether to employ authoritative or permissive methodology.

When a subject declares, "I cannot be hypnotized. My mind is too strong," respond affirmatively, "That's fine. The stronger your mind is, the greater will be the results from hypnosis. We will use your mental power to make it work." Then explain the role of self-hypnosis in every induction. For this person, the permissive approach will work better because he is on guard against being controlled. Once he is convinced that he is always in command of his therapy, he will take pride in taking himself deeper. Underneath his reluctance is usually fear of other people, so speak softly, slowly and "suggest" rather than "command."

You must suit the technique to the subject. The rapid induction style that works wonders for the docile, agreeable person, would, on the other hand, encounter resistance in the strong-minded questioning type who does not like to take "bossy" orders. Here you should apply a slower, permissive, gentle method to gain trust. Make him feel "it happens because *he* wants it." In this way, the subject senses he is in control and he will cooperate.

With the white-collar or intellectual type of individual, it helps to discuss various methods and give the subject a choice. One may like the elevator routine (described below), while another fears and hates elevators. And so with other exercises, such as counting, hand levitation, etc. Some people have little imagination, cannot imagine a balloon tied to the wrist or any of the picture visualization methods, but counting holds their attention. An accountant, for example, relates to numbers; an artist relates to visualization.

Repeated reinduction brings realization of an altered state of consciousness. First, hypnotize the subject to a light or medium level and say, "Each time you go into hypnosis, you go deeper. That's the way it works—deeper and deeper each time . . . wake up now." The operator snaps fingers or claps hands. *Give No Warning.* This action brings with it the realization of a difference in consciousness because of its suddenness.

Then say, *with authority,* "Deep asleep again, deeper than ever, go deeper this time, deeper each time." Continue rapidly with deepening techniques. Awaken the subject. Then, reinduce the trance state once more. State clearly and repeatedly, "Each time you go into hypnosis, you go deeper. Each time you wake up, you will be ready to go back even deeper. That's the way hypnosis really works. Now get ready to go much deeper."

Reinduction (going in and out of hypnosis) within the same session and at successive sessions deepens the trance level. This should be explained in the beginning and restated from time to time. Rapid awakening and reinduction will break stubborn resistance markedly. The subject is compelled to admit something is happening because he notices changes in his state of consciousness from awake to drowsiness. Another form of reinduction within the same trance is accomplished by a simple method. Say, "Now I am going to count in a special way. When I count backward, you go deeper. When I count forward, you awaken a little more. Then, when I resume counting backward, you go much deeper. First, I will count from 10 to 0, and with each backward count, you go deeper . . . 10, deeper . . . 9, deeper . . . deeper and deeper . . . very deep now . . . 6, deeper . . . deeper . . . 5 . . . deeper . . . 4 . . . much deeper . . . 3 . . . deeper . . . 2 . . . much deeper now . . . 1, 0 . . . very deep . . . and now, waking up a little . . . 1 . . . a little more . . . 2 . . . waking up more . . . 3 . . . a little more . . . 4 . . . more still . . . 5, 6, 7, 8, 9, 10 *awaken* . . . now deeper . . . 10 . . . asleep . . . 9, 8, 7, 6, 5, 4, 3, 2, 1 . . . deeper asleep. . . ."

Suggest the subject take up the count himself and deepen his own trance, counting forward and backward. This gives the timid subject a sense of security when he realizes he is participating in the process of self-hypnotic conditioning. This exercise is the beginning of self-hypnosis. Few hypnotists know about this method or realize how much can be accomplished with subject participation. Because it is rather confusing, it requires concentration. The greatest value is the deepening and reawakening procedure which brings the realization of a change of consciousness. This is sometimes referred to as "the confusion technique" because the subject is not permitted time to analyze and intellectualize what is going on with his subliminal thought processes.

APPROACH TO NEW TECHNIQUES

For the difficult subject, a change of scene is often helpful. Another room, chair or couch. Lights dimmed low. If he is fearful, lights turned up. Make the next session decidedly different from the first one—if past results were inadequate. If you haven't used any special effects before, such as flickering lights, or a hypno-disc machine, do so now. Combine them with various body-awareness techniques for pyramiding hypnosis to a deeper state. Most subjects tend to get tired and bored when gazing at an exterior point of fixation such as a light or hypno-disc, which helps speed induction.

THE AUXILIARY HYPNOTIST

Testing and induction phases are conducted as usual. At a given point, the hypnotist calls upon the auxiliary hypnotist to verify the progress being made. Sometimes no progress is evident. However, when such a discussion indicates that there is progress, it invariably implants the *suggestion* of cooperation. Hypnotist #1 says, "He is going deeper, his breathing is slowing up remarkably, he's relaxing wonderfully, isn't he?" Hypnotist #2 confirms this in a positive tone of voice, expressing amazement at the rapid progress of the subject and commending him for his ability to respond. The purpose is to get the subject to think *with the hypnotist and nothing else.* When he thinks "deep sleep" to the exclusion of all other thoughts, he will indeed feel like drifting into a deep sleep.

THE PLACEBO TECHNIQUE

The placebo is sometimes given to a patient by a medical hypnotist in the form of innocuous pills which have no real curative value except in the patient's mind. Such a medication can be given with a suggestion it will cause the subject to go into a deep trance. Pressures with the fingers on nerve points and "passes" are used much the same way. They work because the subject expects them to work. Various "hypnotic areas" can be pressed with suggestions: "As I press your temples, you will feel yourself going deeper. Pressing on these areas causes you to go much deeper." The temples and back of the neck are special points for pressure. Liquid can be sprayed on the back of the neck, giving a cool feeling, at the same time suggesting that the subject go deeper into hypnosis.

CAROTID ARTERY PRESSURES

This method for "instant" hypnotic induction is often overrated, misunderstood and dangerous. Pressing arteries can cause serious damage, even death. Nonetheless, some uninformed hypnotists use this method. Pressure on the carotid sinus causes instant collapse, and sometimes the subject can be manipulated into hypnosis and respond to suggestions. But it has never been proven that this condition is hypnosis. This state, bordering on semi-consciousness, is usually brief. The technique involves a morbid delusion of ego on the part of the practitioner and should be forbidden by law.

GROUP HYPNOSIS

The group setting can provide an ideal way of reassuring the fearful subject. Seeing others who have derived benefits from hypnosis will help the newcomer. Begin the session by asking the experienced members for progress reports. The recounting of positive results will stimulate the beginner's interest and his desire to get into the swing of therapy. Select a good subject and demonstrate hypnotic phenomena such as hand levitation, or rigid arm catalepsy. After demonstrating with one subject, place the entire group under hypnosis using customary techniques. Handling a slow subject in this way works well and prepares him for private sessions with better results.

CONFUSION TECHNIQUES

Recalcitrant subjects often respond to unusual methods that catch them unaware. In producing the various responses such as eye closure, arms rising and falling, clenched hands, hand levitation, etc., rapid suggestions for contradictory actions are made casually, as if by mistake. Reverse suggestion of "the left hand light, the right hand heavy," to the opposite.

Example (hand levitation): "Your left hand is heavy, as heavy as lead, while your right hand is light and floating up . . . your left hand is very light, floating up fast . . . your right hand is heavy . . . both hands are stuck. You can't lift them . . . now they are both floating up . . . now take a deep breath. Your left hand is heavy, as heavy as lead . . . your right hand is light, getting lighter and lighter . . . take another deep breath. Inhale. Exhale. And go deeper asleep. . . ." After a time, resume levitation until response is adequate. The subject will then be glad to return to a consistent pattern of suggestion.

A second example (arms rising and falling): "Your right arm is heavy, it has a heavy book on it, it's falling. And your left arm has a balloon tied to the wrist. It's floating up. Now your right arm feels very light, floating up like a feather on a breeze. Now your left arm feels heavy and is falling down fast, heavier and heavier. Take a deep breath and hold it . . . exhale. Now both arms are rigid."

"Now relax them and go deeper. Your right arm is getting heavier and heavier. Falling . . . your left arm rising . . . the right is falling, the left is rising."

A third example (multiple confusion technique): "Stand over here, put your toes and heels together. Close your eyes and take a deep breath. Hold it as long as you can. Now exhale and take another deep breath and hold it as long as you can. Exhale." The hypnotist stands behind the subject, takes hold of his shoulders, and starts rotating him in a circle, keeping up an emphatic string of contradictory suggestions. Then awaken him without warning time after time, saying, "Deeper each time I awaken you."

"Going to sleep soon, but first, take a deep breath—hold it. Exhale again. Inhale. Hold it. Exhale . . . close your eyes. Start counting aloud backward from 100. Raise your arms straight out. Your right arm is heavy. It has a heavy book on it, forcing it down. There is a balloon tied to your left thumb, pulling it up . . . up. Keep on counting . . . going deep asleep. Take another deep breath. Keep on counting. Your left arm rising up . . . higher and higher. . . . Your right hand rising now, your left arm falling . . . getting heavier and heavier . . . keep on counting . . . deep asleep now. Each time deeper than the time before . . . losing count. Almost unable to count. Wake up. Open your eyes. Now close them again and go deeper. Deeper each time . . . begin counting again . . . legs beginning to grow limp . . . forgetting the count. Hardly able to count. Drop into this chair and go into a deep sleep."

Rapid awakening and reinduction is in itself very effective for deepening the trance. You can, in additon to the reinduction method, combine several confusion techniques. Once you have accomplished disassociation through the postural sway, suggest heavy rhythmic breathing in tempo to the swaying, "As you sway breathe in slowly and deeply; as you sway in the opposite direction, exhale and go deeper."

Giving many commands in rapid succession is especially confusing to the analytical person. This approach gives him no opportunity to rationalize. Taken off guard, he becomes overwhelmed by the rapid change from one directive to another. The rapid induction and re-awakening, plus commands to concentrate on breathing and swaying, soon become too much to think about. When he hears the final command, "Now close your eyes and go into a deep sleep," he welcomes the release from having to concentrate on changing suggestions and drops into a trance level without further resistance.

Before bringing such a subject out of hypnosis, instruct him as follows: "The next time you need to be hypnotized, it will be much easier. Now that you have discovered how pleasant it can be, you will look forward to the experience. All resistance is now gone. You now realize that you have always had inner control and could wake up on your own if you wanted to. You choose to be hypnotized for your own good and, therefore, next time you will cooperate much more."

At the next session, begin by telling him, "Last time you did very well, but this time you will do even better. Each time you are hypnotized, it will be easier and easier and will do you more and more good." This time he will respond to a standard technique more readily. After induction suggest, "Now I want you to go as deep as you did last time by cooperating in this way. Count backwards silently, from 10 to 0, and as you do so, take yourself just as deep as you were before."

You have now involved the subject in helping you hypnotize him.

NARCO-HYPNOSIS: LAST RESORT

In the hands of a skilled medical hypnotist, drugs may prove useful in helping a patient whose resistance stems from phobia or extreme lack of motivation. While it is always best to produce trance naturally and with the patient's cooperation, there are cases where physical or emotional trauma makes concentration impossible. In such cases, drugs such as Sodium Amytol and Sodium Pentothal have been applied with speedy results. However, to avoid dependence on drugs during future inductions, the patient should be told, "In the future, you will be able to enter the hypnotic state when told to do so. You will simply remember how good it feels and be able to return to the pleasant trance level without the future use of drugs."

The proper time to implant this suggestion is before administering the drug, while the patient is still in a conscious state. There is a tendency, in using narco-hypnosis, to overdose. When the dosage is heavy, the subject will tend to drift too deeply into slumber and lose suggestibility. Remember hypnosis is *theta*, the threshold to sleep. Going too deep takes one into *delta*, where suggestibility is lost.

When skillfully and sparingly utilized, results with drugs can be remarkable in saving time and uncovering, as in psychotherapy, deeply buried traumatic material. In cases of drug or alcohol addiction, narco-hypnosis is often indicated because there is a basic reluctance to cooperate in overcoming the addiction. Because such subjects are accustomed to being dependent on a substance outside of their own power, a drug can prove temporarily useful.

During wartime, narco-hypnosis has often been widely used to extract information from captured enemy troops. Espionage and counter-espionage forces also employ this method because of its speed. It has also been used to get weary soldiers back into action. Hypnosis tends to lower the stress, enabling the soldier to temporarily overcome environmental pressure. Practitioners should be aware that there is a difference between trance induction and trance utilization. Realizing the trance to be a period of receptivity, suggestions must be formulated that will be adhered to by the subject in a waking state. Stress reactions must be unlearned under hypnosis and better reactions learned. Carefully formulated suggestions evoke cooperation and promote the fulfillment of the patient's potential.

In psychoanalysis, there have been positive reports of the application of Trilene (Trichlorethylene), a drug used as an inhalant for deepening hypnosis. Spontaneous abreaction of traumatic memory frequently occurs even without specific suggestion or age regression techniques. Trilene is simple to use and, in the hands of a professional, harmless. It leaves no unpleasant aftereffects. The response is fast and brief unless the drug is used repeatedly. While less effective in catalyzing induction than Sodium Pentothal and Sodium Amytal, its benefits as an adjunct to hypnosis for memory recall should be noted.

It has been my experience that using drugs rarely induces hypnosis without the added skill of techniques such as progressive relaxation and suggestion. What can be said for drugs is that they may be of help to some medical people in reducing the time of induction. Their effect is to facilitate cooperation in patients with musculoskeletal tensions of an extreme nature. In cases where patients are not motivated to accept suggestion, narcotics are of little value.

HOW TO USE DRUGS FOR HYPNOSIS

Physicians who frequently use hypnosis inform me that some of the tranquilizing agents can be helpful in decreasing central automatic reactivity and in maintaining a receptive cortical pattern. Meprobamate preparations and phenobarbital may facilitate cooperation in patients with unusual nervous tension problems. Sodium Amytol or Pentobarbital are used intravenously, while Trilene may be administered by inhalation.

When a drug is used intravenously, it is injected into the median basilic vein in the antecubital fossa. Dosage will vary, three to fourteen grains in distilled water, 10 cc or more. The less, the better, keeping in mind always that the real success of all hypnotic technique depends mainly upon the strength of the relationship between hypnotist and subject. From a practical viewpoint, the most important consideration is not so much which technique brings the subject into the hypnotic state, but rather how to adminster the therapy once the receptive state is reached.

In addition to their medical application, sometimes drugs will be used to induce a hypnotic state in order to learn information during a criminal investigation. Where the subject is overly tense and has difficulty relaxing enough to be hypnotized, a drug can sometimes be used effectively (with the person's permission). Sodium Pentothal is sometimes referred to as *the truth serum*. Used properly, it will loosen resistance and bring back forgotten material buried away because of stress. It is not used for interrogating criminals, but rather in working with cooperative witnesses.

The procedure works as follows: after the drug is administered by a qualified person, the physician instructs the subject to count backward from 100. The person's voice will begin to falter, and finally he will stop counting altogether and slump over. His jaw drops; relaxation of muscles to the extent that they become limp is noticeable. Suggestion will produce effective results in some subjects, but not all. Some will merely drift to sleep before the suggestions can work. After sleep, the patient remembers nothing. Others retain enough consciousness to remain in a trance level. At this point, it is wise for the hypnotist to suggest strongly that, hereafter, the subject will go into a deep hypnotic trance without drugs anytime the hypnotist suggests sleep.

Curiously, most subjects swear they were not hypnotized, but simply "knocked out," because their own sense of control was sidestepped by the narcotic. However, if induced a few minutes later, the subject will immediately go into a deep trance and phenomena can be reproduced. This method is extremely efficient. The only value of drugs lies in their effect on the following inductions, which has brought the subject's own state of mind about naturally.

THE USE OF TRILENE (TRICHLORETHYLENE)

Dampen a swab of cotton with Trilene and hold it over the subject's nose while giving hypnotic induction suggestions. Have the subject inhale the fumes and suggest he concentrate on going deeper. Inhalation of Trilene deepens hypnosis rapidly and produces abreaction of traumatic incidents. The degree of realism is extreme and the relief afterward is marked. Suggest that the inhalation of "this pleasant aroma will help you in every way. This is a natural substance, very beneficial in every way."

Explain in advance of administering the drug: "Trilene is a mild anesthetic used in minor surgical cases. Continued use is not recommended though it is harmless and non-habit forming." This method is often used in Great Britain and the Scandinavian countries as an aid to psychotherapy. Some of the results have been remarkable.

When using such drugs as Sodium Pentothal, suggestions of going deeper next time without drugs should be applied at the deepest trance level. Use "signal technique" such as "when I say deep asleep and count backward from 5 to 1, you will go even deeper than you are now. Any time that I say . . . 3 . . . you will go deeper than you are now . . . deeper each time."

EMOTIONAL RAPPORT

Popular misconceptions about hypnosis stem from fear of passing control over to the hypnotist and anxiety about not coming out of the hypnotic state. Operationally, hypnosis produces best results when favorable mental communication is established between hypnotist and subject. Acceptance of the operator requires emotional rapport because most uninitiated subjects are inclined to be fearful and doubtful. Therefore, the professional must inspire confidence and project a genuine desire to help. Emotional warmth is more likely to work in trance induction than dependence upon techniques alone.

While teaching hypnosis to both the lay person and professionals, I have noticed how the application and utilization varies from one practitioner to another. The presence of trust is as important to the success of the hypnotist as it is to that of any other healer. Many people are not suited to the practice of professional hypnosis because of personality limitations. No matter how well they may master methods and techniques, little can be accomplished without the ability to establish empathetic contact with the subject.

In order for the brain to accelerate healing, one must first reach the trance level. Intelligence in other areas has no bearing on the ability to benefit from suggestion. Suspicion and resistance are the most serious deterents, for they create anxiety, which in turn militates against the relaxation of the mind essential to begin the hypnosis process.

Cooperation on the part of the subject is necessary since *no one can be hypnotized against his will.* Therefore, the professional should be less authoritarian and more sympathetic in his attitude. Hypnosis is not a battle of wills between hypnotist and subject. Rather, it is a situation in which the two must work together harmoniously with the best interests of the patient in mind.

The emotions play a strong part in the learning process and, for this reason, we begin suggestion by evoking pleasant emotions in the subject. This can be quite rewarding. Many hypnotic subjects experience deep emotional reactions during early stages of induction. A blissful expression floods the face as stresses melt away. Suggestions given at this time are very effective.

The sensitive hypnotist who is capable of sufficient insight into the personality and needs of his subject can use this open emotional readiness to put the suggestions through skillfully. This is proper use of hypnosis. Freud speaks of "distributions of mental energy." To combine the proper distribution of both mental and emotional energy seems logical. The patient learns to redistribute emotional energies into better channels from negative to positive. This channeling can be dramatically effective, and actually inspire hope where none existed before.

In emotional states, the hypnotist with insight will sense the right moment for implanting suggestions strengthened by the psychic fusion of hypnotist and subject. Whether we speak of the state of hypnosis as regression or as transference, fusion occurs and should be fully utilized to meet the needs of the hypnotized subject. Many subjects who go through the induction stage into medium and deep trance will show a tendency to behave as though fast asleep and seem devoid of emotion. Don't be fooled. The muscles in the face may be flaccid and free of tension, but the mind is alert and feelings can be very sensitive.

FUSION OF BOTH PERSONALITIES

After the initial stages of induction, the subject senses the personality of the hypnotist *whose tone of voice and choice of words convey his sincerity*. With adequate prehypnotic insight, early indications of emotion in the subject can be advantageous. While in this state of heightened self-observation, the subject's inner feelings are aroused through the subjective sense of oneness. He can then be directed to sense his ability in self-mastery and to find new ways to enhance himself.

Freud and Breuer originally held that effective discharge of intense feeling was associated with traumatic events, and that hypnosis becomes a purge of sorts for the patient. When the subject, or patient, is reached on a feeling level, he becomes intensely involved in his own therapy, thereby advancing more rapidly. Sharing the emotional experience with the hypnotist will often produce a speedy curative effect. This varies according to the relationship between the subject and the hypnotist.

Frequently, we find it advantageous to have a subject abreact in order to wipe out negative memories. The degree of suffering will then decrease and he will invariably become indifferent to the trauma in his past. Pointing out each time that the subject has "come through it all" will reassure him considerably. New content can be added, both for abreaction and for ego strengthening.

Direct the subject's abreaction of pleasurable events before the end of the session. This will aid in ego strengthening and build confidence. Positive awakening has a strong posthypnotic effect.

ANXIETY NEUROSIS

Here is an induction technique which is useful in eliminating fears and anxieties. Tell your subject: "Picture yourself descending in an elevator. It's a local elevator, stopping at each floor. Each floor takes you deeper. Feel the car stopping, going deeper all of the time, a feeling of falling down very pleasantly, ever deeper. As the car keeps on going down, you begin to feel a pleasant, safe feeling of descending into a warm, comfortable state of peace and relaxation. All anxiety and tension leave you as you keep on feeling yourself drifting down in the car, deeper and deeper asleep. As you keep repeating to yourself, with the motion of the elevator going down, 'deep, deep, peaceful sleep, everything just fine, feeling happy and well, because I choose to feel that way and know there is every reason for me to feel well and happy, happy, safe and at peace, as the elevator drops down, floor by floor, it is taking me deeper, feeling better and better, secure, safe, contented, and this will last . . . feeling better and better as I feel the elevator descending, floor by floor, almost all the way down now, deeper and deeper into serenity, peace and well-being."

There is one situation where the descending elevator would be the improper technique to use for anxiety, and that is when the fear is one of elevators themselves. In such a case, have the subject imagine instead that he is on an open escalator and "going deeper into better, more secure mental and emotional feeling."

Unusual and Specialized Techniques

Although the major emphasis should be on perfecting a simple induction procedure, once you master a solid foundation, you may wish to expand your abilities into more sophisticated channels. In addition to the standard methods, there are manifold ancillary methods developed by professionals in their practical day-to-day work. This chapter will guide you in the management of the following advanced techniques:

Age Regression

You will guide the subject backward into the warehouse of memories. Used to uncover hidden material and for other recall.

Time Progression

A preview of coming events. Take a look into future possibilities. Used in surgery rehearsals and in self-imagery.

Automatic Writing

A dependable method to tap the subconscious for information. Bypasses the ego and the armor which resists opening up.

Group Hynotherapy

How to conduct hypnosis with a group of people who have various problems. Group regression and progression.

Prolonged Trance Therapy

When all else fails, the subject is kept under hypnosis for several hours or even days. Used in drug addiction cases.

Indirect Hypnosis

Inducing hypnosis without the knowledge of the subject requires a special skill. Suggested for medical use only.

The above methodology can be adapted to a great variety of individual problems. When used appropriately, the results may astound not only the subject but the operator. It is wise to master one technique at a time, although many of them work very well in combination. For example, *age regression* combined with *time progression*, in the same session, would be useful in examining past emotional problems and then taking a look into the future to see how things could be better. They work well together as a negative and positive visualization.

AGE REGRESSION AND TIME PROGRESSION

"Life can be understood looking backward, but must be lived forward," wrote the Danish philosopher, Kierkegaard. Hypnosis gives us a backward look and a forward one, and also *gives us foresight rather than hindsight.*

Age regression under hypnosis can be accomplished in one of two ways: (1) through recall of past events, names, numbers, the subject taps information recorded in the brain or (2) through recall and revisualization, the subject relives the past through "flashbacks." The trained hypnotherapist produces regression easily because all this information, both technical and visual, has been recorded in detail by the brain.

Age regression uncovers reflections from another time without the original emotional trauma. Imagination plus awareness arouses clarity in the brain instead of the old confusion. We are able to observe obsolete emotional patterns and realize that certain old feelings are not suited to new situations. Insight protects us from the past anxieties and projects us into a higher plane as subjectivity gives way to objectivity and an overview of past problems.

Accepting past images without reverting to old patterns of sensitivity involves an attitude of detachment. People who remain linked to old memories perpetually lament "what might have been" instead of considering "what can be" right now. Hypnosis can help illuminate not only the event, but the feelings behind the event. Through hypnosis, behavioral patterns become loosened and dislodged from old ways of thinking.

Clearing out obsolete thoughts is not always easy. They stick like glue, like undesirable tenants who refuse to vacate. Sometimes we need to become adamant, assertive, and serve them with an eviction notice. Habitual thinking forms well-worn paths which become engraved into the brain after much travel along the same route. Through age regression and time projection, one can not only assess past events, but leave them behind and move into the future. Once the mind awakens, old images become obscured and obstructed by new ideas which grow quickly.

PRODUCING AGE REGRESSION

Looking back into one's childhood and earlier years is quite harmless if handled with expertise. For the beginner, I suggest short regressions until you develop the skill. Take the subject back just a few years the first time, and then increase the regression each time you conduct a session.

Here's how it works. The hypnotist directs a dream toward a period of the subject's childhood, going back year by year. Before attempting regression, the hypnotist should have some knowledge and understanding of the subject's personality, and his past, particularly his early experiences. A factor vital to success is the trust the subject has in the therapist. He must be convinced beyond a doubt that his well-being is the most important consideration in the hypnotic situation. At no time should he feel anything but safe, protected, and benefited. The process of regression should be unhurried. If the subject appears emotionally disturbed as he recalls traumatic events, the therapist should not bring him out of hypnosis, but should handle the anxiety then and there. Use the trance level to pacify the subject. Distress will pass quickly with your kindly assurance that the past is finished and no longer threatening.

Before beginning age regression, it is advisable to have the subject write his name or draw a simple picture, i.e., an animal, house, or person. This test is used after regression for comparison of age differential. Regression is then brought about, one day at a time, one year at a time, depending upon the individual case and how long ago the trauma was inflicted. Give your subject time for the remembrances to come forth.

For example, if the subject is about 25 years of age, and you wish to regress him to age 7, take him back to "24, 23, 20, 18, 15, 12, 10, 9, 7." You can skip years, especially if the person is presently much older. (Otherwise, the session would be unnecessarily lengthy.) We tend to remember events by stages of our lives rather than by dates.

Always allow time for each phase to make its impression on the mind before moving back to a younger age. When you ask the person to answer questions, notice how the voice changes, whether the facial expressions are of a younger age. Call attention to birthdays, Christmas, and school terms as specifically as possible. Ask where he is, what he is doing. Give him sufficient time to deepen the trance before beginning regression. If he answers quickly in his natural voice, he may not be reliving the experience, but simply remembering. If he is recalling information, he will say, "I *was* in school" rather than "I am *now* in school." If he is merely remembering, he may mention the teacher's name, "My teacher's name *was* Miss Jones."

However, true regression places him in the midst of the incident and he will say, "I *am* in the first grade. My teacher *is* Miss Jones. She *is* teaching us to write." You will then know that this is a true regression. Should you regress him back to a very young age, he will be unable to speak, but will make noises, and cry or gurgle like a baby. When this occurs, it's best if you have established a nonverbal signal such as lifting a finger.

In cases of age regression to childhood, people who did not speak English until they were older may respond in a foreign language. This is also a sign of an actual regression. In all cases, have a nonverbal communication like a finger movement or movement of a foot to signify "yes" or "no" to questions you may ask of the subject.

Now, reluctant subjects will play a game, role playing instead of revivification. They will act out whatever they believe the therapist requires. This may be a way of avoiding traumatic memories. In such cases, the hypnotist may encounter resistance. This is best handled by slowing down the rate of regression and stopping at a time close to the incident. Later you may gradually return to the desired age. Suggestions given should be well thought out in advance and discussed. Sometimes automatic writing (described elsewhere) can be less painful than verbalizing. This method is speedy and very revealing, and works well in light hypnosis as well as at deeper levels. Several examples are given under *automatic writing*.

EXAMPLES OF REGRESSION

Frank H., 24 years old, was anxious and depressed. He had a fear of subways and of meeting people, and was claustrophobic. Frank had been medically discharged from the armed services. Diagnosed as schizophrenic, he had tried the usual therapies, including psychoanalysis, with no improvement. Responding to hypnotic suggestion well, after three sessions he developed a deep trance. He was regressed gradually to age ten, at which time he recalled violent scenes between his mother and father as well as trouble in school, fear of adults, and hiding in the closet from his father.

At another time, Frank was regressed to age three and spoke in Spanish, which was the language spoken in his home. His voice was a babyish whine, scarcely intelligible, as he described a scene between his mother and father. A violent argument and physical fight took place. Frightened, he ran into the bathroom and hid in the tub. When he tried to come out of the bathroom, the door was stuck. The room grew dark and when he finally got the door open and emerged into the hallway, his uncle was there. He was even more afraid of his uncle than of his father. His uncle chased him down the dark hall. It was suggested he would remember the incident and be able to discuss it fully without pain because, after all, he had survived.

Frank recalled everything and spoke freely. "Isn't it silly to let such a thing upset you for so many years?" he commented. "Look what a big guy I grew up to be, six feet tall and afraid of shadows and quarreling people. How could anyone be so foolish?"

Frank responded to therapy very rapidly after regression. He found a job and eventually married a lovely young woman.

TIME PROGRESSION

Both hypnotic age regression and time progression involve a re-orientation from one's perception of space-time. Progression refers to the artificial hallucination of events of the future. Once a person gains awareness from retrospection, he is better able to deal, not only with his present, but with his future. Instead of restricting his thinking to the way he has been, hypnosis helps him see himself as he could be—as he should be. Visionaries are those who can free their imagination and build a dream to strive for. Imagined situations can later be transferred into real-life situations. Time or age progression projects your thoughts into an unknown space and time—a year from now, five years, ten years—or it might be just a few days or hours. An actress might use the technique to visualize herself on opening night getting a standing ovation. A salesman could use time progression to rehearse his sales pitch and see himself writing a huge order.

During hypnosis, the person hallucinates positive improvements, tests himself in new situations, and tries on the garb of a successful person. While he may still retain his chronological age, he takes a look into the way things might be and develops "possibility thinking." Keep in mind that although some people can be *re*gressed easily because they are merely tuning into recorded information, *pro*gression involves use of the imagination, and the ability to visualize future events not yet experienced. In many cases, confidence in personal fulfillment has not been "programmed" into him by his past experience. His self-image may be weaker than his capabilities warrant. The successful use of "time progression" is based upon the trilogy, *conceive, believe, and achieve.* Each concept is equally important. One may conceive, but without belief, achievement is impossible. Imagining positive events tends to raise positive anticipation, which in turn fires the motivational drive to carry one through to a goal.

A good example is the following case history of a young woman, Jody L., who wanted plastic surgery in order to correct a birth defect. She feared the operation and kept postponing surgery. Under progression, she was told: "See yourself standing in front of a mirror. The nurse has just removed the bandages and you see yourself looking perfectly beautiful. Healed without a trace of scars. You are very pleased at the good results. There are no bruises—no black and blue marks. No redness, no swelling. People are standing around you complimenting you. See yourself clearly. See and you will be what you see."

There is infinite possibility in using imagination in particular situations, depending upon the individual. A skilled therapist facilitates the subject's receptivity to his own inner associations with positive images and integrates this response into action. We do not force moods or feelings, but rather encourage the built-in mechanisms already existing inside all of us. Because belief systems vary, it's well to inquire whether or not the person you are working with is religious, believes in nature, or "cosmic power." Effectiveness can be increased by activating the morals and beliefs already existing in the person.

Dr. William Kroger in his book, *Clinical and Experimental Hypnosis* cites a case history in which progression convinced a subject he should not undergo surgery. While under deep hypnosis, an apprehensive and tense individual who came for consultation on the advisability of having a vasectomy, was told that the surgery had already been performed, and that it was now five years later. He was told to think and feel the emotions and sensations of a man who had had a vasectomy. The doctor then asked him, "How have you been feeling since you were sterilized?" He replied, "Oh, Doctor, I haven't had a good night's sleep since my operation. It's made me very tense and nervous. This isn't the time for me."

After dehypnotization, he was advised to postpone surgery until certain meaningful and deeply repressed material could be worked out with a psychologist. Afterward, he was ultimately able to accept the consequences of the proposed surgery. He was also able to achieve greater personality integration because of the insight he gained under hypnotherapy.

In a similar way, rehearsals of surgery, childbirth, dental work, and other procedures which might involve apprehension on the part of the patient are useful in the elimination of anxieties. A lively imagination plus positive anticipation combine to prepare the subject for the best possible results. Surgical rehearsals are a certain antidote to the jitters that so many patients complain of prior to the operation. I use a technique called *The Yes or No Technique*. Here is the verbalization: "Picture two screens, like T.V. or movie screens. One shows a sign reading *yes* and the other a sign reading *no*. On the *YES* screen see yourself having had the operation. Everything has worked out just fine. The results were even better than you expected. Now take a look at the other screen. You have decided against the operation. What are the consequences? Take a look at your two choices—*yes* or *no*. Which one makes more sense to you? This preview will help you make up your mind. The decision will be the best one at this time."

UNCOVERING AND DISCOVERING SECRETS

Many people bury the most important information deep inside the subliminal caverns of their minds. Take the case of Kenneth R., a business executive, married and extremely conservative. His aim in life had always been to be successful, yet no matter how much he earned, Kenneth always considered himself a failure. By the time he discovered hypnotherapy, he had already had two nervous breakdowns. The first occurred when he was still a college student. Anxious and worried about living up to the expectations of his parents, he was filled with so much fear that his life became unbearable and he attempted suicide. His second breakdown occurred following a business disaster when he had to declare a bankruptcy. Kenneth was in his middle forties at this time and was institutionalized for his breakdown. Upon his release, he began seven years of psychoanalysis that he said did not resolve his feelings of depression. Many medications were tried with no appreciable success. Finally, someone suggested hypnosis.

Kenneth was a resistant subject from the start, having lost all faith in therapy. After four weeks that included four one-hour office sessions and the use of a cassette self-training tape that he played at home three times a day, Kenneth entered a light hypnoidal state. His case is important because there is the tendency among hypnotists to give up too soon and label a difficult subject as "nonhypnotizable." With persistence, almost every human being can be helped to some degree by hypnosis.

Although Kenneth was not a deep subject, we were able to produce some regression to a time before he had his first breakdown. He was handed the pad and pen for automatic writing.

"Write down, just as thought occurs to you, anything that may explain whatever is bothering you."

AUTOMATIC WRITING

Automatic writing is one of the most fascinating and valuable tools of hypnosis. Yet few hypnotherapists utilize this phenomenon. Many of them are under the misconception that automatic writing requires the deepest stage of hypnosis, somnambulism. This is far from the truth. Automatic writing even occurs at nonhypnotic levels such as "doodling" while a person is distracted on the telephone. Nonassociated scribbling is often filled with symbolic images and can reveal a great deal about the "doodler."

Material produced in this manner may reveal trauma buried under many layers of self-deception. Automatic writing brings out the truth, and, when combined with hypnosis, offers a method of uncovering information vital to a patient's recovery. Sometimes the subject chooses to draw pictures rather than write words. Sometimes the revelations come forth as disjointed syllables which need to be interpreted later. In any case, important, helpful insight will be forthcoming no matter whether you are working with a deep or light subject.

I have found it useful to work with a large artist's sketch pad and a felt-tip pen. The large pad is appropriate because many people tend to write much larger than normal when hypnotized. Perhaps this is because they "open up" more or revert to a more childish manner of scrawling. The writing is done with closed eyes, and the larger surface assures the operator that the results will be legible. A soft-tipped pen is needed because when in a trance state most people feel very light-handed and if you use a pencil or ordinary pen you may not be able to read the material.

Regression is often used prior to automatic writing. The subject is first inducted to as deep a level as possible. This usually requires two sessions. He is then guided to a particular time or event.

The trance depth necessary for producing automatic writing and regression is largely a matter of opinion, depending on the degree or rapport between operator and subject. Take time to explain how it works. Confidence and self-assurance help a great deal. Begin by showing examples of other people's writings under hypnosis. Explain: "Mary worked out her problems so much faster after she wrote these words. John found the right kind of job through the symbols in this drawing."

VERBALIZATION FOR AUTOMATIC WRITING

After locating the time or event about which the subject is to write, you bring about a sense of disassociation in his writing hand. (Be sure to check before induction whether your subject is right-handed or left-handed.) "As I stroke your hand, you will begin to feel it becoming numb, losing all feeling. Your hand feels light and detached from the rest of your body. Your hand is being controlled by a nerve which goes directly to your brain where the hidden information is stored. You no longer have conscious control of your hand. Your brain is feeding memories directly to your hand. Your hand has the information and is able to write it down easily. Even if the information was once painful, it doesn't bother your hand. Your hand has no emotions; it is automatic like a robot hand. Your robot hand gets the information from the computer brain and writes it down on the paper. Your hand will write only the truth. You will not think or question what is being written. Start writing answers when you hear my question."

At this point you direct the subject's mind to the area of trauma and ask short questions such as: "Where are you?" and "How do you feel?" Allow sufficient time for the subject to think and write. As the subject is writing, suggest: "After hypnosis is terminated, you will understand and be able to interpret what you have written." Repeat this several times.

After the session, the written material is evaluated. The subject is questioned about what he really meant when he wrote the information. Sometimes the words will be symbolic of deeper meaning. Very often the words will be abbreviated or transferred into symbolic shapes or objects such as a star, box, or other geometric design. A great deal of time is saved by this direct technique.

AUTOMATIC DRAWING AND DOODLING

In some cases, automatic drawing or doodling has certain advantages. For instance, where a language barrier exists or there is regression to an age before the subject learned to write, you might say, "Draw me a picture of how your father looked at the time," or, "Just let the pen doodle anything it wants to do." The results are often surprising. In the case of Alvin H., his childhood experience had been so painful he had difficulty recalling that period in his life. When he was told, "Do a cartoon strip representing the four worst things that happened to you," he portrayed himself as a dog being beaten by his father. Alvin was not an artist. The sketches were executed crudely, but the content was very powerful. At first he explained the dog this way: "My father would not let me have a dog. I was afraid if I brought one home he would beat it." Then he corrected himself: "No . . . the dog is really me. I was treated like a dog by my father, who had a terrible temper."

Interpretation of the results in automatic writing and drawing depends on an established, trusting relationship between therapist and subject. Rather than assuming you have the answers, it is best to ask the subject, "What do these writings mean to you?" When handled properly, the after-talks help to clarify not only events but hidden attitudes.

THE "AS-IF" OR SUBSTITUTION METHOD

When normal techniques of automatic writing or doodling fail to elicit the necessary communication—when the paper remains blank— try this. Suggest that the subject is merely an observer, examining a person with problems. Tell him: "Write down on the paper what is wrong with this person. You know him better than anybody else does. Look inside his head and see what he is thinking and write it down." Tell him he is an assistant to the therapist and is investigating the problem. "Allow your hand to write out a report on this person. You want to help him because he is really a nice person who needs help."

Virgil T. at 14 years of age, was having trouble in school. Although he had a high I.Q., he was noncooperative and a poor student. Virgil had a history of smoking, drinking, and drug abuse. His parents had forced him to come for a session in hypnosis. He stubbornly refused to communicate. When I attempted automatic writing, the only time his hand moved was to draw small circles . . . zeros . . . Virgil was trying to tell me something.

The substitution method worked like a charm. I suggested, "Write 'as-if' you are an observer investigating a boy with problems in school. Let your hand write about what causes this boy's trouble." Virgil readily responded with the following: ". . . trusted . . . he wants to be trusted . . . he is afraid . . . teacher insults him too much . . . he's cutting classes. . . ."

After the session, he opened up to the therapist and explained that his father was old-fashioned, and that he could not turn to him for advice. The father was invited to attend the next therapy session, and frankness and openness developed between father and son. This case history is an example of how communication can be increased through automatic writing rather than having the subject speak under hypnosis. In some cases, speaking rouses the subject and brings on feelings of resistance.

AUTOMATIC WRITING AS A TECHNIQUE IN THERAPY

Peter was a 38-year-old man who had been an alcoholic for sixteen years. He had failed to receive help in psychoanalysis. Alcoholics Anonymous didn't appeal to him. Shock treatments, faith healing, medication, and all kinds of other cures were tried to no avail. Peter was no puny nipper; he was a three-bottle-a-day man and it didn't matter to him what brand or type of liquor he imbibed.

Peter was a difficult subject. Hypnosis, with and without Pentothal, had been tried by a medical hypnotist but without success. After ten sessions of hypnosis using automatic writing, he was finally developed into a good subject. When Peter was asked to recall a time when he was 16 years of age, he wrote: "It's closing in, closing in, the street is closing in." What he had been referring to he did not recall, but rather spoke more freely about his other problem, which centered around a travelling phobia which kept him from going more than a block from his house. He had had several epileptic seizures, beginning at age ten, and he feared being overcome by a seizure in public and so stayed home most of the time. His fear would cause acute panic in him.

At his next session, Peter was hypnotized and he was regressed to age ten. He was asked to write about what happened at that age that had upset him. He wrote: "I stole money from mama's handbag. I am running . . . running . . . she is closing in." This time he recalled the original experience as well as the feeling of terror which had overcome him. He cried throughout the one-hour session, but remained at a deep trance level. We were able to reconstruct his entire neurotic behavioral pattern later in a private counseling session.

As a small child, he had occasionally stolen small sums of money from his mother's handbag whenever he felt rejected or unloved. Later he would suffer pangs of guilt and fear of punishment should his thievery be discovered. One day after being scolded by his mother for problems in school, he took the largest amount so far, a dollar bill. Afterward, Peter was running down a dark, narrow street when he was suddenly overcome by extreme anxiety and had his first seizure. His mother never confronted him with the fact that she knew he was stealing. Had she done so, the disturbance in his personality may not have become so deeply engrained into his nervous system. Perhaps she felt it would "just go away in time." It didn't. Peter became worse.

After his first seizure, he developed agoraphobia, fear of leaving the confines of his house. He would not step off his front porch. This lasted until he was an adult. In fact, his first hypnotic session was conducted in his home because of his phobia about travel. At the first session, he was trained to expect to leave for just one hour, so that he could visit the hypnotist's office. After being cured of agoraphobia through hypnosis, he tried many other therapies to no avail and later returned to hypnotherapy to overcome his addiction to alcohol. Finally, Peter learned self-hypnosis, which he now practices every day, and he has remained in good mental and physical health ever since.

One problem Peter was unable to resolve was his distaste for work. During hypnosis, he would awaken from a profound trance if he were told he'd feel well enough to find a job. In this case, Peter is a classic example of the fact that a hypnotist cannot always force a subject to accept a new image.

Jason R., 26 years old, suffered from primary impotence. Though he was physically healthy in every respect, he could not remember ever having an erection. He explained that in spite of his inability to function, he often felt strong sexual desire for intercourse with women but inevitably would end up masturbating with a flaccid penis. This had been his practice since adolescence. While he had intense sensation in the penis, the flow of circulation was psychologically shut off. Jason was referred to me by his urologist, who explained that he could find no evidence of any organic disturbance.

After three conditioning sessions, he reached sufficient trance depth for regression techniques to be employed. Jason was regressed to the age of 9, at which point he raised his hand as a signal to me that some information was forthcoming. I placed a large writing pad on his lap and a felt-tip pen in his hand, and Jason wrote in a childish, 9-year-old scroll:

"I am taking a shower. Dad is shaving at the sink, or maybe brushing his teeth. I say, 'Dad, come over here. I want to show you something.' He comes over and I point to my penis, which is hard. I ask him, 'How come it does that?' Dad laughs and says, 'Throw some cold water on it and it will go away.' Dad gets the glass of water from the sink and pours it over my penis and the erection goes away. Then dad goes into the kitchen and tells my mother and they both have a good laugh. I wonder what's so funny about me. Something must be wrong because they hush up as soon as I come out of the bathroom."

Once the original trauma was isolated, Jason's therapy proved very effective in removing the repressive block interfering with his sexual response. Many of the other techniques described in this book were also used, with excellent results. After six sessions, Jason awakened one morning with an erection and soon after was able to transfer this ability to lovemaking during the evening hours. He has since married.

GROUP OR MASS HYPNOSIS

Because people are generally more susceptible after witnessing an induction performed with someone else, follow this procedure:

1. *Test for suggestibility* using any of the methods described earlier. The *Hand Rising and Falling* test is the one I prefer.

2. *Select the most responsive* subject (or subjects) to use for a demonstration in front of the rest of the group.

3. *Demonstrate an induction* with the suggestible subject(s). One of the speedier inductions will be sufficient to prove the point.

4. *Proceed With Group Induction* following the simple instructions which follow. The technique works with ten to ten hundred, easily.

Demonstrations are useful in convincing skeptics in the group that the phenomenon of hypnosis is for real. However, in working with a large group (hundreds or thousands), there will always be a percentage who will not allow themselves to be hypnotized. They will watch with a fascinated expression as the rest of the audience goes into trance. This does not indicate that they are less hypnotizable, but rather that they are not ready at this moment in time to cooperate in the induction. It is wise to say to a large group, "Those of you who would prefer to watch may do so. However, if at any time your eyes should grow tired, just close them and join the group and relax with us."

Stage hypnotists often follow the procedure outlined here. They rely on selecting the most agreeable subjects in the audience and after demonstration proceed with a routine similar to the following:

"I want every one of you to take a deep breath, breathe in, in, in, in, *hold it, hold it.* O.K. Now exhale. Let it all out. . . . Now, in a few moments I am going to ask all of you to close your eyes, and after you have closed your eyes, I am going to have you take five deep breaths. . . . After you have taken five deep breaths, you will hold the *fifth breath*, while I count backwards, 5, 4, 3, 2, 1, . . . When I reach 1, you will be deep asleep and will not be able to open your eyes. Remember now, you will hold the *fifth breath*, while I count backwards 5, 4, 3, 2, 1 and then *deep asleep*. . . . Now, all of you close your eyes. Good. . . . Now:

> Number One: "Breathe in, in, in, hold it . . . hold it . . . exhale . . . exhale."
> Two: In, in, in, in, and out, out, out, relax deeply."
> Three: *"Breathing in all the way in, now exhale out, out."*
> Four: "In, in, in, and out, out, out."
> Five: *Take a really deep breath, hold it, hold it. Five, Four, Three, Two, One, Exhale Completely!!*
> *Deep . . . Deep . . . Asleep . . . You Will Remain Deep, Deep Asleep Until I Awaken You . . . You Will Find This Experience Restful and Self-Enriching. The Deeper You Go, the Greater the Benefit to You. Now, Get Ready to Relax From the Top of Your Head to the Tips of Your Toes."*

You now proceed with deepening techniques such as progressive relaxation, countdowns, etc. Group or mass hypnosis is no more difficult than individual hypnosis. The routines are the same after you eliminate the original resistance by demonstrating with a highly suggestible subject. Group hypnotherapy is a marvelous aid in handling juvenile behavior modification, improving study habits in classrooms, in drug rehabilitation, obesity, insomnia, and in pain clinics. Hypnosis in a group is also a practical solution for preventing mental illness because it is lower in cost than individual therapy and eases the practitioner's case load.

Group hypnosis dates back all the way to the Egyptians. Many ancient people performed group rituals which were hypnotic in nature. Mass chanting and hypnotic meditation to the steady beat of drums was widely accepted as part of the religious healing arts. Healing with the mind predates medical practice and is still used in many primitive societies with some surprising results.

Just as the healer in ancient times, the hypnotist moves among the group, touching each subject's shoulder and whispering individual suggestions into each subject's ear. The suggestions begin as soon as the entire group has reached at least a light-to-medium trance level. Then the operator goes to each individual and reads from the card the subject is holding. (Experience has taught me not to depend on memory in giving suggestions to a large group.) Each person is told in advance to write their suggestions on a card and hold the card as they are inducted into the trance. As you approach each subject, you are verbalizing as follows: "Now as I speak to each of you and touch you upon the shoulder, you will go deeper. The rest of you will use the sound of my voice to go deeper." When the problem is one which the subject is shy about, such as sexual dysfunction, the suggestion is whispered directly and very softly into the individual's ear to respect his privacy. However, when the suggestion can benefit everyone and is of a general nature such as improved learning or better sleep, it is spoken in a moderate voice.

Some disturbances are universal, and group suggestions will often include Confidence Building, Improved Self-Image, Better Organization, Healthier Personal Habits, Serenity, Faith, Cheerfulness, Tolerance, Freedom from Fear, Decisiveness, Setting Goals, Independence, and Financial Success.

In addition to building better inner images, the group approach is ideal for positive brainwashing that rids the mind of unwanted, obsessively negative images such as Confusion, Procrastination, Anger and Hostility, Indecision, Guilt, Nervous Tension, Pains, and Irritability.

The average length of time needed for good results is from 1½ to 3 hours. When working with individuals, you will need from forty minutes to an hour to achieve proper depth of trance level.

GROUP RESPONSE IN AUTOMATIC WRITING

The following events transpired at a hypnotherapy group session. Ten people participated, both male and female, aged 21 to 43. The subjects had been previously conditioned in private sessions to reach medium and deep trance levels. The object of the group was to train them in memory and recall so that when automatic writing took place they would be ready. There were four group sessions in which regression and automatic writing were utilized.

First Session. While under hypnosis they were told (collectively) that they were to recall a time at which they were first made aware of their particular problem. They would then focus on the circumstances and people connected with the original cause of the problem. The technique for regression was as follows:

"As I count backwards from 43 years of age, see yourself growing younger with each count. Those of you who are younger than 43, join into the countdown when you hear the number representing your age." I counted down to 21, the age of the youngest member of the group, and then continued the regression, "21, 20, 19, 18, (and so on)." They were told to signal when they remembered a traumatic incident by raising a forefinger. I then placed a writing pad and pen in each person's hand. When everyone had pad and pen, I instructed them to write their names. Most of them wrote in large childish script or printed.

Second Session. After repeating the above procedure, seven out of the ten began writing meaningful information. Of the remaining three, two were still insufficiently deep and the third sat with her eyes closed weeping and unable to communicate. Examples of the positive writing follow:

Alice B., age 30, was an asthmatic and hoped hypnosis would lessen the severity of her attacks. She wrote part of a sonnet by Shakespeare which expressed the death wish. One word stood out clearly: "suffocation."

Margie V., age 21, weighed 85 lbs., although she was 5 foot, 6 inches tall. Her condition, known as anorexia nervosa, began when she was 19 years of age and a newlywed. She weighed 125 lbs. when she married, having been on a diet when she originally weighed 135. Margie did not write words; she doodled. The drawings resembled sticks. Some of the sticks were assembled into people. Her later writings were to the point.

Albert M., 31, was embarrassed when he revealed that his problem was enuresis (bed wetting). He had rarely had a dry night since he was an infant. Traditional approaches had been tried with no results. He was an excellent subject. "The house is too cold," he wrote. He explained later that as a child he had lived near Buffalo and in a house with little heat in the winter. He had become conditioned to sleep through urination rather than get up to go to the toilet in the cold.

There were less interesting responses from the remaining members during this session. Two of them had routine overweight problems.

Third session. There were now eight people in the group. The young woman who had been unable to communicate was referred to a psychiatrist for analysis. One of the other people decided he was unable to work in group and returned to private sessions. Alice B., the asthmatic, wrote profusely of her first attack, blaming her mother for not allowing her to date her first boyfriend. She released a tremendous amount of hostility. Margie V. revealed she was trying to turn her young husband's sexual drive down because he "comes on too strong. Now he's afraid to touch me." She smiled as she wrote this.

Hank D., a homosexual, had been unable to write anything at the first session. Now he wrote, "I feel healthy and normal this way. As a child, I knew I was different." He later told the group that he visualized himself as bisexual even as a very small child. He had had a vision of himself as a person with breasts and a penis.

Fourth Session. By this final group session in automatic writing, all eight people had mastered the art and were doing self-analysis with supervision. One of the group members who had not demonstrated any particular ability to visualize said that he had regressed all the way back to a previous life. Victor W. wrote, "Rough sea. I am going down. Dead. Year, 1807." He described to the group a scene that contained a pirate ship and himself as assistant to the ship's cook. This rather amused me, because in the many years of practicing hypnotherapy, I have listened to hundreds of reports of reincarnation as a result of hypnotic induction. However, most of the reports are of past lives as prominent people. Queens, kings, presidents are the most popular, making one wonder how much of the report is hallucination and wishful thinking. In Victor's case, however, seeing himself merely as an assistant to the cook gave his story some sense of authenticity. While there is no way to prove reincarnation, those of us who have worked with hypnosis for many years do not rule out the possibility, since there have been similar writings reported by hypnotists in various parts of the world.

This group was also taught techniques of self-hypnosis that they used to good advantage in many different ways. I asked them each to write to me several months after working in the group so that I could list the improvements they made. Here is a list of the ways in which hypnosis and self-hypnosis improved the lives of these ten people:

"Learning French for a trip to Paris."
"Helped me learn how to dance."
"Sleep better than I did before."
"My sex life has improved. More stamina."
"Overcame biting my nails and snoring."
"Keep my temper under control much better."
"Get along better with my co-workers."
"Hypnosis worked for painless dental work."
"Lost some more weight. Don't eat sweets."

PROLONGED TRANCE THERAPY

Extending the length of the therapeutic trance to several hours or even days can be extremely useful in breaking entrenched behavioral patterns. Dramatic short-term recovery is possible in many situations, e.g., lowering stress where there is excitation from shock, aiding the drug addict and alcoholic during the withdrawal period, and improving cases of extreme obesity where eating patterns must be radically altered in a short period of time.

The subject is hypnotized to a suitable level and told he will not awaken until instructed to do so. "You are going to relax and 'sleep it off.' When you wake up much later, you will feel as if you have had a full night's sleep. Only this time you will wake up without your old problem. You will wake up as if you are reborn—a new person without the old problem." During the interview, he is instructed on how to cooperate to help himself in the procedure. He is told that the longer he stays in trance, the better he will feel; the further he goes into hypnosis, the further he will go forward correcting his problem.

Proper suggestions are discussed with the subject. He is then told to start a long count (1,000 or 500 down to 0), each count to take him deeper and deeper. While the subject is silently counting to himself, the operator proceeds with progressive body relaxation. This is done very slowly, with long pauses and lapses in the voice so that the subject will become accustomed to periods when he keeps himself under by counting. Prolonged trance works best with a preconditioned subject who has been trained to enter a medium to deep level. Otherwise the subject will keep coming out and the effect will be lessened. Keep in mind that after an hour or two, he can open his eyes and still remain in hypnosis. This will be necessary for periods of eating and going to the bathroom. However, the eyes are only opened intermittently and never except when the hypnotist gives the command.

In cases where the hypnotic trance is prolonged for many hours or days, an auxiliary hypnotist is advisable. Tapes and records will also prove useful. You can prerecord some of the countdown routines and various deepening techniques to use when you need to take a break from the program. It is best not to leave the patient listening to tapes longer than fifteen minutes at a time, as there may be a tendency to lose some depth. Human contact is far more effective in achieving results, because the subject senses the emotional rapport and concern of the operator. The duration of the therapy varies according to the condition of the subject.

Time distortion plays a vital role in the degree of recovery, as a few case histories will demonstrate.

George Z. suffered from a combination of several serious problems. Not the least of these was a serious drug addiction that had kept him in a state of extreme apathy for almost five years. As a war veteran, he was transferred from one hospital to another. All treatment, both medical and psychological failed to help him overcome his total lack of self-esteem. In addition to his drug dependency, he also had violent episodes and been arrested for assault with a dangerous weapon on three separate occasions. His last arrest was for threatening his mother with bodily harm if she did not provide him with money for his drug habit. His mother contacted the hypnotherapist during a period when her son was out on bond:

"There is so little time for him to be helped. Soon he will be sentenced and put away. Can you do something quickly while he's available for treatment?" Prolonged trance therapy was decided upon as a means for accelerating his improvement. George responded immediately to this suggestion: "Space out. Just like you do when you are high on drugs. Only this time, we are working with nature to cure you of all need for the junk. You will come out clean and free of the habit. Are you willing for this to happen to you?"

He readily agreed. George loved to be hypnotized. He felt relief in turning his problem over to someone else, even if it was only for several hours. George was kept under for ten hours with the help of two hypnotists and several recordings. Music was also used in the background. In selecting music, pick something that is soft, slow, and sounds like a lullaby. Lyrics are contraindicated because they draw mental concentration away from the suggestions. Because of the long duration of this therapy, we recorded his personalized suggestions and played them when we needed a voice rest.

George progressed into the induction rapidly by the use of "awakening and reinduction techniques." Because this was his first experience with hypnosis, all sorts of methods were employed. Standard as well as specialized methods kept taking him deeper at each induction. He remained in the trance state during the entire time, which included his brief breaks to eat, stretch, and wash up. Here is the verbalization given just before a break.

"When you hear the count of 3, you will open your eyes and remain in hypnosis. You will do exactly as you are told until you are instructed to close your eyes once again. You are permitted, upon opening your eyes, to walk immediately to the bathroom and then return to your chair where you will be fed some nourishment. When you finish your food, you will immediately be told to close your eyes and go deep asleep. Now get ready to open your eyes and remain in hypnosis. One, 2, 3, eyes open . . . stay under. Go to the bathroom and come back."

When George was reinducted, he immediately slipped into the deepest level of hypnosis. It was firmly suggested that he would feel healthy and strong and disgusted with all drugs, and that he would become a helper in the drug rehabilitation movement to assist young people to avoid all the suffering he had been through. After the fourth induction, he signaled with his forefinger that he agreed to this suggestion.

When George was finally awakened at the end of the ten-hour period, he was amazed that it was already dark out. We had started the therapy at 10 A.M. and, by 8 P.M., the auxiliary therapist and I were feeling a bit exhausted. George, however, felt chipper and filled with energy. He could not believe that ten hours had passed. It seemed to him that the passage of time had been accelerated, condensed into just an hour or so. His memory of the experience was vague, but his attitude had clearly changed. It touched us emotionally to see him put his arms around his mother, who had come to see that he got home alright. At that moment it seemed impossible to imagine that just a few short months before he had made a threat on her life. Such is the nature of the mind distortion which accompanies the abuse of drugs.

When George completed his jail sentence, he visited the therapy center where he had received his prolonged hypnotherapy. He joined a group therapy session which was in progress at the time. In addition to participating in group sessions, he now goes out with a woman, works part-time, and is a volunteer in a teenage drug rehabilitation center.

When some people suffer the shock of an accident, the trauma may remain with them for a long time. Charlene T. was a stewardess who had the misfortune to be working on an airliner which crashed upon landing, killing dozens of people. Charlene was deeply depressed and complained of persistent nightmares about the crash. In addition, she was terrified of flying and because this was her means of livelihood, she had been out of work for two years.

"I've got to snap out of it and get back to work soon," she confided. "My bank account is running dry. Please do what you can to speed it up."

Charlene was a preconditioned subject. She had attended both group and private sessions. One hypnotist was used, with a cassette tape during rest periods. The following techniques proved successful: regression back before the accident, progression forward to a happy, safe career, and signal reversal from negative thoughts to positive ones. We also used the *directed dream technique* to wash the nightmares out of her memory.

Another case of prolonged sleep therapy is that of Elise R., age 34. Problems: mental confusion, which rendered her unable to concentrate on her work, and compulsive eating. Though Elise knew every diet, she could not stick to one more than a few days. She had been through six years of analysis. After several sessions of hypnosis, she was still unable to control her emotional eating habits.

One day, while under hypnosis, another client arrived early and I escorted him into an adjoining room. I instructed Elise meanwhile to listen to my voice and keep going deeper, even though she might not fully understand my words.

"You will not care to listen," I told her, "but the sound of my voice will take you deeper, no matter what I am saying to the other person. You will not awaken till I place my hand on your shoulder and say, "Wake up now." Elise was told to keep implanting the positive sugges-tions that she would have no desire for fattening foods and would eat only the minimum amount. At the termination of the one-hour session she seemed much deeper than ever before, though I had not addressed myself to her directly. She was indirectly keeping herself in hypnosis using the distant sound of my voice. Elise remained under hypnosis for four hours by this method. I repeated the technique four times, and she was finally able to conquer her compulsion and to work out her other disturbing problems as well. Eighteen months later, her recovery seemed complete.

Benson T., age 26. His problems included a fear of meeting new people, anxiety regarding work, and claustrophobia. Benson was dis-charged from the army and listed as disturbed. Many diagnoses had been made regarding his case. He was called schizophrenic, paranoic, and a lobotomy had been recommended by army medics.

After three sessions utilizing regression and automatic writing, Benson was placed in prolonged trance in the same manner as Elise. Tape recordings were employed as a supplement to live suggestions. He remained in trance from three to six hours daily for five days. At the end of that time, Benson was strongly motivated to find suitable employment. Since, he has gotten married and has persevered in the same job for more than a year. Now is free of anxiety, gets along with people, and is so well-adjusted that he is considering raising a family.

Anne B., age 35, was terrified of dental work. She required six prolonged hypnotic sessions, lasting four hours each. In addition, she had ten sessions in group hypnosis. The results were very positive. She developed great self-confidence and learned how to administer self-anesthesia through autohypnosis. At this writing, Anne, a recent bride, tells me that she will transfer her knowledge of local anesthesia to painless childbirth, if and when she becomes pregnant.

INDIRECT HYPNOTIC INDUCTION

It is possible to induce the hypnotic state in very susceptible subjects without their awareness. Some dentists use this approach on children by telling them, "When you hear the drill, close your eyes and make believe you are watching your favorite T.V. show. Any time I tell you to wash your mouth, you will do so and then close your eyes and go back to watching your favorite show." All doctors are strategically in a good position to practice indirect hypnosis without the problem of resistance because they often represent to the patient an authority whose opinion is not to be questioned.

Indirect hypnosis should only be used in cases where overt induction will raise fears and anxiety that would interfere with the treatment. If the hypnotist wants to induce the hypnotic state without discussing it with the subject, he must avoid words typically associated with hypnotic induction. Words such as "sleepy or drowsy" can be circumvented substituting "relaxation," "concentration," or "meditation." Many clinics use hypnosis techniques under the guise of *behavior modification*. There are dentists, doctors, and psychiatrists who use substitute terms in cases where a patient might be afraid of hypnosis. The patient might be told he is being "sedated" or that the physician intends to use "psychosomatic induction," or "narcosynthesis."

The basic principle of disguised hypnosis is based on a common misconception that hypnosis is synonomous with nighttime sleep. The prospective subject assumes he will become drowsy, fall asleep, be unable to hear the operator, and will not remember anything when he awakens. This is only true of a small percentage of highly susceptible subjects. In about seven out of ten cases, the subject remembers easily.

The truth is that hypnosis is more similar to the waking state than it is to nighttime sleep. The main difference is that, under hypnosis, the subject is highly suggestible and tends to be agreeable to the commands of the operator. This same suggestibility can be achieved without direct reference to the term, "hypnosis."

APPLYING THE INDIRECT METHOD

The success of the induction lies in studiously avoiding words that may have a disturbing meaning to the subject. Prepare the induction by eliminating any stress factors, making sure the subject is as comfortable as possible. Begin the induction by using one of the standard tests for suggestibility such as the *arms rising and falling test*. Call the test, for example, *power of imagination*. You can use this test both in group and with individual inductions. Conduct the test with the subject standing facing you as you demonstrate. After the test, tell the subject, "You have a fine imagination. Now we are going to relax and use your imagination to get rid of fatigue and emotional irritations." For some subjects, you merely have to tell them you are going to teach them "meditation," and they will proceed to induct themselves without any reluctance.

Suggest eye closure by saying, "You will be able to use your power of imagination much better with your eyes closed. Close your eyes so that you avoid the interference of other images." From this point on, you can advance to other procedures being careful to substitute other words for "deep sleep" and hypnotic terms such as "suggestion." Substitute expressions such as "pleasant tranquillity," "emotional serenity," "free-flowing feeling," and "spiritually uplifting" work well as deepening phraseology. Instead of "suggestion," talk about "improved self-image."

An alternate disguised technique is to refer to the experience as "*alpha* mind-control," telling the subject he will learn to control his own mind. Another substitute term is "natural biofeedback technique." After all, what's in a name? It's the results that count!

The Trained Brain
Eliminates Pain

Hypnosis is effective as a medical adjunct both as an analgesic and an anesthetic. Hypnotic suggestion alters the way messages of pain are perceived, processed, transmitted, and interpreted by the brain and central nervous system. From the temporary, localized pain, experienced at the dentist's to the chronic pain of cancer patients, hypnosis offers new hope in alleviating suffering.

Headaches, backaches, arthritis, rheumatism, angina pectoris, sciatica, menstrual cramps, labor pains, and accident injuries are but a few of the numerous ailments which respond to the methods described in this book. For more and more people, hypnosis has proven to be a boon in lowering the threshold of pain and lessening the need for drugs.

How does hypnotism work as a painkiller? Let's consider migraine headaches. The classic migraine patient complains of painful throbbing around the head and eyes. Visual distortion—spots or an aura of flashing lights—are also often cited. Vascular disturbance inflicts its misery by dilating the blood vessels around the head. This stretching of the blood vessels creates a pounding sensation that causes severe pain. Under hypnosis, the patient is told to visualize himself relaxing and to see the congestion in his head drain away into other areas of the body. "Picture your hands turning rosy red as the blood moves from your head into your hands."

Jean G., age 45, complained of headaches for ten years. Every known means of relief had failed. Doctors pronounced Jean organically healthy, except for "nervousness." Under deep hypnotic trance, probing failed to reveal any underlying cause of her migraine problem other than stress. She was hypnotized seven times in bi-weekly sessions and given suggestions of relaxation and general well-being. Jean was told her headaches had no valid cause, but were simply habits which were correctable. Her first session brought some relief but then she complained of a headache before her second session. She almost gave up therapy because she expected to be relieved instantaneously after the first session. A friend of hers experienced speedier results, which had led her to believe that one session would be sufficient. She didn't realize that people vary in their ability to respond and that what is suitable for one may not be adequate for another.

Jean came for the third session and afterward felt much better, so she continued for the full treatment, which lasted twelve sessions. She persisted in studying hypnosis after her headaches were completely eliminated to improve her memory and recall. Highly impressed and pleased with the results, Jean decided to return to professional writing, which she had given up several years prior when the headaches had disabled her.

Writing gave Jean renewed feelings about life. "Without some creative activity, my life was just one big headache," she said. "Now everything is opening up. I feel life has no problems, only challenges."

THE BRAIN MANUFACTURES IT'S OWN PAINKILLER

Scientists have long been aware that the brain is the center of pain perception. They are learning more every day. Among the newest information is the knowledge that the brain gives forth a morphinelike chemical responsible for the lessening of pain. Imagine, an incredibly potent painkiller available to everyone, able to relieve the most excruciating pain, with no harmful side effects. Best of all, there is no fear of possible addiction, and your brain's chemistry is with you at all times. This natural substance is two hundred times as powerful as morphine. It is called *dynorphin,* one of a family of exciting brain chemicals called *endorphins.* These chemicals are a major part of the body's defenses. Evidence suggests hypnosis releases endorphins from the brain during trance.

Although endorphins are still under investigation, we know they are part of a collection of approximately fifteen brain chemicals called peptides. Many others probably are lying dormant, awaiting discovery. The secretion of these chemicals is believed to profoundly affect our emotions and behavior. This may explain the general feelings of well-being experienced by the person who meditates or uses hypnosis regularly.

Some people produce more natural painkiller and, therefore, have a lower threshold of pain than those who inhibit the flow of this vital substance in themselves. Expectations of suffering seem to affect the degree to which we lessen or increase our own discomfort. The discovery of the brain's narcotic manufacture raises hopes that we can diminish the use of the addictive painkillers that have entrapped so many people. Neuroscientists discovered this new information in their search for the mechanism by which drugs such as heroin and morphine produce a state of euphoria and deaden pain, thereby causing addiction.

Scientists suspect these natural narcotics attach themselves to certain areas of the brain, producing a chemical reaction with positive results. Hypnotherapists believe that, with successful application of the principles of hypnosis, the brain can be trained to produce extra secretions of painkiller without added stimulation by drugs.

HOW TO PRODUCE ANESTHESIA

Strategies for controlling pain vary to a great extent, depending upon the individual. If the person is highly hypnotizable, the operant may decide to use one of the speedier methods. Here's one that works well: ask the patient to visualize a local anesthetic being injected directly into the painful area. Then say: "The pain is becoming less and less. You have now been anesthetized. Numbness is taking over." This procedure is especially useful in dentistry. Here the dentist tells the patient to open his mouth and close his eyes. Dentist, after tapping the gum: "I have just injected Novocaine into the right side of your mouth. Your jaw is becoming completely numb. This numbness will become even stronger when you hear the sound of the drill. Nothing will interfere with the nerves becoming number and number. When I count backward from 10 to 0, the pain will be gone."

When the drilling is finished, the doctor will say: "The nerves in your face will now return to normal. When I count from 1 to 5 and say, 'wide awake,' you will open your eyes and there will be no aftereffects of discomfort."

A pill or ointment may be suggested as a substitute for the injection. Another technique: "Imagine the nerves that lead into the area controlled by switches in your brain. See your hand turn the switch and the pain is turned off."

It is a truism that pain is perceived in the mind and central nervous system, rather than in the skin or muscles at the exact site of the problem. Conclusive proof of this is illustrated by the phenomenon of the "phantom limbs." The Phantom Limb Syndrome is a bizarre complication that sometimes occurs following surgical amputation. The patient feels sensation in a part of the body that no longer exists. A surgeon described his patient's reaction after amputating his left leg at the knee:

"I feel a painful tingling in my foot," the patient said. "It feels as if it's still there." He complained of calf muscles aching. This reaction is explained as a conditioned reflex based upon a mental image. The thought of his injured limb produced the pain. In return, the pain then reproduced an image of the missing part. Anticipation is a fundamental part of cognition. Anticipating depends upon previous experiences that are stored in the memory warehouse. As a result of expectation, pain and body image become linked together in an automatic reflex.

Treatment consists of teaching the patient self-hypnosis. He is taught to relinquish his unreal memory of the limb and to use self-imagery as an aid in adjusting to reality. Hypnosis is also used in such cases to train the patient to relax and comfortably accept the prophylactic replacement. Hypnosis also facilitates cooperation before surgery. It can be employed to promote better sleep, bed rest, and stimulate appetite and general recovery after surgery.

The sensitive physician knows you do not limit treatment merely to parts of the body, but attend to the emotions as well. Hypnotic suggestion is invaluable in altering the patient's outlook on his misfortune, encouraging cheerfulness and expectations of improvement.

HELP FOR THE CANCER PATIENT

There are many ways in which the cancer patient can be helped through hypnosis. To begin with, it helps in controlling emotional depression, and building confidence in recovery. Patients report relief of the nausea resulting from radiation treatment and chemotherapy. In addition, where surgery is indicated, hypnosis lessens the need for anesthesia. In many cases, cancer patients treated with hypnosis get enough relief from pain that their need for narcotic drugs is substantially reduced.

Dr. Frank Lawlis and his wife, Dr. Jeanne Achterberg, of the

University of Texas Health Science Center in Dallas, studied the results of mental imagery on ninety cancer patients and reported that, in the large majority of cases, the mental visualization of healing aided recovery. The researchers teach patients to envision their internal disease process and then to picture the forces of their bodies overcoming the disease. They stress the importance of the patient's understanding how the body functions in both a healthy and diseased state. To sharpen their imaginations, Dr. Lawlis guides his patients through individualized relaxation exercises. In some especially difficult cases, he uses his self-hypnotic system in conjunction with drugs and other medical treatment.

A victim of cancer, who claims to have achieved complete remission, described his visualization this way: "I imagine I am surrounding the cancer cells with white light and then I talk to them mentally as you would to troublesome people. I tell the cells they must stop their activity and go somewhere else. They are unwanted."

This subject believed he could influence his own healing, and perhaps his strong belief had a positive reaction. This phenomenon appears to have enough validity to provide an avenue for future exploration in the same way religious healing now commands the interest of researchers. In all areas of healing, a self-helping attitude on the part of the patient brings hope and can certainly do no harm.

Some years ago a group of hypnotists volunteered their services to terminally ill cancer patients at the Memorial Hospital in New York City. They reported that some of the patients who had not been able to move their limbs because of pain and weakness responded so well to hypnotic suggestion they were able to get out of bed, dress, and see a movie in the hospital theater. While they were beyond complete healing, their last few months were made more bearable by the regular visits of the therapists who trained them to use self-hypnotic suggestion to lessen the pain and discomfort of their condition. For many terminally ill people who have grown immune to the effect of painkillers, hypnosis offers relief as a last resort measure.

In some hospitals in Europe tapes are used for terminally ill people to ease their suffering during the last few months. Joyce Slone, a psychiatric nurse who practices hypnosis, reported that such is the practice at The Institute of Suggestology in Yugoslavia, where patients can tune in on healing or reconditioning tapes while they are convalescing. The doctors there claim regression of serious diseases based on mental reconditioning.

THE PAIN OF DENTISTRY

The use of hypnosis as an adjunct to the practice of dentistry is no longer controversial. Trained hypnodontists are now making full use of its many benefits. The skilled hypnodontist carefully applies the techniques, encouraging hypnosis where practical while, at the same time, employing traditional methods.

The bravest person among us may shudder at the thought of a trip to the dentist's chair. For this kind of patient, dentists find hypnosis a valuable tool in making the experience less fearful as well as less painful. Hypnotic anesthesia has made dentistry possible for many who heretofore were unable to submit themselves to the needed treatment. Not only do the techniques cause treatment to be tolerable for the patient; the dentist is also relieved of undue strain in handling difficult patients.

The value of a psychosomatic approach as an integral phase of dental practice has been proven not only to lessen the pain of drilling, but also effective in allied work such as orthodontistry, periodontistry and other special areas. There is more to hypnosis than merely putting the patient "to sleep" and performing on a numb subject. Drugs could do that. Hypnosis is used in a more important way—to relax the person emotionally, thereby eliminating stress and apprehensions. Hypnodontists cite a special advantage over injecting anesthetic. There are no side effects such as numbness and mood changes, which often accompany the use of drugs. Also, self-hypnosis can be taught to difficult patients who can self-administer autosuggestions in the few minutes prior to treatment, while they are in the waiting room.

Where children are concerned this is especially important, because a pleasant experience conditions the child to future visits without the usual fussing. This can make the difference between a healthy mouth and a lifetime of dental problems. Dentists have told me that the more squeamish the patient, the easier he is to hypnotize. The stronger the distaste for dental work, the stronger the motivation to avoid pain and discomfort. Therefore, the patient opts to cooperate as an escape.

The science of hypnodontia has spread to such an extent that a special organization exists, The American Society of Psychosomatic Dentistry. This is an association of ethically minded dentists who have been trained and certified to apply hypnosis in dentistry. The members recognize the psychological reactions of each individual in relation to his treatment. The dental application of hypnosis was begun early in the year 1948, many years before the American Medical Association recognized hypnosis as a valid medical adjunct, by a group of dentists in the northwest, working under the leadership of pioneer Thomas O. Burgess, Ph.D, a clinical psychologist often referred to as the "father of dental hypnosis." The organization is now national in scope and publishes the *Journal of The American Society of Psychosomatic Dentistry*. The mystic confusion surrounding hypnosis has worn away and now this scientific phenomenon is applauded for its many successes.

RELIEF FROM CHRONIC BACKACHE

Many sufferers of back ailments tend to be fatalistic about their problem. "The doctor said I just have to live with it," is an expression we often hear. This sort of mental reinforcement makes it difficult to convince the troubled person that a cure is possible. Negative thinkers have sensitized themselves to endure needless mental and physical anguish. Some are driven to the edge of suicide due to the excruciating pain affecting not only a specific nerve, but their entire nervous system.

Dr. William S. Kroger, in his book, *Clinical And Experimental Hypnosis*, says: "There is an 'organ language' which the body uses to voice its protest. The choice of the organ system is determined by the focal area in which the conflict occurs."

Thus, expressions such as, "carrying a load on my back," "get off my back," "pain in the ass," and "pain in the neck" all become an emotional base for localizing discomfort, which indeed may lead to pain. The more the negative expression is verbalized, the greater its power as a conditioning force. We are all influenced by choice of words and the emotional–physical impact which they deliver.

Relieving pain of psychosomatic origin begins by helping the afflicted person gain awareness of his unconscious habit of emotional reinforcement. Dr. Kroger recommends using both posthypnotic suggestion as well as teaching the patient self-hypnosis and autosuggestion. Pain removal by a hypnotherapist always requires the patient's permission, because symptom removal may cause the unaware individual to shift the symptom to another area.

After standard induction to as deep a trance level as possible, mobility is suggested in the following way. The patient is told to move the pain from its entrenched position. "See it shifting . . . drifting . . . up and down . . . then to the front . . . up through the respiratory system and, finally, breathe it out with the next outgoing breath. Expel the pain out of the body completely . . . never let it return . . ."

Some therapists suggest: "Visualize the pain as a blue mist. Picture an opening in the area of pain and, as you exhale, see the blue mist exiting out of the opening in the troubled spot." Instant removal of pain is possible, providing the subject is medium to somnambulistic. The hypnotist places his hand directly on the painful area and says, "My hand is a sponge . . . ready to soak up all your pain. You will give it to me and I will throw it away because you don't neet it. Now as I count from 1 to 3, the pain is gone . . . one . . . going . . . two . . . going . . . three, take a deep breath and blow it out . . . release the pain permanently . . . three . . . going . . . going . . . all gone!"

ANOTHER VISUALIZATION

"Picture your back as twice as wide as you normally think of it . . . also twice as long. Get the feeling of wide, open spaces . . . lots of space for the muscles, nerves, shoulder blades, and vertebrae to float around in . . . wide open back . . . feel the spaciousness. Now imagine the nerves in your back branching out of the spine in knots."

The patient sees his pain in knots. Then he is told to visualize the knots unraveling, the muscles opening up no longer gripping the nerves. After he awakens, he feels free of pain. The suffering person must then be taught how to use self-hypnosis to remove the pain should it return another time.

In cases of arthritis, one of the most common sources of human agony, pain often disappears during the very first hypnosis session because arthritic pain is to a great extent a result of tension, and when the muscles are relaxed during hypnosis the pain is definitely eased. To aid in the remission of any illness, the patient is trained to envision his internal organs fighting the disease. He learns to see images of his body having overcome the ailment. The images do not have to be medically factual, as long as they are believable to the subject. Imagination is stronger than reality when belief and hope are present.

CHILDBIRTH

Patients who have experienced hypnotic anesthesia for childbirth are unanimous in their approval. Hypnosis and the use of self-hypnosis are fast assuming a dignified position in the area of obstetrics. By using these methods, a large percentage of pregnancies can be carried through the early stages of delivery without the use of sedation or anesthesia. However, in the second stage, some degree of medical analgesia is sometimes resorted to, depending upon the individual case.

Women are becoming cognizant of methods to control and relieve pelvic pain that do not depend upon noxious drugs and other such agents. Hypnosis may not ever supplant drug anesthesia; however, it can serve as an important supplement to methods already in use. There are a variety of reasons why a pregnant woman may elect to use hypnoanesthesia rather than drugs. Very often fear is the greatest motivator.

"I am terribly afraid of the pain of childbirth," said Clara Z. "When I discovered I was pregnant, I was terrified. I felt I couldn't go through with the birth. I heard about drugs they could give me, but that made me even more frightened of being unconscious. Then a friend told me about a hypnotist who helps people get rid of fears of things like flying and elevators. So I went to see him."

One of the things that convinced this young woman to use hypnosis for her delivery was that with it she could be conscious and involved in the birth process. Her anesthesia was administered by a trained hypnotist. However, many women learn the art of self-hypnosis and lessen their own pain by managing labor in a more relaxed way. The patient who chooses hypnoanesthesia must be trained in advance of delivery in the physician's office. It works best if she attends a series of sessions which act as rehearsals for the eventual birthing experience. Hypnosis works to eliminate the discomfort of labor, but does not impair the sensations and pleasant emotions of the experience. Free of pain and anxiety, the mother is fully aware and can enjoy her baby's first cry. Instead of pain, she feels the contractions merely as a tensing of the abdominal muscles.

Rhythmic breathing is an important part of this training process. Among the suggestions given are the following: "Breathe deeply as you were trained to do in your practice sessions. Concentrate on the rhythms of your breathing, the rising and falling of the lower diaphragm. As you feel a muscular contraction of labor, begin to pant in short breaths. Count the number of short breaths that you take between each contraction."

Focusing the patient's attention away from the pain and directing her thoughts into counting and breathing tend to lessen anxiety, and the sensation of pain becomes diminished. Hypnosis also reduces anxiety, speeding up the time between each stage of labor. Many obstetricians use hypnosis as the sole anesthesia in most of their cases. Dr. James A. Hall of the University of Texas Health Sciences Center in Dallas says, "Hypnosis can be coordinated with labor so that the beginning of each contraction is a signal for the patient to relax deeper into a hypnotic trance. The end of each contraction leads her to come out of the hypnotic state and communicate with her physician."

In other words, contractions and depth of hypnosis are harmonized by this method. An important postnatal hypnotic suggestion is for accelerated healing and the return to normal activity as quickly as possible and without complications. It has been found that, through the use of hypnosis and self-hypnosis, the usual moaning and crying of women in labor has been eliminated.

MENSTRUAL PAIN

Doctors tell us there is no valid explanation why some women have cramps and others don't. Sometimes doctors will tell a young woman, "Your condition might improve after you've had a baby," which isn't very practical to the single woman or the sixteen-year-old who may be suffering every month with her period. There are many prescriptions and over-the-counter painkillers that claim to offer relief from menstrual pain. However, some of these products can be dangerous, as witnessed by the fact that the Federal Drug Administration has banned several of them.

Self-hypnosis is especially effective and more practical than going to a hypnotist every month in order to prevent the recurrence of menstrual cramps. In fact, a woman can avoid the onset of cramps by giving herself the autosuggestion that she will have a normal, natural flow without discomfort.

"Glove anesthesia," which involves the focusing on numbness in the hand, works remarkably well with menstrual cramps. The person simply places the hand which has been anesthetized over the pelvic area and concentrates on transference of numbness to that area. One young woman who studied self-hypnosis with me created the following fantasy which works very well for her in removing pain from any part of her body:

"The first thing I do is relax and go into my space, my "center"— then I imagine myself shrinking into a tiny little nurse and I visualize myself inside my own body locating the source of the pain. I see it as a warm, red area. I then imagine myself placing an icepack on the pain and cooling it off."

Her visualization was simply a matter of mind over matter. I have since described the technique to other people suffering from internal pain, and they have reported back with positive results. Testimonials to the therapeutic effectiveness of self-hypnosis have become commonplace.

Skin Reflects Inner Emotions

The psychosomatic etiology of such skin disorders as eczema, alopecia areata, dermatitis, warts, psoriasis, and pruritus has long been established. Silently, spontaneously, our skin reveals inner feelings we would sometimes rather conceal. The condition of the epidermis reflects the underlying mental mood because skin and nerves are closely connected by sensitive, responsive tissue.

Because of this link, hypnotic suggestion has been able to produce various sensory effects upon the skin, such as blisters, numbness, and sensations of extreme heat or cold. The nervous system is capable of directing emotional force to concentrated areas or organs of reception. This may be why vast numbers of young people are troubled by skin eruptions at a time when they are very vulnerable to emotional upset. Just when the facial appearance is of greatest concern, the emotions reflect negative inner images. Acne is one of the most distressing skin reactions influenced by psychosomatic factors. Because at times the emotions can trigger or perpetuate this ailment, dermatologists often send people to a psychologist or hypnotist for a combined cure, mental and physical.

Many psychologists believe acne may be aggravated by a sense of insecurity about the approaching responsibilities of maturity. Thus, sometimes emotional adjustment proves to be more effective than medication. Hypnosis can be very helpful in creating greater awareness of this kind of problem in the patient. There have also been cases of acne clearing up quickly with the aid of a hypnotist who suggests aversion to picking at the lesions: "Any time you can think of picking at your face, you will visualize an ugly scar and stop instantly. You will then see your face becoming clearer and clearer."

One of the remarkable uses of hypnosis is in alleviating the distress of itching. Irritated thinking increased the itching feeling.

Because so many skin disorders are psychosomatic in origin they are therefore changeable. Deep neuromuscular relaxation, combined with suggestions given during the therapeutic trance, often brings speedy results. I have seen skin lesions heal before my eyes within a one-hour period of hypnosis. One of the techniques employed in the correction of acne and other skin disorders is the "mirror technique." Seeing oneself free of the unwanted ailment spurs the imagination to carry out the envisioned improvement.

Mental messages move quickly through the nerve passageways. Imagination tends to set off a physical response. We all have experienced skin reactions to our emotional feelings. Fear may cause "goose pimples" and body hairs to stand on end. Embarrassment may create a rosy blush for some, and an uncomfortable flush for others. Anxiety increases perspiration and stress often aggravates skin itching.

In cases of chronic itching in which there is no apparent physical cause, repeated verbalization aimed at symptom removal helps a great deal. Tell the hypnotized subject, "Your skin feels smooth and comfortable. See it looking perfectly clear without blemishes. Remember you have no reason to scratch. There is no itching . . . just a smooth comfortable feeling."

Suggest that the fingers are becoming very heavy, like lead, and therefore unable to scratch even if thoughts of itching do occur. Once you stop the person from picking on himself, remarkable improvement will occur in cases of psoriasis, eczema, hives, and acne. When the mind accepts a more positive attitude, physical reactions become self-protective rather than self-destructive.

EMBARRASSMENT TRIGGERS BLUSHING

The blush has long been the province of the poet, associated with the charm of innocence. Shakespeare loved the blush. Henry V, while pressing his courtship on Katherine, pleads, "Most fair Katherine, will you have me? Put off your maiden blushes. . . ." And Desdemona's father describes her ". . . of spirit so still and quiet that her motion blushed at herself."

Webster's Dictionary is clear on the subject of the emotional link involved: "Blushing . . . a reddening of the face, especially from shame, modesty, or confusion." Blushing is more than a physical reaction of blood rushing to the face. It is psychological. We blush when the inner self is unexpectedly touched by a thought which unearths a secret feeling we have tried to keep hidden. Regardless of emotional stimuli, blushing may be attractive at 14, but a nuisance at 40—especially for a man in our macho society. When young people are unable to resolve problems of stress, they become older people with hangups which are really hangovers from the past.

Leonard R. was a sales promoter for a cosmetics firm. Public speaking was not easy for Leonard. Throughout his youth, he had fought shyness. He diligently took all the prescribed courses, and read all the advertised books. Still, whenever he delivered a promotional spiel to an audience, he sweated profusely and his face grew red. His colleagues became accustomed to his flushes. He was always described as the man with "the ruddy complexion." Everyone seemed to accept Leonard's red face except Leonard.

"How can I stop this stupid blushing?" he asked at this first therapy session.

"A good place to start is to find out the original cause—the situation that triggered your uncomfortable feelings."

Under my guidance, he regressed and discovered the cause of his problem. Each time he made a mistatement about his product or exaggerated its worth, a sense of guilt, which he associated with lying during childhood, brought about the blushing. Regressing further into his past, Leonard remembered that, even as a small child, his mother would say, "I can always tell when Leonard is lying. God paints his face red so everyone will know."

Leonard was finally able to laugh at this recollection from his childhood. "What a silly reason for blushing during a sales promotion!"

Awareness opened his mind to the uselessness of his outgrown psychosomatic symptom of guilt. What is suitable as a reaction in childhood is seldom fitting for the mature person. Most of the problems of immaturity are due to situations where people are grown up physically, but are still thinking and feeling as children.

HIVES AND REPRESSED ANGER

Ramona L., a 42-year-old grade school teacher, broke out in huge, red welts whenever she repressed her anger. Explaining that her condition worsened whenever she felt aggravated by her students, Ramona showed the beginnings of insight into her condition. For many years, however, she had been convinced the hives resulted from food allergies.

"I used to think it was tomatoes, potatoes, strawberries, or cucumbers. I went on a rigid diet. Still, nothing helped. I even tried psychoanalysis—five years with no luck. Finally, my medical doctor suggested I call you for hypnosis."

At her first session, Ramona mentioned her addiction to tranquilizers. "It's the only way I can tolerate the wild brats I teach." In addition to the hives, her doctor suggested she be taken off tranquilizers and instructed to stick to a sensible low-calorie diet that he provided. During the middle of her third session, Ramona reached a deep trance level and we explored the source of her aggravation. To tap the warehouse of her recorded early memories, I suggested:

"Visualize the time and the situation that first caused the welts to appear. Who are you with? What is happening? Concentrate on your feelings and notice how your skin reacts."

As I spoke, I watched her arms closely. Within minutes, angry welts flared up. Though Ramona was in a deep trance, a look of amazement spread over her face. At this point, I reversed the image. "Now picture yourself completely healed. You are strolling in the country with a pleasant breeze caressing your clear skin. You look good and you feel so relaxed. Your skin is perfect."

Serenity melted the muscles of her face. I stared at her arms and said, "The welts are growing paler and smaller. The skin on your arms as well as your entire body will soon be perfect . . . the welts are growing smaller and paler . . . smaller and paler. . . ."

The hives vanished even faster than they had appeared. I discovered that Ramona was able to turn her hives on and off by focusing her mental power on a negative or positive visual image.

The impact of what had happened under hypnosis convinced Ramona she had control over her body's reactions. Now, whenever an annoying situation occurs, instead of feeling anger, she knows how to reverse her disturbing emotions. She is conditioned to smile, take three deep breaths, and think of a solution to the problem.

Two years have passed since Ramona's last visit to my office. She has been practicing self-hypnosis and autosuggestion as described elsewhere in this book. During her last telephone call, she informed me, "I have been using self-hypnosis to control my weight, improve my sleeping habits, and reduce my tensions. Also, I have been able to discontinue using tranquilizers and medication for the hives. I don't let anger get under my skin anymore," she said, (which demonstrates the high level of her awareness), "I just let it all roll off my back!"

ECZEMA AND ANXIETY

Nick D., a 29-year-old waiter, suffered from recurring eczema for eight years. Whenever the rash appeared on his hands, his employer asked him to stay home until the condition cleared up. If you are thinking maybe Nick didn't like his job, you are right. But he never dreamed there was a connection between his resentment at being in "the servant business" and his breaking out in a rash. His frustrated desire to do something more suitable to his talents and ego resulted in eczema.

Nick tended to be absent-minded, often forgetting part of a customer's order. Misplacing objects in the kitchen caused the chef great annoyance and Nick was often chastised. He soon decided to study electronics in the evening. He didn't do very well as a student, finding it difficult to concentrate even though it meant getting away from being a waiter.

When I questioned him, he described himself as lacking the self-confidence to succeed at something new. "And besides," he rationalized, "I need the money I earn as a waiter to live on." Nick was trained to give himself the following autosuggestions through self-hypnosis:

"I will enjoy my work and remain relaxed. My hands will stay clear . . . no more eczema. Excellent memory . . . both as a waiter and for studies."

After four sessions of hypnosis and daily self-hypnosis with the use of a tape, Nick reported a diminishing of the eczema and an outstanding improvement in his memory. About this time, his uncle opened a restaurant and Nick became the manager, a position of authority which he enjoyed immensely. His eczema has disappeared completely.

PSORIASIS AND REJECTION

One of the most interesting case histories is that of Marcella B., a 27-year-old recreation worker in a day nursery. Though it was a hot summer day, she wore a scarf around her head, a blouse with long sleeves, and slacks to cover the lesions on her legs. Only her crusty eyebrows revealed the extent of her condition. Marcella rolled up her trouser legs and took off the bandana to show me, and said, "I've had psoriasis all my life. I've tried everything. Even psychological counselling hasn't helped me. I don't have much faith in anything. I don't think anything can help. Frankly, I'm trying hypnosis only as a last resort."

She explained with tear-filled eyes how parents of children where she worked asked her whether psoriasis was contagious. The only positive factor, she explained, was that during times when she was very relaxed the condition seemed to clear slightly.

Suggestions of relaxation, confidence, and faith were given Marcella. Although she was a resistant subject, after five or six sessions she finally reached a level deep enough for subliminal communication. I worked with her for six months, one one-hour session a week. At home, she listened to a tape recorder of positive suggestion twice a day in between her sessions with me. We were encouraged during periods when the psoriasis would completely clear up, then disappointed when the condition returned when we least expected it.

We decided to tap the deeper recesses of her mind for the earliest manifestation of the disorder. Age regression was used, followed by automatic writing.

Marcella's memory uncovered important material. Here is her story as revealed under hypnosis:

"I am 5 years old. I am at a summer camp with lots of other kids. We are in the recreation building. The boys and girls are playing a game. All the little girls put one shoe in a pile. Then the boys come in, choose one shoe, and try to match it to the right girl wearing the other shoe. Bobby got my shoe. He said, 'Oh, no, not her. I don't want her for a partner. She's too fat and ugly.'"

When Marcella came out of trance, I asked, "Do you think you were fat and ugly as a child?"

"Not really. Actually, I was a cute, little, chubby girl. But Bobby hurt my feelings and I cried hysterically. No one could console me. My parents had to take me home from the camp. I brooded about his remark for years afterward, feeling rejected. I still cry when I think about it."

"What has this to do with your psoriasis?"

"I still think of myself as fat and ugly, and feel unworthy of the attention of a nice looking guy. My bad skin keeps everyone away from me." Had she ever dated, I wondered?

"I never went out with boys in high school or college. They all shunned me, even the girls did. I had very few friends."

"How do *you* evaluate yourself?" I asked, "Say, on a scale from 1 to 10."

"At the bottom of the list—zero. I'm afraid to even look into the mirror. What I see disgusts me. I remember when I lived back home with my parents, every time I took a bath and saw my body in the mirror I had a crying fit all night."

Marcella was, in reality, a beautiful young woman. Her features were regular and delicate. Her full smile revealed perfect sparkling teeth. Though her scalp was covered with crust, her hair was thick and luxurious. Her figure was full, shapely and well-proportioned. She hid her body under loose, old-fashioned, homely clothing, anything to discourage the attention of men. Only her shoes were new and bright—perhaps a holdover from her experience as a child in summer camp.

I remember the joyful day when Marcella reported that her elbows and lower arms had completely cleared. She came in with her arms exposed in a revealing blouse. Her scalp had begun to clear. She admitted the positive results of hypnotic suggestion and within two weeks all the scales fell off. We were elated. However, a dramatic setback occurred that left Marcella feeling devastated.

She had visited her parents' home in Jersey to show them her remarkable recovery. Lo and behold, upon awakening and looking into the old bathroom mirror, she regressed back to her old memories, and noticed signs of redness returning to her legs and arms. At that moment, Marcella gained a deep awareness of the power of self-imagery. She left her parents' home feeling depressed, but felt better after discussing the connection between her emotions and her skin problem. Fortunately, she was able to remove the lesions once again through hypnosis. Six years have passed and Marcella is free of psoriasis.

REMOVAL OF WARTS

Reports from other hypnotists corroborate my own findings that 60 to 70 percent of warts cases respond positively to suggestive therapy. The deeper the hypnotic trance, the sooner one sees good results.

At 17, Mark T. had six warts on his right hand and several on his buttocks. His mother had come to me for help in solving a weight problem. During her last visit, she said, "I wonder if you can help my son. He broke out in warts when he was about 13. He may not tell you, but he also has warts on his buttocks close to the anal opening. The warts appeared soon after he was molested by a pervert while playing in the schoolyard." This case proved to be one of the strongest convincers that warts, like other skin blemishes, are closely linked to emotion and imagination. Mark was hypnotized three times and suggestions were made that the warts would diminish, then disappear and never return. His warts became smaller after the very first session. They were all gone by the third. Two years later, I called Mark to check and he reported the warts had not reappeared.

Josephine B. called me on the phone to complain she had developed warts on her hands and knees as a result of watching television. While at first this may appear preposterous, further questioning disclosed she had been watching a daytime serial sponsored by a wart remedy company. Repetitive suggestions during the commercials relating to the ugliness of warts had a reverse effect. She assumed the problem instead of the cure.

Because her warts were mentally induced, a learned condition, once Josephine relaxed she was able to unlearn the condition. After five hypnotic sessions, all the warts had dissolved. She still watches her favorite T.V. show, but knows enough about indirect hypnosis to protect herself from the harmful suggestions. Every time she sees the commercial, she tells herself, "This is not meant for me. I don't have warts and I don't want them."

The most unusual and fascinating case involving warts is that of Janie, a beautiful 16-year-old girl. Shy, lacking self-confidence, Janie behaved like a 12-year-old rather than like the young lady she was. The first time I saw her she was wearing a tee-shirt with a picture of a frog painted on it. Her habitual pose was with her head hung low, and her hands crossed and tucked into her armpits. Upon examining her hands, I saw the worst case of warts I had ever seen. They covered her fingers, wrists, and reached up toward her elbows. The right hand and arm were considerably worse than the left.

Fortunately, Janie proved to be an excellent subject, intelligent and cooperative. The first session showed slight improvement. At the second session, I decided to dig out the source of the problem. Age regression was used with verbal response.

"Why do you wear a frog on your shirt?" I asked.

"Because I love frogs. I think they're cute."

I took her back year by year, having established a signal so that when I mentioned the year when she first got the warts, she would raise her finger and then speak. Regressing to 8 years of age, Janie said, "I am playing with a frog and he just wee-weed on my hands. Everybody tells me I will get warts."

"Why do you still like frogs?" I asked.

Janie spoke in a baby voice, "I have a book and it tells how a frog turns into a prince if you treat it good."

When Janie came out of hypnosis, we talked about her relationship with boys. She was very immature for a sixteen-year-old and frightened about sex. The warts were one way of holding back her maturity. But, most important, she clung to the warts as a way of identifying herself with her imaginary prince. "I used to think that when a cute guy who looked like a prince came along, he'd recognize me by my warts and know I like frogs. I know it sounds silly but that's the way I used to feel."

Janie not only got rid of the warts, but also her misconception that life was based on fairy tales. Now she can understand herself, and her feelings toward the opposite sex much better.

GROUP THERAPY AND WARTS

Several adults who were attending group hypnosis for other purposes such as weight reduction and smoking also had warts and skin blemishes. Warts disappeared after multiple suggestions that related to the group's overall program. While some warts took longer to diminish and required reinforcement at home through self-hypnosis, all warts and skin blemishes vanished eventually.

There are numerous cases of warts being removed through suggestion without using hypnosis. As a child, an elderly aunt told me, "Prick the largest wart with a pin and then hide the pin where no one can find it." I did this and three warts disappeared miraculously overnight. Perhaps this was the beginning of my staunch belief in the power of suggestion. I know now that what the mind gives, it can also take away. My aunt had indirectly hypnotized me as a child, preconditioning me to expect good results. A dependable law of the mind is that anticipation brings its own reflection. *Conceive, believe, and you will achieve.*

SKIN STIGMATA—PASSION AND PUNISHMENT

The term *stigmata* is derived from the early Greek language and originally referred to the branding with hot irons of captured or fugitive slaves. After the crucifixion of Christ, the term stigmata took on a special meaning. Religious writers describe stigmata as the reproduction of the wounds that Christ suffered on the cross upon the body of a worshipper. Many of the authenticated cases involve saints, monks, nuns, and other ascetics. The most famous case of stigmata is that of St. Francis of Assisi. When he died in 1226, his followers examined his body and were amazed to discover that, in addition to the wounds, he bore fleshy formations that looked like nails. The *miracle* of St. Francis had great impact and after his death there was a dramatic increase in the number of reported cases of stigmata. Are stigmata caused by a miracle or by man's imagination?

Even the church leadership is beginning to wonder. The Catholic World Dictionary warns, ". . . care must be taken that the stigmata are real and due to genuine holiness and not self-deception or the result of mental suggestion." One thing seems certain; other kinds of symptoms may be seen for some time prior to the appearance of the overt wounds. All stigmatized people on record give evidence of mental and emotional anguish before the actual physical demonstration takes place. The unresolved question is this: if stigmata are regarded as a miracle, why is it that an hysterical emotional condition is a necessary prerequisite for the onset of the phenomenon?

It is also interesting to note that the nature of the wounds varies from one individual to another. Depending on the person's visual conception, the shape of the punctures might be square, round or oblong. There may be a great deal of pain and/or bleeding—or none at all. An explanation for the wide variability may be found in the fact that in many cases the stigmatists tend to reproduce the kinds of wounds found on a particular crucifix which they have seen. There have also been cases where stigmata appear and disappear during repetition of passionate prayers. *The conditioning effect of prayer is akin to autosuggestion and the state of meditative contemplation is similar to self-hypnosis.* These factors point to a strong possibility that stigmata may be psychosomatic in origin.

Stigmata are not confined to the Christian religion alone. Dr. Von Arnhard, a writer on religious history, speaks of frequent stigmata found among Moslem ascetics who immerse themselves in the sacred contemplation of the life of Mohammed. These stigmatics respond to their inner images and emotional stress by reflecting the wounds suffered by Mohammed during the battle for the spread of his faith. Instances of spontaneous stigmata among other religious sects have also been reported. The case that I will now describe is that of a modern young Jewish man of 24 who strongly identified with the agony of Christ.

I met Joseph during my most recent visit to London, when I was teaching self-hypnosis to a group of young people as an alternative to drug addiction. One of the students referred to him as "a Jesus freak." He called himself Joseph St. John, and considered himself a latterday saint. Joseph was tall, thin, and looked much older than his years because of the expression of pain etched into the lines of his face. A long, white robe reached to the tops of the sandals that covered his bony feet. His hair flowed down his back, as did his beard over his chest. Joseph could have stepped into a Cecil B. DeMille epic and played the part of Jesus without the help of a speck of makeup. As he stood facing me, he fingered a heavy, baroque cross, which hung from a chain around his waist.

A teenage girl, Lynn, had spoken to me about Joseph the night before. Now they both stood there—she, embarrassed; he, distrustful. She explained, Joseph and I live together. Although we love each other and sleep in the same bed, our relationship is just spiritual. Joseph is sexless. There have been times when I try to arouse him, but he turns away from me. He claims he is celibate because of his religious feelings, but I know something physical is worrying him. He gets terrible pains in his sex organs. Once when he started to warm up to me, he actually went into convulsions of agony. His hands even swelled up one time when he gave me a massage."

I asked Joseph if he had been to see a medical doctor and he assured me that he had had a complete physical examination and the doctor told him there was no organic cause for his pain. At my urging, Joseph had his doctor call me, and in the course of the conversation, he suggested I try hypnosis. I knew that in order for hypnosis to prove effective, Joseph would have to relinquish his need to suffer, that he would have to free himself of the guilt-punishment syndrome. And, most important, he would have to give up his identification with Christ's suffering on the cross.

Joseph responded well to testing for suggestibility and concentration and proved to be an excellent subject for hypnosis. After four sessions, the swelling in his hands was noticeably diminished and the genital pain had lessened. However, he and I both knew that there was a deeper cause of his distress. With his doctor's permission, I decided it would be helpful to regress him to the first time he felt genital pain in order to alleviate the image triggering his painful flare-ups.

Since my time in London was limited, I arranged to see Joseph every day for one hour. By the second week, he was ready to turn his inner telescope backward into time. We arranged for him to signal me when I mentioned the age where the problem started. When I counted back to 13, he raised his hand. I placed a large writing pad in his lap and handed him a pen.

"Write whatever comes to mind. Tell the truth. The truth will set you free of pain. Explain how your problem got started." With eyes closed and deep in hypnotic trance he wrote: "My real name is Joseph P. I live in Great Neck, Long Island. I am in my 13th year and my parents are upset. I am supposed to be confirmed and have my Bar Mitzvah, but I was never circumcised because I was a sickly baby and that's why they put it off. Now my mother tells me I have to have my tonsils out, but while I'm unconscious the doctor circumcises me instead.

While he wrote, I repeated in a monotone: "You are healthy. You are normal. There is no reason for pain; therefore, you feel no pain."

He paused at one point and drew a cross and wrote under it: "My mother crucified me and castrated me."

I questioned him about the redness and swelling of his hands.

He answered, "Before I was circumcised, I masturbated. My mother used to make remarks about my dirtying the sheets."

"When did you start to identify with Christ?"

"While I was still in the United States. I told my parents I had renounced the Jewish religion. I felt my real religion was to admit my pain to be the pain Jesus suffered for mankind."

"Why are you celibate?"

"I have given up the love of the flesh for the love of God."

"What kind of a person were you before you identified with Christ, when you were Joseph P.?"

"An honor student in art college. I had a one-man exhibition in a gallery at the age of 16."

I suggested he had two choices: He could continue to suffer pain in a life of celibacy without a woman's love and other fulfillment, or he could give up his painful, martyred self-image and live life as Joseph P., a young, talented artist. Joseph finally decided to forfeit the pain. After almost two months of daily hypnotherapy during which time he also listened to conditioning tapes at home, he finally made the change-over. I often wonder how much of human sexual dysfunction originates from self-denial and stigmatic punishment.

One happy day, Joseph arrived at my hotel and I hardly knew him. He wore a plaid shirt and jeans instead of his usual religious costume. His hair and beard were neatly trimmed. Not only had his facial expression changed, but even his voice was different. His girlfriend, Lynn, was with him. They brought me gifts and a painting Joseph had done to express his feelings after his first sexual experience without pain. At this moment the picture hangs over my typewriter. It is filled with both religious and sexual symbols, proof that the two are often intertwined.

I have since learned that Joseph and his girlfriend, Lynn, are back in the United States and that he has made contact with his parents. It is hoped that a greater awareness and closer communication has developed among them all.

Sexual Dysfunction and Hypnosis

Larry S., 33, had a high sex drive and a low self-image. While women aroused him to the point of frenzy, he always ended up feeling frustrated. Fearing criticism, ridicule, and ultimate rejection, he resorted to masturbation to the exclusion of female companionship.

When Nancy came to work in his office, Larry, a bookkeeper, had difficulty keeping his mind on any figures other than Nancy's. Still, he lacked the courage to ask her for a date. Instead, after staring at her all day, he'd return to his apartment at night and give in to his only sexual release, thereby satisfying himself. Having become conditioned to the sensation of his own hand, on the rare occasions when Larry had attempted sex with a woman, his overanxiety caused him to lose control. Even so, he decided to try one more time.

One day, he mustered his courage and asked Nancy, "How about having dinner with me tonight?"

"I'd love to," she said, wondering what had taken him so long.

They spent an enjoyable evening together, until the moment of truth came. Nancy, being a warm-blooded girl, invited Larry to her apartment. As the elevator went up, his libido went down. He wondered and worried: "Will I be able to follow through? Will I be able to hold an erection long enough to satisfy her?" In wondering and worrying, Larry predicted his own downfall. Of course he did not perform adequately. All self-predictions come true. It is impossible to succeed if you expect to fail.

UNDERSTANDING HUMAN SEXUALITY

Sexual fulfillment is composed of an interweave of emotional, mental and physical responses—in that order. On this, most experts agree. Psychological factors precede physical manifestations. Therefore, it is only natural that hypnosis should play an increasingly positive

165

role in the correction of such problems through mental persuasion. The inability to function seldom begins in the flesh but rather in the flash of images in the mind. The "fantasy of failure" takes over.

We perceive our bodies in three ways
1. What we are taught in childhood
2. What we imagine through fantasy
3. What we feel through our senses

Too often, we have been conditioned to view our sexual flesh as less than perfect. Because of this we have to use corrective imagery and sensory awakening to restore proper feeling and function. Hypnosis trains the patient to change his inner view and explore his real feelings. Negative memories, no matter how distant in the past, tend to lower pleasurable sensation because of the extreme vulnerability of sexual tissue to thought. In no area of human function is response to thought so immediate.

It is the responsibility of the therapist to teach the subject how to convert negative repressive images into positive, releasing ones. After training the subject to overcome his or her inadequacies, self-hypnosis should be taught, so that the subject can remain in control at all times. Suggestions and techniques are then applied during actual sexual experiences.

The variety of psychogenic sexual disorders which respond to hypnotic suggestion include:

Male Problems	*Female Problems*
Premature ejaculation	Disinterest, analgesia
Inability to get an erection	Clitoral exclusivity
Fetishes (fur, leather, etc.)	Inability to reach orgasm
Fear of penetration of vagina	Fear of pregnancy

In addition to the problems peculiar to gender, there are also some that affect both men and women. Both need to develop better sexual communication in order to prolong and intensify the pleasurable experience of intercourse.

SEX PROBLEMS WHICH AFFECT BOTH GENDERS

Overactive or Underactive Sex Drive
Inhibition, Anxiety, Sense of Guilt

Fixation on (or Rejection of) Masturbation
Disgust and Aversion to Oral Sex
Compulsive Promiscuity, Absence of Emotion
Latent Homosexual Desires, Transvestism

First, it should be noted that both men and women have problems functioning sexually sometimes. It usually happens when the mind interferes, thinking in ways that cause feelings of insecurity. When a man is trying too hard to impress a woman with his prowess, or a woman is worrying about her looks or whether she will become pregnant, the mind shuts off feeling.

I would like to draw an analogy between the state of consciousness experienced during sex and that which occurs during hypnosis itself. In both instances, there is an intensity of mental concentration combined with physical relaxation. When either is missing in lovemaking or in meditation, we remain in *beta,* which interferes with the free flow of fantasy. And without fantasy we cannot exclude environmental intrusions.

It is also important to know that there are physical factors that can cause sexual dysfunction. These include diabetes, obesity, drinking, and the use of assorted drugs prescribed for high blood pressure and depression. The most common cause of sexual problems, however, is psychological: the expectation of failure. The pianist who thinks about his fingers too much finds that by the time of the concert he has stiffened up. The skater who worries about falling takes an unplanned slide.

Some people silently tell themselves, "I can't." But inside every "I can't" person is an "I can." Too many people give up on themselves in despair.

LACK OF SEXUAL CONFIDENCE

Charles K. arrived late for his appointment and apologized profusely. He explained that he felt great embarrassment in discussing his sexual problem with a woman therapist. Why then, I wondered, had he chosen me?

"I figure that if I can talk about it with you, maybe it will help me get over being so nervous with other women." His face was flushed and his hands were restless. Charles responded to routine questions haltingly, as if he was carefully considering his answers before taking a chance on offending me. I asked about his childhood.

"What I remember as most painful is being teased and ridiculed about my nose, the way it sticks out at a funny angle."

Charles turned to show me his profile. I thought to myself, "A little pointed, but so what? Doesn't look too unusual. . . ." Out loud, I said, "Your nose seems to suit your face. It may have seemed too large when you were a child, but obviously you grew up to fit the nose. After all, nobody's perfect. A bit of difference makes each of us distinctive and more interesting."

He was not placated. "My father used to call me anteater! And my sister nicknamed me 'frankfurter nose.' Some of my close friends still call me Frank instead of Charles. I know my family didn't mean to be cruel, but by the time I was fifteen I had a bad inferiority complex. I was convinced girls were laughing at my nose every time I heard someone giggle."

Charles nervously avoided answering direct questions about his sexual difficulties. Finally, in answer to my direct question, "How has your nose affected your sex life?" Charles lowered his eyes and said, "Well, I'm 28 years old and I'm still afraid to ask a girl to go out with me. I'm especially worried about talking to strange women. Even when I know them, like I do my sister's friends, I still feel they might say something nasty about the way I look."

As mentioned above, therapists often find that hang-ups are really hangovers from past negative conditioning. Hang-ups, like hangovers, can be eliminated by removing the source of the problem. Just as negative self-images are learned, so can they be unlearned and a better sense of self established. I explained to Charles that before he could feel confident about a woman liking him, he would have to begin by liking himself. He had two choices as far as his nose was concerned: he could learn to live with it or have some plastic surgery. Under hypnosis he wrote, "Love me. Love my nose." Charles was developing a sense of awareness. He began to realize that a sense of self-worth doesn't depend on the size of one's nose or the size of one's penis or the size of one's breasts. Rather, it stems from how you feel about each part of yourself, and whether you accept or reject the total image.

A similar case of low self-esteem was that of Iris D., a beautiful young woman who was self-conscious about her breasts. Although she had worked professionally as a high-fashion model, her experiences in intimate relationships had convinced her:

"I'm just not sexy. I'm a turn-off. Men have told me that I'm built like a boy. Sure, the faggy clothes designers love my body, but the guy I want tells me to get implants."

Iris didn't get silicone implants. She decided to get a new boyfriend who likes her just the way she is.

After many years of working as a sex therapist using hypnotic methods to help my clients, I have heard every kind of cop-out for sexual malfunction.

"I'm losing my hair. Women like men with hair." Nonsense. Some of the world's greatest lovers have been hairless or balding.

"My teeth are crooked. I have a lousy smile." So what? Good-looking teeth are often made by a dentist. There are many balding, crooked-toothed people with pointed noses who have good sex and enjoy living. They simply see themselves as worthy of a loving relationship.

FEMALE ORGASM

Sadie S., 26, though married five years, had never reached orgasm. Before long, both Sadie and her marriage deteriorated. Her husband, Alex, began to stay out late with the "boys." When she confronted him, he complained, "It's your fault. It's that you don't have any interest in sex. You should go talk to your doctor about it."

Sadie took his advice and her gynecologist proposed hypnosis when he could discover no organic reason for her disinterest in sexual intercourse. After ten sessions of private hypnotherapy, she finally achieved the ability to respond to the point of climax. Her marriage is now stabilized, and instead of going out with the boys, Alex invites the boys to his home to meet his wife, who has a new attitude not only about her sexual self but also about her own appearance.

Sadie was so delighted with the results she sent her sister, Rose, who had similar problems, to me. Rose complained that sex was an ordeal. She not only could not reach an orgasm, but felt pain upon penetration. I explained that this was a result of her tension and not because of the size of her vagina.

"I guess that's true because I gave birth four times and one of my babies weighed almost ten pounds."

In probing into the reasons both Sadie and her sister Rose resisted sexual pleasure, we discovered that their upbringing had inhibited their normal reflexes. They were unable to "lean back, relax, and enjoy it." However, now that her sister Sadie had achieved orgasm, Rose was already ready for good results. And because positive expectations bring their own rewards, results were speedier with Rose. After just four sessions, she reported improvement to the point of clitoral orgasm and was still practicing her posthypnotic suggestions for total orgasm.

Here are the suggestions which worked well for the sisters Sadie and Rose: "Relax and allow pleasant feelings to flow. Sex is healthy and proper. Nothing to be ashamed of. More and more sensation with each sexual experience. Easy orgasm without straining. Better each time." They were instructed while under hypnotic trance to practice self-hypnosis regularly, especially before sexual intercourse, as a means of preparing the mind and the nervous system for a pleasant experience.

AVOIDANCE OF SEX

One of the most common difficulties underlying sexual inadequacy in both male and female are feelings of fatigue, sometimes real, sometimes imagined. We have heard the proverbial jokes about women who are perpetually tired or complain of a headache. These days, this kind of an excuse is equally common among men. Weariness often has a common origin—fear of failure to satisfy or be satisfied. Some people become mentally exhausted just thinking about sex. Behind the exhaustion is the concept of sex being a burden rather than a source of joy.

In the case of nonresponsive women, fear of sex may be complex. Fear of pain, penetration, and pregnancy head the list. There are also fears relating to attractiveness and possible rejection because of imperfections such as small breasts. Some women are so embarrassed by overt sexuality that they suppress sensual urges and live their lives with tremendous amounts of residual tension, which ultimately results in a variety of physical ailments. Pelvic congestion is not peculiar to the female. Behind a man's complaint of feeling too tired may also lie a repression of fears.

One of the great fears which plague men is the fear of failure to perform adequately, which for many means the inability to get an erection or to sustain the erection long enough to satisfy his mate.

Without confronting and correcting the problem, many couples develop a hidden hostility toward each other which spreads into the rest of their life. Intercourse for them becomes a battle rather than an exhilarating experience of love.

OVERWEIGHT AND SEXUAL INHIBITION

Remember Florence, the overweight wife? Her real problem wasn't her appetite; underneath her constant gorging lay a deeper sense of emptiness. She felt unloved and unlovable. The cold fact was that she couldn't warm up to her husband's sexual advances. While he complained of her "frigidity," she complained of his lack of emotional feeling for her. Meanwhile, her disappointed husband kept struggling and failing to sexually arouse her. Florence was far from frigid. Her sexual potential for pleasure was simply lying dormant, waiting to be awakened.

Florence had fallen into a pattern familiar to many overweight women, one of accommodating without participating. Lack of spontaneity and sensous involvement turns women into spectators, detached from their own antics. Sometimes sex amuses them, but more often it bores them. As bystanders, they become strangers to themselves and their sexual needs. Florence was one of these women, afraid of partaking in the exchange of pleasurable feeling. A sense of unworthiness because of her weight stood between her and the intimacy she so badly needed. She continued to suffer from self-perpetuating, psychic masochism, unable to surrender to pleasurable sexual sensation.

Florence had fallen into the habit of being totally inactive, both during foreplay and intercourse. "I would just lay there and let him do his thing." Later Florence would learn that inactivity suppresses sexual feeling, while active involvement spurs orgastic sensation. She would discover through hypnotherapy that sex is more than physical. Later she would learn to correlate sensual and emotional pleasure, but now Florence was like a young, innocent child. She longed to be pleased, but was unable to permit herself to relax and enjoy intimacy. She used her obesity as a shield of armor to keep her from becoming really close to her husband. Invariably, after a disappointing sexual experience, she would steal out of bed, and quickly and quietly devour everything she could find that was edible.

"Once I ate a whole loaf of bread and two jars of peanut butter at one sitting," she confessed, "and I wasn't even hungry that night."

After Florence lost the excess weight, she also lost her sexual inhibitions. Her hunger for food was transferred into a hunger for sexual/emotional closeness. Her center of pleasure had moved from oral gratification to the sexual gratification of maturity. As she became more confident in her body, she developed stronger sexual feeling and, after several months of therapy, finally reported that she was able to achieve orgasm. "I can enjoy sex in any position. I'm not ashamed to get on top, which used to upset me because I felt so enormous."

However, improvement didn't just happen. Florence worked at it diligently. Most people find that when they lose some weight, even five or ten pounds, there is a definite improvement in their sexual energy. While all fat people do not necessarily have a sexual problem, overweight definitely interferes with mobility and the sexual self-image. The middleage spread doesn't just happen to women. A man spreads, too. When he does, straining for intercourse with an overtaxed, sometimes overfull stomach can strain the heart, and cause other serious physical problems.

THE INADEQUATE MALE

Tolstoy said, "Man survives earthquakes, epidemics, the horrors of disease and all the agonies of the soul, but for all time his most tormenting tragedy has been, is, and will be—the tragedy of the bedroom."

Sexual deprivation and malfunction are habits that are learned. As such, they can be unlearned, and self-fulfilling habits can replace them. Some people go through their lives without sexual fulfillment because their relationships with others is frought with nervous tension and expectations of defeat.

The need for self-actualization is basic and, without a satisfying sex life, one is never totally fulfilled emotionally or physically.

Take the case of Murray A. Murray was 43 years old and a widower. He married young, and his only child, a daughter, was 21. She soon left home and became a wife. Murray, a successful business-man, traveled all over the world, then returned to his palatial home alone. This was difficult for Murray because he did not enjoy being a loner. Women interested him, but though he made attempts at attracting them, it was more talk than action. His conversations never culminated in pillow-talk. When a woman hinted at sex, or showed too much warmth, Murray cooled off. He made excuses to avoid sex, pleading he had to leave for an appointment, promising to call again. But he never kept his promises. Though sexually inclined and sexually deprived, he fled the confrontation. Why was Murray avoiding a successful relation-ship with a woman?

Murray was short, stout, and insecure. Alongside his bulging wallet dangled a miniscule penis. Afraid he could not satisfy a woman, he wasn't going to take the chance of being humiliated and rejected. When it came right down to it, Murray felt he'd never make the grade, so why even attempt it and be insulted?

When Murray came to me for help, he admitted he hadn't been to bed with a woman for six years, ever since his wife had died. "Life is passing me by," he complained. "Without sex, I don't feel like a man." Murray was miserable, unhappy, lonely. After six months of recondi-tioning, Murray's confidence increased. During a group session, he began to notice Marion. Marion had the bad habit of being too aggres-sive toward men. Luckily, Murray needed some of her outgoing per-sonality in order to balance his lack of confidence.

One night, Marion sought him out after the group therapy session. She invited him to a party and taught him to dance. She drew him out, humored him and, before long, they were attuned to one another. Marion saw substance in Murray, recognized qualities she liked in a man, and his money wasn't bad, either. With kindness, gentleness, and patience, she bolstered his ego and built his confidence. His insecurities dissolved in her warmth, and Murray became a total person again. It is interesting to note that the small size of Murray's penis turned out to be an asset. Marion's reason for hypnotherapy was vaginismus, which made penetration difficult.

ACCEPTING RESPONSIBILITY FOR SEXUAL HANG-UPS

Blaming others is a surefire way to hang on to hang-ups. Only by admitting a problem exists and accepting responsibility for it can the remake job be done. Positive suggestion under hypnosis is a powerful tool for reshaping sexual reflexes. Hypnosis brings mind-control through thought-patrol. With it, you can lift your libido as high and as wide as your imagination will allow. Sexual satisfaction is self-cultivated, but for some the link between expectation and experience has never been established. Such people need to be taught by the therapist that the most erotic part of their sexual apparatus is the mind.

The mind has greater power than all the drugs, alcohol, and marijuana in the world. Those who learn mind-mastery over their bodies can reach unimagined heights of ecstasy. The basic reason that hypnosis has proved to be so dramatically useful in solving sexual problems is that both hypnosis and sexual intercourse take place in an altered state of consciousness called *alpha-theta*. Sexual foreplay requires the same level of concentrated thought as the hyponoidal trance. Sexual intercourse leading to orgasm requires a depth of focused attention similar to that required for a deep hypnotic trance. Because of this correlation, when you train the brain to enter hypnosis, you are also preparing the subject to function better sexually.

For the man who lacks sustaining power and the woman who has difficulty reaching a climax, the effects of hypnosis seem miraculous. It is the difference between chance and choice. You can choose to improve upon mediocre sex and raise fulfillment to a new dimension. If the man is too fast, hypnosis slows him down. If the woman is too slow, hypnosis speeds her up.

Some people fall into the self-defeating trap of blaming their sexual problems on their mates. Janet F., attractive and intelligent, complained about her husband, "He is warped. His sexual desires are brutal, unnatural."

Janet had undergone five years of psychotherapy with some slight improvement. However, she still suffered from anxiety, was confused, and unable to cope with a marital relationship. After questioning her in some detail about her husband's sexual behavior, I discovered that his so-called "brutal, unnatural desires" were for oral stimulation. She felt oral sex was degrading and an indication that her husband looked down upon her.

"He treats me like I'm a hooker or some bimbo he picked up in a bar. He uses four letter words and that turns me off. I want to be talked to with respect."

After conditioning Janet to a deep level of hypnosis, she revealed an insecure childhood with parents who were not only cold to each other but indifferent and insulting to her.

"They were always telling me I would never amount to anything. They said I was stupid. When I would dress up for a date they would say 'you have too much makeup on. You look like a hooker.' My father once said, 'you're a bum just like your mother.' He would accuse me of chasing men, call me worthless, sinful."

Janet, like so many other young people, carried out her parents' negative prophecy. When she was 17, she ran away from home and found a job in a massage parlor. After a period of drug use and prostitution, she broke away and landed a job in a department store as a sales clerk. It was here that she met her future husband whom she married on her twenty-first birthday. Now, after five years and the birth of a son, the marriage was falling apart and so was Janet.

After six sessions, she reached a somnambulistic level and was regressed. The following exchange occured:

Hypnotist: "You are going back in time. You are now 26 . . . going back further . . . now 25 . . . feeling fine as you go back in time . . . 24, everything very clear, 23 . . . further back, 20 . . . you are getting there . . . 18 . . . you are there 17 . . . now, concentrate . . . tell me where are you and what are you doing?"

Janet became very agitated. This was the year when she had run away from home. Tears ran down her cheeks, although her body remained perfectly still. She was crying while in trance. I considered bringing her out of trance, but decided instead to comfort her at the level she was in. I softly stroked her shoulder and whispered that this would all soon be gone and everything would be wonderful, without problems. Then suggestions were made that she would be able to reexperience leaving home without being unduly upset emotionally.

"See your past as if you were watching a T.V. show with a flashback that is interesting but not disturbing." Reassured, she became calm and was guided into a deeper stage of revivification. She began to speak out loud at my suggestion.

"I've made up my face like a slut, the way they always say I am. Too much lipstick and mascara and my hair is puffed up. Tight sweater to show my bust. Tight skirt to show my rear end. A man named Tom is waiting down the street. He's going to give me a job in a massage parlor. So what . . . everybody says I'm bad anyway."

When Janet was aroused from the trance, suggestions were given that she would view the regression as a valuable experience in clarifying her past and bringing her an awareness of the causes behind her present behavior. She was greatly relieved, saying, "Well, I understand what was wrong with my parents now. They were using me because of their own hang-ups. And I also understand why I'm so uptight about my husband wanting oral sex. It reminds me of a time in my life I would like to forget."

Janet and her husband had several sessions of joint marital counseling with me. During this time, I taught them self-hypnosis techniques for mutually satisfactory sexual intercourse.

SEX OFFENDERS

In cases of antisocial sexual behavior such as child abuse, incest, and rape, hypnosis holds out new hope of eliminating the problem at its source. There have been reports by state corrections officials in Connecticut who have been treating sex offenders with hypnotism combined with electric shock treatment. Because shock techniques are considered controversial, they are only used in extreme cases. However, to date, the results have been extremely positive, without any detrimental side effects. Commissioner of Prisons John R. Manson was quoted as saying: "Not one of the many convicts treated in the state program has so far been recharged with repeating further sex offenses." The program was set up for hardened sexual offenders with records of repeated attacks upon children.

When asked to describe the hypnosis-shock program, state officals said that only volunteers participated. The inmates were first hypnotized and then given suggestions of negative aversion in relation to sexual thoughts about children. They were then given positive suggestions to respond to thoughts about mature women. They were shown slides of nude women and children. When they watched the slides of women, the voice of the hypnotists suggested normal response and feelings of arousal in the future under the proper circumstances. However, when a child's picture was flashed on the screen, the convicts received an electric shock in the genital area. The shock was startling and unpleasant but not so severe enough to do physical damage.

The inmates were then hypnotized again, both in private and in group, and put through an imaginary sexual experience with a child. During the visualization, fear and horror were evoked and emotions of shame, guilt and disgrace were emphasized. The process was repeated until the inmate could no longer associate sexual pleasure with children because his reflexes had been reversed.

Hypnotherapy is also used to trace events back to the original root of the problem. Regression to childhood may be employed and, in several cases, the therapist has discovered that similar offenses had been committed against the prisoner when he was a child. A mental cleansing procedure takes place along with reeducation aimed toward desensitizing the molester away from children. He is then sensitized to respond normally to mature females when he leaves the prison.

Once the disturbed person learns hypnotic principles, he begins to avoid the feedback of unwanted reflexes. Eventually the convicts are taught how to do self-hypnosis and eliminate the troublesome signals permanently. The conditioned patterns which caused the difficulty in the first place are replaced by a better frame of reference.

HYPNOSIS FREES ACCUSED

In Philadelphia, a witness under hypnosis corroborated clues leading to the arrest of a 36-year-old plumber suspected of being the "jogging rapist." William Gray was charged with seven counts of rape and ten attempted rapes. Police say Gray jogged up to young girls, asked them the time, and then assaulted them. After an extended period of searching, police were unable to track down the suspect. Then one day, a woman walking a dog heard a 16-year-old girl scream. She then saw a man jump over a hedge and flee in a car. After being hypnotized, the witness was able to fill in a precise description of the man, what he was wearing, and the car in which he fled.

A major problem facing attorneys today is that people can't remember what they have seen and become emotionally disturbed when questioned. Defense Attorney Douglas Combs, who practices in Kansas City, described how a poorly educated Mexican-American, Jesse Flores, was cleared of rape and murder charges through hypnotic techniques. Attorney Combs stated the client was charged in the death of Margarita Haro, a 17-year-old girl. "The evidence was overwhelming, a defense attorney's nightmare."

The state alledged that the teenager, an acquaintance of Flores, drove off with Flores after an argument with her mother, who opposed the relationship. Three days later, Margarita's body was found in a roadside ditch. An autopsy showed she died of a skull fracture. Flores claimed he didn't kill the girl. He was very nervous and spoke with difficulty. Much of what he said was incoherent, rambling, and emotional. His attempts to explain made him appear guilty. Combs enlisted a clinical psychologist who used hypnosis to interview Flores in his jail cell. The psychologist recorded the interview on video tape so it could be studied by the attorneys.

"At the conclusion, we had the missing details we needed to reconstruct what really happened," said Combs. "It turned out there was no commission of a crime." The girl had fallen or jumped from Flores' car. Flores stopped and found the girl was breathing. He then placed her in his car, intending to take her home to her mother. On the way, he realized she was bleeding and he removed some of her clothing to see how badly she was injured. Flores then panicked and, afraid of facing the girl's mother, left the girl and ran off. When the District Attorney viewed the tape, he ordered a polygraph test which backed up the statements Flores had made under hypnosis. The judge then dismissed all charges against Flores and he was freed.

HOMOSEXUAL TO HETEROSEXUAL AND VICE VERSA

According to the Masters and Johnson survey and the Kinsey Report, there are more heterosexuals repressing homosexuality than the other way around. Sexual confusion and misconception mirrors the confused world around us. Most homosexuals prefer their choice of life-style and have no intention of changing. There are some isolated cases, however, in which a homosexual may decide to become a heterosexual. Contrary to popular misconception, this is entirely possible through hypnotherapy. The following case, while not typical of homosexuals in general, illustrates the power of the mind in determining the nature of one individual's sexual activity.

Hollis G., an actor, 28 years of age, wanted to give up his

homosexual life-style, "settle down, marry, and have children." He appeared sincere and well-motivated, and in the initial stages of therapy quickly gained insight into the origin of his sexual behavior. He didn't believe he was born to be homosexual. In fact, he was one of the rare homosexuals who felt uncomfortable as a nonconformist.

After six months of biweekly sessions, Hollis developed an aversion for all sex and remained celibate for several months. Then, for a period of weeks he lived a bisexual life-style which culminated in the woman winning out, and he settled down for six months in a devoted hetero-sexual relationship. He reported his success to me and told me of his plans for marriage. His behavior at this point indicated a complete reversal in sexual activity. An excellent subject, Hollis produced re-markable examples of automatic drawing and self-directed dreams. There was recurring theme in his dreams and fantasies that indicated a highly critical attitude toward his intended wife. In speaking of her in a conscious state, his reports were glowing; however, after periods of self-hypnosis he would report that he was troubled by anger, only toward his fiancée, but also toward his mother and sister. One day, while in trance, he spontaneously regressed to the age of seven. When he came out of the trance he told his story.

"At the age of seven, I had a close friendship with the boy next door. We really loved each other." Hollis became very emotional as he recalled his childhood feelings. "His name was Wally and we used to play around sexually. Nothing much. Just touching and measuring our penises to see who was bigger. My sister was watching us from the closet where she deliberately hid. She told my mother, who banished Wally from the house. I was never allowed to speak to him again."

In spite of the anger Hollis felt toward his sister and mother, he gained a great deal of awareness from the recall of this experience. He was most determined to break with his homosexual past and marry his fiancée. Hollis persisted until he finally believed that his homosexual behavior was symptomatic of a deeply rooted neurosis that could be traced to his early relationship with his sister and mother. Because he believed this to be true, it was true for him. He believed that his was an acquired behavior resulting from psychological rather than physical causes. Added to this was a strong religious need to be accepted by his church members.

Hollis and his girl were married in a church wedding and soon after she became pregnant. At last report, they had been married for four years and were doing well.

HYPNOTHERAPY FOR SEX PROBLEMS

DIFFERENTIAL RELAXATION

Instead of using the standard progressive relaxation technique, (from the top of the head to the tips of the toes), begin by suggesting that the subject focus his or her awareness upon the pelvic area. "Imagine a powerful magnetic force shining over the pelvic area into the flesh of your genitals. All negative stress will be converted into positive energy and stored in your sexual center for future use." Now proceed to relax the subject from his or her toes up to the magnetic force that is transmuting the negative current into positive sexual power. Next, start at the scalp and carry the energy down to the pelvic area: "The magnet is drawing all the tension from every part of your body and changing it to super sexual energy." Repeat the exercise several times.

SPECIAL BREATHING TECHNIQUE

Instead of the usual "with each breath you drift deeper and deeper," here is a sexual breathing exercise borrowed from ancient yoga technique. It is called *the magic cycle.* Suggest: "As you breathe in, imagine that you have a tube that carries oxygen and energy down through the center of your body into the pelvic cavity. As you exhale the air, visualize a misty stream of warm air coming out of the opening of your sexual organ (penis, or vagina). As you breathe in this important life force (*Prana*), you are breathing in sexual power for (control, orgasm, a stronger erection, etc.). As you breathe out, you are expelling all your problems, tension, and stress. Visualize a stream of refreshing cool air flowing into your nostrils, warming up inside your body, and drifting out of your sexual opening, warm, moist, and very pleasant. With each breath your sexual confidence and ability grows stronger and stronger."

A DEEPENING TECHNIQUE

In addition to standard routines, such as countdowns, the following method combines deepening with autosuggestion: "The deeper you go into self-hypnosis, the stronger your sexual improvement will grow. Tell the subject to repeat to himself silently, as you speak out loud, the above suggestion, changing it to first person, "The deeper *I* go into self-hypnosis, the stronger *my* sexual improvement will grow." Combine "hetero-hypnosis" and self-hypnosis with the following technique, "As I count backward from 50 to 0, you count forward from 0 to 50. This will take you much deeper. *Both your counting and mine will double your sexual improvement.*"

FANTASY AND SELF-IMAGE

The subject's normal, healthy body image may be eclipsed due to repetitive sexual failure. You will get good results by training the subject to improve his or her inner self-image. "See yourself standing nude in front of a full length mirror, looking good and feeling healthy and happy. Look into your eyes and tell yourself you are attractive, normal, and improving with every experience." The suggestions may vary according to the specific problem. Another very effective technique is: "Imagine you are sitting in a movie theater where a very erotic film is to be shown. You are the star, the director, the writer, and the audience. Picture yourself behaving without your old problem. You are naturally virile and responsive. You have no guilt, no embarrassment. After you have successfully completed the best sexual experience of your life, take a bow. You were great. Hear the applause. Tell yourself, 'I have everything it takes to turn that rehearsal into the real thing.' And next time, you will do even better. Each time you will improve."

TAILOR-MADE SUGGESTIONS

Suggestion, when believed and accepted by the patient's subconscious, becomes internalized. Therefore, the suggestions should be formulated with the subject before induction. Posthypnotic suggestion is carried forward by the patient into the next sexual encounter. Phrase the suggestion in the first person and tell the subject to mentally repeat the phrase as you speak out loud. For men it might be: "I can restore full potency and have long-lasting control." Or, "I am sexually confident. What the mind caused, the mind can cure." "I will regain my youthful virility. Sex is right at any age." Keep the suggestions short and to the point. For women, try these: "I am sexually normal. I have everything it takes to reach orgasm." "I enjoy sex without guilt or embarrassment. I will experiment freely." "I enjoy the feeling of the penis. There is no pain, no anxiety." Train your subject to practice positive autosuggestion at all times. Clearing the mind of negative anticipation requires affirmative reinforcement before, during, and after sexual intercourse.

SENSORY AWAKENING

Sensuality can be markedly increased. Orgastic sensation can be intensified by internalizing images and suggestion. Every picture and every thought has an inner message of its own. Inhibiting blocks can be dissolved and pleasure heightened. Because people use only a speck of their sensory potential, expect outstanding results in this area. Suggest: "All of your senses will harmonize in intensifying pleasure and creating better function. Your sense of sight. Your sense of hearing. Your sense of smell. Your sense of taste and touch. All will combine to make each experience more fulfilling in every way: mentally, emotionally, physically, and spiritually. You will feel pleasure more and more deeply and completely."

TRAINING THE SEX MUSCLES

Thoughts cause a chain reaction as every idea sparks an emotion, which, in turn, reacts on a particular muscle of the body. Thoughts of pain, such as those that occur to the fearful, nonorgastic woman, can cause vaginismus, a tightening of the sphincter muscles, and prevent penile penetration. Other women lack muscle tone, which is an obstacle to their reaching orgasm and decreases sensation for the male. Men, also, need to learn how to train their sex muscles. For premature ejaculation, muscle flexing increases staying power. Hypnotic training increases staying power. Hypnotic training accelerates this important control. When your subject is in medium or deep trance, suggest: "Tense your sexual muscles as if you are holding in the urge to urinate. Focus on keeping this contraction until you count to 5. Contract the muscles as you breathe in. As you exhale, relax the muscles, counting from 5 to 0, slowly." Then tell your patient to rest while he counts to 10. Repeat the training several times, then explain: "Feel as if you are drawing together extra circulation and sexual energy. You have frontal muscles, anal muscles, and muscles at the base of the penis or inside the vagina. Flexing this group of muscles will bring you greater tone and control."

REGRESSION WITH AUTOMATIC WRITING

The hypnoanalyst may find it necessary to uncover the root of the problem in order to clarify the patient's understanding of why the dysfunction exists. The process requires a medium to deep trance level and usually involves four to six conditioning sessions. Regress year by year; "You are now 25, 24, 23, 22, etc." Go slowly, taking enough time for the subject to visualize himself in a sexual embrace. Suggest: "When you come to a situation which negatively affected your function, raise the forefinger of your right hand, and I will give you a pen and pad, and you will explain how your problem originated."

Hypnosis Meets New Challenges

The use of hypnosis is rapidly spreading into areas long considered out of bounds. Once looked upon as a parlor stunt and then only reluctantly accepted by the medical and psychological professions, today its use is widespread among all sorts of respected people. Hypnotic practice is widely used not only in hospitals and psychiatric clinics, but in jails, in the courtrooms, in sports, in the schoolroom, and even inside churches and synagogues. Judges, lawyers, and police officers have come to recognize hypnosis to be an excellent investigative tool, a reliable aid in memory recall and rehabilitation of criminals. Proponents cite case after case in which information gained through hypnosis led to the solution of difficult criminal cases.

The Chowchilla, California kidnapping case may be the best known example. Under hypnotic induction, a school bus driver recalled a license number that led police to the kidnappers who had abducted a busload of schoolchildren. Extremely useful in piecing together the forgotten information that helped to convict the kidnappers, hypnosis was also used as psychotherapy for some of the children, who were greatly disturbed by the experience. There are no limits to the variety of ways in which this fast growing art can be utilized.

An increasing awareness exists among sports figures that self-images improved during hypnotic trance can make the difference between being a winner and an also-ran. Hypnosis can also produce increased concentration and communication inside the classroom and makes the work of a teacher much easier. Inside prisons, psychologists are using it as an aid in retraining prisoners to become socially useful citizens. Specialized methods are employed as a wedge with which to enter and understand the criminal mind, and as a means by which changes and solutions can be discovered.

CRIME AND LAW ENFORCEMENT

Judicial attitudes regarding the use of hypnosis to obtain evidence are mixed. Certain states have yet to admit information gained in this manner. However, it wasn't too long ago that presently accepted forms of evidence such as fingerprinting, breathalizers, ballistics, and hand-writing exemplars were undergoing the same kind of critical scrutiny. Now, even mechanically produced evidence from lie-detection machines is commonplace in criminal trials all over the country.

Tapping the unknown areas of the subconscious still worries some diehards and conservatives. However, many agencies (including the FBI) find that hypnotic investigation fills a void, solving the problem of how to get people to remember what they've forgotten. Modern day investigators point to the stunning success with what they term, "a new weapon—hypnotism." In fact, law officers are cracking open some of the most baffling of their previously unsolved cases. Hypnosis has become a boon to the overworked and understaffed police departments in many urban areas.

In New York City, the police department has appointed its own official hypnotist, and his success in solving difficult criminal cases has won him nationwide acclaim. Hypnosis has proven to be the magic key for unlocking the frightened minds of the countless witnesses who have blocked out important details after viewing a disturbing crime. The information is there, but the confused person cannot recall it when tension gets in the way.

Sgt. Charles Diggett, the New York Police Department's official hypnotist since 1976, declared, "Our subconscious minds automatically bury the painful parts of the experience. Otherwise we'd never be able to get over it." Sgt. Diggett has been called in to help solve 113 cases since the program was officially introduced. New information turned up in 62 percent of the cases, directly resulting in arrests. In the case of a young man whose uncle was shot, the teenage boy's description under hypnosis was so detailed that the homicide detectives realized he knew the suspect personally. After hypno-induction, the teenager was easily able to select the man's picture from mug shots.

In Los Angeles, both the Police Department and the FBI are using hypnosis with equally startling success. Lt. Dan Cooke of the Los Angeles Police Department stated: "We have ten lieutenants who have been specially trained as hypno-investigators. They are employed extensively in many of our cases and are loaned to other cities throughout the state." Dr. Martin Reiser, Director of Behavioral Science Services of the L.A.P.D., is also Director of a fast-growing organization called *Law Enforcement Hypnosis Institute*, where he trains investigators from all over the country in the use of special hypnosis techniques such as time regression and revivication.

Dr. Reiser tells of a small boy who saw his father murdered and hastily scribbled the license number of the fleeing killer's car. "The boy had transposed two digits and was unable to report the number correctly. Under hypnosis, he remembered the license and an arrest was made." Dr. Reiser says that hypnosis produced information in nearly 80 percent of the 350 cases in which it was used. "More and more agencies want to get people trained because hypnosis works and is very cost-effective."

The FBI seems to agree. "It is a magnificent way of interviewing and relaxing a person to tell what they have witnesed," said Special Agent Supervisor, Dr. Patrick Mullany, Senior Psychologist at the FBI Academy in Quantico, Virginia. "We have four special agents who are licensed, certified hypno-investigators, and believe it is a valid way of getting information."

Lt. Harry Haines, Chief of Detectives in Concord, California, also uses hypnosis with excellent results. He commented, "People give better, more vivid descriptions than they can under a normal fully conscious state." He also made the following important point: "Hypnosis is only used on witnesses and victims. We never use it on suspects. Obviously, you would not hypnotize somebody into making a confession. And, of course, we only hypnotize witnesses with their full consent."

Can an accused murderer be convicted by "memory-jogged testimony?" Here's a case in point. Mrs. Dyanne Quaglino was struck and killed by a car that sped away without stopping. A witness and tire tracks led police of Santa Barbara, California to the car that was involved. Later, they traced the car to Myron Jenson, who had sold the questionable vehicle to another person several months prior to the accident. But to whom? They found the man's name, but Jenson could not remember what the man looked like. Detectives showed him a picture of their murder suspect, the dead woman's husband. Jenson was at first confused. He said the photo seemed to ring a bell, but he wasn't positive. After hypnosis, he was sure. Jenson's testimony was the crucial element in Mr. Quaglino's conviction on a charge of first degree murder.

Here's a reverse application of police hypnosis. Weekly hypnotic trances are helping a group of sheriff's deputies to relax from the everyday pressure of being cops. A hypnotist conducts "tension relaxation sessions" with the Lee County Sheriff's Department of Fort Myers, Florida. In a typical session, hypnotist Robert C. Ward instructed twenty-five hypnotized deputies to "feel relaxation flowing through your face, shoulders and body." He explained, "One of the side benefits is that police are able to leave their jobs behind them and go home to be a good father and husband rather than a tense police officer who might be irritable and take it out on the family. It also helps them ward off headaches, ulcers, and premature aging—all caused by tension."

One deputy reported, "I'm generally more energetic and pleasant to be around after hypnosis. I feel more like getting back to the job and tackling problems, and also sleep more peacefully."

JUDGE HYPNOTIZES DEFENDANTS

Judges are also becoming involved in applying hypnotic techniques. Here is one judge who uses it to set criminals on the right path. Judge F. E. Robertson of Grant County, Washington, reported in a newspaper story: "I must have hypnotized 34,000 defendants over the past 25 years." Judge Robertson has helped people overcome emotional difficulties, drinking problems, and even physical ailments.

He recalled one of his most difficult cases: "A young boy with criminal tendencies was sent to me by authorities who asked me to try to keep him from getting into trouble again. After some hypnosis therapy, the boy never was in trouble with the law again. Instead of becoming a criminal, he went on to become one of the best wrestlers this state ever produced."

Some prisons around the country are beginning to install rehabilitation programs which include self-hypnosis classes. At San Quentin prison in California, a woman hypnotist, Jeanne West, has conducted classes in self-hypnosis for inmates, with outstanding results. These classes are biweekly and last for four hours with thirty to forty men attending. The inmates have learned how to relax, adjust to the food (which had caused problems), and to utilize their time to better advantage. They learned self-anesthesia for dentistry and surgery. Two members of the class are studying for the ministry. Another is a teacher's aide. Others have become active in community programs. Several have blossomed into creative writers, poets, and painters. One inmate has married and is working in the family business. All the men have the highest praise for hypnosis and say it changed their self-image for the better, giving them more confidence and self-assurance. They also have stopped blaming others for their predicament and are able to accept responsibility for their misfortunes.

The program at San Quentin received a great deal of positive publicity all around the world. The British Broadcasting Corporation interviewed the hypnotist and prison-classmates via Telstar.

Although hypnosis has been previously employed in correctional institutes in lecture format, this was the first time anywhere that self-hypnosis was taught in classes on a regularly scheduled basis. The governor of California attended the graduating class and expressed his praise for the remarkable results. Let's hope it spreads to institutions all over the world.

SPECIAL TECHNIQUES IN CRIMINAL INVESTIGATION

Before information can be obtained from a witness, victim, or offender, a trusting relationship has to be established between the hypnotizer and the hypnotized. This requires breaking down barriers of anxiety which are always present and interfere with the gathering of information. Relaxed, pleasant conversation should always precede induction techniques. Once induction is accomplished, the subject should be tested for depth of trance. If the level is merely hypnoidal or light, very little real information will be obtained. Another session may be necessary in order to achieve sufficient depth for meaningful interrogation.

Questions should be formulated in advance, so they are concise and require the minimum in the way of an answer. Preparation is important as confusion on the part of the questioner will also confuse the hypnotized person. Time and age regression are employed after basic questioning in order to bring about revivification, which goes deeper than direct answers.

The operator asks the person to go back to the time and place where the incident occurred and to relive the experience. This may tend to be traumatic, so tell the subject: "You are merely an observer. This will not upset you in any way. You are merely watching a flashback as in a movie. You feel no emotional involvement."

The question is often asked of me: "Can the person fake hypnosis? Can a subject lie?" The answer is the same as that given to questions about polygraph machines. *No*—not if the operator is experienced, submits the subject to testing, and double checks the results. It requires adequate training and consistent practice to acquire the necessary skill and expertise.

CLERGYMEN ARE NOW USING HYPNOSIS

Until lately, hypnosis has been feared and condemned by the clergy, who have usually been poorly informed about this vital therapy. A book circulated among church people, *Diabolical Religion of Darkness* by Jess Pedigo, asks: "Are you aware that demons have admitted Satan as the source of power behind hypnotism?" In still another book, *Angels of Light* by Herbert E. Freeman, hypnosis is grouped with ESP, Ouija boards, cults, psychics, clairvoyants, astrologers, mediums, seers, and fortune tellers. The book's premise is that power derived from only two sources—God or Satan—and concludes that because none of the above can be associated with God, they therefore must be directed by Satan. The book ignores biblical teaching, which tells us all healing power is derived from God, that He created man a creature of choice with the ability to choose between good and evil. When we examine what is happening to all religious sects today, it is obvious that some new attitudes are sorely needed.

Surveys point to the fact that most people have turned away from traditional religion. Seventy percent of the Catholics, 75 percent of the Protestants, and 80 percent of the Jews in the U.S. no longer attend regular religious services. In a recent inquiry conducted by Father Edmund Nadolny, a priest, the question was asked, "Why are people staying away from church?"

Using radio, television and the news media, he reached over five million people. Based on twenty thousand replies, the main reason was indicated to be that people felt their clergyman church to be out of touch with present day problems.

Fortunately, we are now experiencing a remarkable change in the attitude of some theologians, who are beginning to apply techniques of hypnosis in many important ways in order to help members of the congregation. The Rev. Francis R. Duffy is an example of how to

combine ministry with "power-of-mind" techniques. A native of Philadelphia, Father Duffy became interested in hypnosis in 1962 when he
was chairman of the Social Sciences department at Duquesne University in Pittsburgh. His interest was triggered by his concern for students
who tended to do well until confronted by examinations.

Father Duffy, 63 years of age, has used hypnosis, not only in
pastoral counseling, but also for emotional, mental, and physical problems. He has helped over 2000 persons of all ages throughout the
nation to kick the smoking habit, and overcome stuttering, fingernail
biting, enuresis (bed-wetting), obesity, and shyness.

"Every now and then," Father Duffy said, "somebody suggests
that I, as a priest, am doing something reprehensible by practicing
hypnosis. My answer is that two popes long ago authorized twilight
sleep, which is deep relaxation reached through hypnosis, for women
during childbirth, and that authorization still remains.

At Parks College of Aeronautical Technology, Rev. J. J. Higgins, a
Jesuit priest, uses hypnosis to help students overcome exam jitters.
Father Higgins has employed this technique for more than seventeen
years with about one sixth of the college's 600 students and in the
process has had some spectacular results. Father Higgins has the bless-
ing of his Jesuit superiors.

MENTAL ATTITUDE AND SPORTS

Can a hypnotist help your game? Can you visualize yourself coming in
with a par for 18 holes, whipping your toughest tennis rival, and getting
one strike after another at the bowling alley?

Sports-minded hypnotists say that if you can "conceive and believe, you can also achieve." Your body will do anything you ask it to
do as long as your request is reasonable. All physical activity is mental
in origin. Professionals are the first ones to admit this. Leading professionals in many sports say it may be as much as 80 percent mental.
Hypnosis can give both top professionals and rank amateurs an extra
edge. Hypnosis spurs the potential to make anyone more than mediocre.

Stage hypnosis has fostered misconceptions. Many people have
come to believe that to have success with hypnosis, a deep trance is
required. That's the stuff that comes from old Bela Lugosi movies. Self-
hypnotic tennis or golf is relaxed concentration and has nothing to do

with a deep trance. In sports, hypnosis trains the participant to have total, acute awareness. Most of all, it magnifies positive expectations.

The athlete not only brings his racket or his club into competition, he also brings his personality. Winning becomes not just beating the other fellow, but feeling like a winner inside. Many coaches of football, baseball, or basketball teams talk to their players about "psyching up." The self-hypnotic factor can make the difference between being the victor and being the victim in a competitive match.

George Foster of the Cincinnati Reds hit more home runs than anyone else in the major leagues for a period of time. Hypnosis turned out to be his secret assistant. Whenever George was troubled, he concentrated at the plate, and went into his special self-hypnosis routine. His hypnotist, Dr. Robert Bernstein from Indianapolis, trained him to live up to his highest batting potential.

"George had a problem concentrating, which caused him to hesitate when he was at bat. He needed to talk to someone outside the baseball team about this problem. George was hypnotized to have mental awareness at all times. He can be compared with a pianist who becomes too involved thinking about the individual movements of his fingers on the keyboard rather than relaxing and playing instinctively. George simply needed a mental nudge to get back on track."

It required only a short session to put George Foster's batting average back on the beam. His batteries recharged, he forged ahead to win.

A United Press International report from England tells us about Gary Player's victory in the British Open Golf Tournament by four strokes. Gary says, "By using self-hypnosis, I put myself in a state of perfect concentration out there and was confident all the way." Carol Semple won the British Women's Open Championship to become the first American in twenty-five years to win two successive titles. "I suffer from nerves in the big matches," she says. "I have a cassette tape I play to prepare myself. I listen to the reassuring voice telling me how to relax, concentrate, and play a round of winning golf." Miss Semple, hugging her trophy, gives thanks to her hypnosis cassette tape.

A Hollywood, Florida hypnotist, Cheryl Weisberg, describes her sessions with a group of women tennis players: "I had them lay down in a dark room while teaching them progressive relaxation exercises. Once the body is relaxed, you can be sure the mind follows. When you reach that point, we build a channel of communication between the subconscious mind and the physical movements of the body. Once he or she develops the knack," Miss Weisberg says, "a tennis player can induce self-hypnosis in just three minutes." She suggests such an interlude once a day, especially before a match.

Former San Francisco quarterback, John Brodie, goes into hypnosis and imagines in slow motion the enemy defensive line. This gives him the opportunity to study responses carefully in order to enhance his own performance.

Gary Rees of the University of Miami Swimming Team is also a booster of hypnosis. He specializes in long-distance events in which swimmers are often weakened by fatigue from lactic acid build-up. Under hypnosis, visual imagery becomes the antidote to fatigue. Rees imagines how his muscles look under a magnifying glass. "I see the lactic acid as milk or thick cream running over my muscles, which I picture as a red cobblestone street. I then envision a magical spray counteracting the lactic acid, washing it away like a mist."

An added problem for the long-distance swimmer involves sucking in wind. Rees says he used visualization to make every breath count more for energy. "I imagine my lungs so enlarged they fill my entire body. I see oxygen as a white cloud filling up my whole hollow self . . . my body reacts as if I have all the oxygen and air I need because every breath is magnified by my mind."

GAMBLING—LOSERS BECOME WINNERS

Do you want better odds at the casino? Here's a tip from professional gamblers who say, "Psyche yourself up!" Good winning streaks depend upon good mental attitude as well as on luck. The difference between being a constant loser or a consistent winner is the degree of concentration you bring to the game. Hypnosis increases one's ability to focus attention upon what is happening at the moment. It strengthens retention, and improves memory and recall of numbers, cards, and rules of the game.

Certain games are easier to beat than others. Mechanical devices such as slot machines and wheels of fortune are not responsive to mental power because of computer programming. Chance rather than choice is the determining factor. Therefore, play the machines long enough and you're bound to be a loser. However, with the heightened awareness derived from hypnosis, you can dramatically improve your chances at blackjack, baccarat, and the crap table.

Learn the subleties of the game you wish to conquer, but don't be fooled into thinking you can alter the system which favors the house. True, you may be able to influence the percentage of winning, but not the built-in odds against you. The most important tip from the professionals who use self-hypnosis is, "Know when to quit." A message of insight, or psychic hunch, will be delivered at the right moment when you have trained yourself with autohypnosis.

It may sound a bit wild, but reports indicate hypnosis can make you a better horseplayer. Masters of self-hypnosis do not lose their shirts at the race track because they are less likely to be reckless. Most players, when on a losing streak, become desperate and take unnecessary risks in order to recoup. Trying too hard to win becomes a negative force while a calm, self-confident attitude helps one win. The law of averages proves that the more frequently a person bets, the greater his chances of losing. Therefore, bets should be well-calculated. Apparently, professional horseplayers are successful because they have studied their subject well, and the acquired knowledge leads them to make only spot plays based on information rather than emotion. They never risk money on a horse unless the horse has a better than even shot at winning.

How does this relate to hypnosis? While hypnosis cannot give you knowledge about a given sport, it can unlock latent, subconscious talent, releasing hunches based on information. Having applied self-hypnosis, you are in complete control of your feelings while at the track, so if your horse loses one day, you don't panic, and still have confidence in the same horse next time. Regardless of the odds, the professional will bet until the horse wins again. Self-hypnotized players do not become overexcited by winning or terribly depressed by defeat. A calm, businesslike attitude is usually maintained. The horseplayer's only concern is the amount of profit he can make by betting. According to studies conducted by psychologists, confidence and positive anticipation bring about a higher percentage of victories.

THE COMPULSIVE GAMBLER

An epidemic of gambling, both legal and illegal, is sweeping the country. In addition to gambling conducted by privately owned enterprises, many states have set up lotteries to boost their dwindling coffers. At least forty-four states are involved in some form of legalized gambling, from casinos and bingo to jai alai and lotteries. Television game shows add to the indoctrination. Reports indicate over half of the United States population is engaged in some form of gambling. The states are to blame for much of this increase although they excuse themselves by pointing out that gambling is a dependable source of revenue. This situation has brought about a surge in the number of compulsive gamblers in the U.S., which is now estimated to be between six and nine million.

There is a correlation between the urge to gamble and other problems such as sexual inadequacy. Here's why. The gambler tends to believe he can compensate for feeling like a loser in one area by being a winner at another game. Gambling gives him the semblance of a thrill, the excitement and glamour which is missing from his life. For the person suffering from sexual dysfunction, gambling may be a substitute in that it provides a nervous build-up of tension and anticipation followed by a quasi-orgastic release when he wins or loses.

In the end, compulsive gambling proves to be a form of self-punishment just as being a chronic loser at sexual-social relationships does.

A TYPICAL CASE HISTORY

Clifford P. chewed the stub of a cigar while he agonized over his compulsive need to gamble. "The more I lose, the more I find reason to go back and play again. I'll bet on anything: horses, sports, whether it will rain. I even bet against myself . . . whether I'll put on my left or right sock first."

Clifford readily admitted he was sexually impotent at times. "If I have to choose between making it at the game tables or making it with a woman, I'd rather shoot craps."

He told about the time a friend in Las Vegas had introduced him to a beautiful showgirl. After buying her a few drinks, he found himself in bed with her. He had walked out of a poker game, rather than admit to his friend that he was less interested in sex than poker. Now here he was, unable to get an erection with one of the most beautiful young women in Vegas.

"Please don't tell my friend," he pleaded. "Let me go back to the game, and I'll send you a nice present."

I asked Clifford why gambling was so important. "I trip out on gambling," he explained. "I fantasize about being a really big winner. I imagine myself going off on a fantastic vacation, first class . . . building a monument to my parents . . . or a hospital in their name." Meanwhile, in reality his gambling had already cost him his business, his marriage, and the respect of his children.

Clifford was ready to be helped through hypnosis. We not only eliminated his urge to gamble, but corrected the basic source of his insecurity—his sexual inadequacy.

Louis T. was so compulsive a gambler, all he had to do was see a picture of a horse and he'd rush to the track to place a bet. Outside of holding back the barest amount of money for existence, Louis gambled most of his earnings away. No amount of logic could convince him to quit.

One day he confided to a friend: "I don't have money for rent, for food, or for medicine. I haven't eaten a square meal in three days. I'm desperate."

"Louis, do you mean to tell me you're stone broke? Not even betting money?"

"Oh, I got betting money, but I don't have money for rent. . . ."

Here is the self-hypnosis routine which helped Louis overcome gambling. Under hypnosis, he would deliberately imagine the following scene: "I am arriving in Las Vegas with a big sack of money, *one million dollars*. I see myself entering the gambling casino, moving from table to table, and holding onto my sack of money without betting a cent."

Louis was training his brain to resist temptation. "I picture myself leaving the casino, going to my room and counting my money. Hooray! I'm a winner! I didn't lose a cent. Then I reward myself. I see myself going out on the town, spending the money on more satisfying things. I see myself wearing a new outfit, driving a custom-made car, escorting a beautiful girl, living it up, and having a great time, like a winner, instead of being depressed, like a loser."

TEACHING AND LEARNING DISABILITY

We are all aware that students complain about anxiety associated with testing and examinations, and the fear of failure contributes to the shutting down of mental responses. On the other hand, hypnosis speeds up the learning process and acts as a stabilizer for the emotionally insecure student. Pinpoint concentration helps us to assimilate, retain, and recall information. This can make the difference between success and failure in any learning experience.

Self-hypnosis is helping novices in police academy work. Postal workers are memorizing schemes. Nurses use it in their training. Actors in learning scripts. Musicians in perfecting scores. Salesmen in practicing their pitch. Even politicians can sound believable through self-hypnosis. Anyone can build confidence and assertiveness and project a more pleasing personality.

Teaching through hypnosis is done in three stages:

1. Before hypnotic induction, the material is read. The teacher makes sure it is understood. Questions are answered.

2. The students are then relaxed into a suggestible hypnotic state. While hypnotized, information is repeated and reinforced with auto-suggestion.

3. After coming out of hypnosis, the student follows posthypnotic suggestions of retention and recall. It is wise to include suggestions of improved study habits and stronger motivation to succeed.

LEARNING LANGUAGES

Hypnosis has long been recognized as a valuable aid in the learning of languages. Hypnosis can also be employed in recalling a language once spoken and forgotten with the passage of time. Lost or buried knowledge can be dredged up from the recesses of the mind and reactivated. Many language courses are now beginning to feature accelerated learning through the use of hypnotic techniques.

A friend, Clarisse T., who teaches Spanish in a community college, invited me to participate in her class to determine if hypnosis would be useful in speeding up the learning process. She was concerned with increasing class attentiveness as well as their ability to recall the material and use it in every day conversation.

We began our experiment with a lesson by Clarisse in the proper pronunciation of Spanish vowel and consonant sounds. I then hypnotized the group using basic induction methods, beginning with progressive body relaxation and positive suggestion, and ending with posthypnotic suggestion. Most people drifted into a light to medium trance, which is sufficient for learning a language.

Clarisse proceeded to read out loud from the Spanish textbook. She asked each student to repeat certain key words after hearing them pronounced correctly. They responded in unison in monotonous singsong voices, indicating that they had drifted deep enough to bypass emotional response and work with the rational higher mind. The first group session lasted two hours; one hour was devoted to inducing trance and the other hour was used for study and memorization.

However, at the second session, all five subjects relaxed into a suitable trance level within twenty minutes, and the rest of the time was devoted to learning the language. Results were impressive. Suggestions of hyperacuity and hypermnesia were implanted into the subconscious to work posthypnotically.

Upon awakening, the group was tested for retention of the material covered in the session. Each student reviewed what he had learned and, by so doing, contributed to the general knowledge and progress of the group.

Clarisse and I were pleased to discover the length of learning time was reduced by two thirds. Upon further experimentation, I have since learned it is not only the depth of trance that brings positive results, but motivation and expectation. Thus, if a student believes he is a poor hypnotic subject, results will be better if he concentrates on the suggestions instead of forcing depth of hypnosis. As a result of this work, *all students learned a minimum of 200 words per session without difficulty*, regardless of trance depth.

Allison R. was especially well-motivated, eager to learn Spanish quickly so she would be able to speak the language better on her visit to Mexico. Allison amazed the group by being able to gather a working vocabulary of 3000 words within five two-hour sessions. Two factors contributed to her success:

Allison was strongly motivated, looking forward to kindling a romance with a young man she had met in Mexico on her last trip. At that time, she could not speak any Spanish. Now her romantic feelings spurred her to be able to communicate with him. The other positive factor was the hypnotic training she had received for weight reduction some months prior to her language studies. Once a person has been conditioned to hypnosis, he can always be reinducted if he so desires.

Barry H. and John H. were brothers, aged 23 and 21, struggling to achieve passing grades in the first and second year of college. They came to my office together to share the session. Both complained of difficulties in concentrating in class and on their homework. Barry, the older brother, described himself as a procrastinator, "I put off till tomorrow what I should do today." John worked diligently, but believed he was less intelligent than Barry. Being two years younger than his brother, John never seemed able to live up to his older brother's level.

They shared one thing: severe apprehension about tests and a fear of flunking out of college. On the positive side, both young men were strongly motivated to improve, and cooperated with hypnotic techniques. They were agreeable and flexible, and after an eight-week course in self-hypnosis during which they came for two hours each week, their memories improved as well as their powers of concentration and their self-confidence. They were ultimately delighted to earn excellent records, rising from C averages to B-plus and A.

In addition to bettering their study habits, Barry's and John's program of improvement included cutting down on watching television and curtailing the use of cigarettes, marijuana, and alcohol.

Jerry B., age 14, looked younger due to his short stature and childish facial expression. He was failing in a parochial school that he bitterly hated. He seethed with rage as he described real or imagined abuse by his teachers. His antagonism had increased to the point where he was unable to study at all. Jerry missed classes periodically and turned in blank pages instead of homework. His mother managed to get him to come to me for therapy on the threat of sending him to reform school. Jerry confessed he had destroyed his report card rather than have his father punish him for poor marks. I noticed Jerry's fingernails were bitten down to the raw skin.

"What seems to be the problem, Jerry?" "I hate this school," he said. "They are too strict and the teacher insults me in front of the class. She said I was not only short in body, but short in brains. I stayed out of school for five days."

Nothing his parents could say diminished his anger until they agreed that he could transfer to another school at the end of the semester. Meantime, Jerry joined a six-week hypnosis course twice a week in which he learned to concentrate with renewed interest on his school work. His mother says he is now doing fine in the public school, working hard to catch up to the level of his peers. The hypnosis group in which he participated consisted mostly of adults. Discovering that adults had problems gave him an awareness that people are more alike than different. The older members of the group encouraged him to keep trying and cited problems of their own teenage years. Jerry took great pride in living up to the expectations of the group and was not a disappointment to them.

THE CASE OF UNEQUAL TWIN BROTHERS

Chuck H., ten years old, was in the third grade and considered a poor student. His twin brother, Clark, was in the fifth grade and doing well. Chuck had failed to get passing grades in his second and third term. His confidence was shattered from constantly being compared to his brother. His comprehension and memory were low. Two preliminary sessions were necessary to develop the trance state, which was medium. At his third session, this conversation took place. I asked, "How was your school work this past week?" "I brought my test papers to show you," Chuck said. "I'm doing a lot better. You told me I would be able to concentrate and now I'm able to understand the teacher most of the time."

"That's fine, Chuck. Today you're going to write down the suggestions you want to improve by. Now that you know hypnosis works, we can proceed to accomplish much more."

I handed Chuck a pencil and pad, and without the hesitation or confusion that bothered him at the first session he wrote: "First, I want to learn faster, catch up to my brother. Second, better concentration and remember my work. Third, be good at doing the times tables and long division."

I proceeded: "Chuck, just lean back and relax all over. Now you know how to relax easily so close your eyes and let your muscles feel loose. Think about your arms getting very heavy . . . pleasantly heavy. Your legs heavy . . . relaxing all over . . . as I count from 5 to 1, let yourself go deeper with each count. Just give in and let it happen.

"Now concentrate on your right hand . . . soon you will feel your hand getting lighter and lighter . . . it feels tingly as you concentrate on it. Just keep listening to my voice, concentrate on the meaning of all of the suggestions I am about to give you. There's lots of time . . . no pressure . . . repeat each suggestion I give you 10 times. Count the suggestions off on your fingers . . . First suggestion . . . 'I will learn faster, catch up to my brother.'" I paused and watched his fingertips count off ten repetitions. Each of his three suggestions were implanted in the same way.

I continued. "It is becoming easier and easier for you to relax and concentrate on every word I say to help you . . . you are learning to use your bright and intelligent mind . . . better and better. (Praise accelerates results, especially when working with children.) Now I am going to press your fingertips gently, and this will take you deeper and deeper because you want to go deeper and deeper to learn faster and faster. Each time you study with this method, you will learn to follow positive suggestions. As your studies improve, you will love your schoolwork more and more. You will help yourself grow up to be a fine man with an excellent education. Your schoolwork is becoming very interesting . . . everyday more and more interesting.

"Now as I count backward from 20 to 0, you will go deeper, much deeper into trance, concentrate on the count and feel so deeply relaxed and comfortable. Twenty, 19, 18, 17, 16, 15, 14, 13, 12, 11, 10, 9, 8, 7, 6, 5, 4, 3, 2, 1. Much deeper. Listen closely, with all of your concentration, and repeat the next suggestion, and accept it fully.

"Learning fast . . . repeat this suggestion, pressing your fingers down, one at a time . . . the little finger of your right hand . . . learning fast . . . each time you repeat it, it makes a more lasting impression in your mind . . . and you let yourself go deeper . . . learning fast."

Each suggestion is repeated, with a few deepening techniques between suggestions. It helps children to repeat the suggestions aloud. Some verbalize inaudibly, forming the words with the throat, lips, and tongue.

Speaking while in trance has a tendency to cause some subjects to lose depth, especially in the lighter stages. This should be left to the discretion of the hypnotic operator. After all of the ideas have been implanted, further suggestions of well-being and confidence in the method working are instilled. The subject is then awakened.

After the trance state is suitably developed, whether medium, deep, or somnambulistic, the subject can open his eyes without awakening when told to do so, and can read and memorize rapidly. The subject matter can be read by the hypnotist or the student can be instructed to open his eyes and read himself. Suggestions of hyperacuity and hypermnesia will result in speeded-up learning.

Sometimes a bad self-image contributes negatively to scholastic attitudes. Susan T. was 17 and 40 pounds overweight. Though of normal intelligence, she was failing in Algebra, History, and Latin. Her poor study habits included eating junk food and watching television while supposedly doing her homework. Obviously, both eating and watching T.V. are distractions from the concentration necessary to memorize homework. Susan complained of a lack of incentive. She just did not care about learning. Her mind was involved with her appearance and with feelings of social rejection.

I decided to include suggestions on weight loss and appetite control. After losing the first 5 pounds, she began to apply herself to her studies. At last report she was 15 pounds lighter and had received an A on an algebra test.

Howard M., 16, had a history of playing hookey. On two occasions, he had run away from home when pressured to attend school regularly. As a result, he was a poor reader, sullen toward his parents, and generally had no direction or goals in his life.

"What do you really want to do?" I questioned while he was under hypnosis. He mumbled something about a guitar.

Upon awakening, Howard revealed that he had asked for music lessons from his father at the age of 13 and had been refused. I arranged a deal between him and his parents. He would have the money to rent a guitar and take lessons for a limited period of time, provided he applied his energies to his schoolwork. After six months of doing well in his music and other work, his parents bought Howard his own guitar and the difference in his attitude toward school, and his parents, changed considerably.

LEARNING DISABILITIES

It is important for parents to be alert in spotting learning problems as early as possible, the best time being before the child enters school. However, one should not necessarily see a developmental difference between one child and another as serious. A single symptom of slow learning could merely represent a temporary quirk. What may appear to be slow for one child may be normal for another.

If parents perceive marked slowness in a child's responses and learning development, they should bring their concern to the attention of a pediatrician who understands the variances of mental and emotional development in children. When in doubt, do not transfer your anxieties to the child, because worry about normalcy simply compounds the problem. Children with learning disabilities, even those who are mentally retarded, are often good subjects for hypnotherapy. High intelligence is not a requisite for hypnotizability. Most children with problems are uneducated, rather than unable to *be* educated. Many have simply not been taught to learn and study properly. Hypnosis teaches them how to tap their unexplored assets. The results are often immediate.

Concerned parents can contact The Association For Children with Learning Disabilities (ACLD). They have 750 chapters across the country and can guide you to the proper kind of assistance. Information is available on diagnostic clinics, special school programs for children and parents, professional counseling, hypnotherapists, and so forth.

A brief description of some of the learning disabilities which respond to hypnotic suggestion follows:

Ataxia. Abnormal (meaning below average) muscular control of various parts of the body. The absence of orderliness. This can be worsened by emotional stress, causing lack of coordination between thoughts and feelings.

Dyslexia. Inability to read printed or written words with understanding. Often associated with impairment of comprehension and too much pressure to learn. Hypnotherapy lessens the stress.

Dysgraphia. Difficulty with writing. Lack of coordination among mind, eye, and hand. Often linked to the child who cannot write spontaneously, but can copy from printed material.

Dyscalculia. Inability to grasp mathematical concepts with normal teaching. Sometimes improvement is speedy when an alternative method, such as hypnotic visualization, is taught.

Hyperkinesis. Abnormally increased motor activity; constant movement without apparent purpose. Can also refer to excessive verbal responses—fast rambling speech and constantly interrupting.

Hypokinesis. Abnormally quiescent state, unresponsive, tendency to withdraw, inattentive to stimuli. Low energy and disinterest in surrounding activity. Stimulation of nerve centers through suggestion.

Perceptually Handicapped. Inability to recognize or to become aware of certain words, objects, and other data through the senses (sight, hearing, touch, taste, and smell). Sensory awareness used.

Strephosymbolia. The reversal of symbols as in reading and writing. (Was for saw, for example.) Revolving screen is visualized under hypnosis.

NERVOUS CHILDREN HAVE SCHOOL PROBLEMS

Sometimes children are classified as having learning disabilities when, in fact, they are unable to concentrate because of stress and anxiety. The trance is a state of relaxed learning without the intervention of pressure or coercion. Fortunately, most children respond favorably to hypnotic suggestion because they are less critical of the procedure. Even emotionally retarded and brain-damaged children can improve, because hypnosis increases alertness and builds belief in oneself. Children who are hypnotized learn from three to five times faster and with less effort than they would normally. Proof of new learning must always lie in results, as you will note in the following case history.

Reginald S. was 12 years old and several years behind his age group in reading and arithmetic. His problem was first diagnosed when he was seven as *strephosymbolia.* In addition to his reading and arithmetic problem, Reginald stuttered, a clear sign of the nervous tension he was suffering. As the only child of college-educated parents, he felt especially pressured to succeed scholastically. After several months of hypnotic training to help him relax physically and emotionally, he learned to compensate for his visual limitations and is now a top student. To assure his continued improvement, Reginald was given the posthypnotic suggestion that his mother or father would be able to place him in a trance by the key word *improve.* This is best in cases where the parent-child relationship is a good one. Even then, suggestions should be written out and accepted by the child in advance. This approach engenders trust—not only that the hypnotist who develops trance in the first place is sincere, but also that the parent will not take advantage and slip in suggestions against the child's wishes. In other words, the child is given a feeling of security.

SPEECH PROBLEMS

Speech disturbances often begin when children have school problems. When Don started stuttering at 5, his folks said, "He'll outgrow it." At 20, Don still stuttered after eight years of analysis and three speech therapists. Working toward a career as an architect, Don knew stuttering would limit his advancement. He was especially nervous in the presence of authority figures such as parents, teachers, and prospective employers.

Socially, Don was also inhibited. Although unusually handsome and well-dressed, he had never dated. Stuttering became worse around girls. His only attempt at sex was with a prostitute with whom he could not function because of nervousness.

Fortunately, Don proved to be a cooperative subject, as is the case with many stutterers. I found his breathing to be spasmodic and irregular. Under hypnosis, therefore, Don was trained to breathe fully from the diaphragm, to let his voice flow smoothly with the exhalation of air. One's pattern of breathing is always an indication to the therapist of underlying tension. Shallow, spasmodic breathing is associated with fear and anxiety, while deeper diaphragmatic breathing is characteristic of greater harmony of the internal rhythms of the body.

Stutterers must first master the art of smooth, controlled breathing, and hypnosis is extremely effective in this regard.

Since stuttering is a manifestation of deeply rooted tension, we worked out a complete relaxation and reconditioning program. The suggestions given to him under hypnosis included the following:

"I will remain relaxed under all circumstances. Increase confidence, poise, be at ease with women. Breathe deeply and speak slowly and freely. Every time I speak, I sound better and better."

By the second week, Don's friends began noticing he was more at ease. He slowed down—taking time to think and breathe before speaking.

At his third session, Don discussed the possible reason for his problem, mentioning that his father and mother had divorced when he was a small child. However, he was unable to recall any specific traumatic incidents which might have contributed to his distress.

During the fifth session, I suggested *automatic writing* as an uncovering technique to find the reason for his problem. When he was in as deep a state as he could achieve, I set a large writing pad on his lap and placed a felt tip pen in his hand, directed the automatic writing as follows:

"What happened to cause you to stutter? Let your hand write the answer. Your hand will write. Your subconscious mind knows the answer and wants to help you. Soon your pen will begin to move . . . now . . . it is moving . . . begin to write . . . what caused you to stutter in the first place? Continue to write until the truth reveals itself. This will give you insight and understanding . . . think back to the first time that you stuttered . . . make believe it's happening right now . . . who are you with?"

Don wrote slowly in small cramped letters, hardly legible. When the pen fell from his hand, I knew there was no more material forthcoming at that time. One of the words Don wrote was "*wore.*"

"What does this unfinished sentence mean? 'My mother . . . *wore*?'" Upon awakening, Don was amazed. He recalled a violent scene he had witnessed at the age of 5. His mother had returned late one night and his father started an angry argument. At one point, he struck his mother and Don awakened hearing her scream. He heard his father call his mother "whore." However, in writing the word, Don had left out the letter "h" in an attempt to conceal the shocking truth from himself. As a small child, he had not realized the meaning of the word, but the violence had shattered his sense of security. For years after the incident, he suffered from nightmares, and became fearful and submissive in his behavior. It was at this time that he remembers stuttering for the first time.

After his revelation, Don seemed better able to relax. Even his speech was more relaxed. It is now two years later, and he speaks clearly and without difficulty. Don continues to use self-hypnosis to improve his learning habits and to remain relaxed and confident when dating women.

Glossary
Additional Uses for Hypnosis

The following list is compiled from my own files and the case histories of other professional hypnotherapists and physicians. Also included are some of the uses reported by students using self-hypnosis.

ABRASIONS. Bruises and sores are soothed and encouraged to heal with positive suggestion under hypnosis and/or self-hypnosis.

ABREACTION. A technique used in psychoanalysis by which forgotten thoughts are brought forward to conscious awareness and relived.

ABSENT-MINDEDNESS. The tendency to be occupied with one's own thoughts to the exclusion of outside events. Withdrawn and forgetful.

ACCIDENT-PRONE. Liability toward involvement in mishaps causing pain or injury. Largely due to mental-emotional states of confusion.

ACCOUNTING. Rapid calculations as well as greater efficiency. Attention to detail and ability to ignore outside distractions.

ACNE. Adolescent skin eruptions respond favorably to hypnotherapy because of stress factor. Anxiety is lessened, self-image improved.

ACTING. Memorizing lines and cues. Poise. Accept difficult direction. Feel the part. Become the character. Improve timing.

ACUMEN IN BUSINESS. Efficient planning. Organize bills and paper work. Discipline yourself to work. Originality of ideas.

ADAPTATION. The ability to adjust to altered living conditions. New location, climate, job, change of vocation. Marriage—divorce.

ADVERTISING. Set up better work schedules. Creativity in promotion. Increase sales. Meet deadlines. Insight in making deals.

AGORAPHOBIA. An abnormal fear of being in open spaces. Anxiety about leaving home or being in unfamiliar surroundings.

AIRPLANE TRAVEL. For crew, alertness at the controls. For fearful passengers, confidence, relaxation, sleep throughout trip.

ALCOHOLISM. Affecting over 50 million Americans, even 12-year-olds. Hypnosis brings about permanent cure in weeks or months.

ALLERGIES. Overreaction to substances such as pollen, dust, and animal fur resulting in inflammation of nasal passages reduced and soothed.

AMNESIA. In cases of lost memory or identity, hypnosis helps in recall of names, numbers, and places. Used for finding lost documents.

ANALGESIA. Pain relief. Produced by developing localized insensibility. Analgesia can be retained by postsuggestion. Helps arthritis, bursitis.

ANESTHESIA. Loss of sensation is accomplished in order to permit painless dentistry and surgery. Hypnotist often assists during operations.

ANGER. This seething, destructive emotion can be channeled into positive, constructive energy with increased inner direction.

ANIMAL TRAINING. Quick thinking, patience, an attitude of alertness and courage. Transferred to the animal by trainer's inner control.

ANOREXIA. Total lack of appetite results in severe emaciation. A hysterical condition, extremely responsive to hypno-suggestion.

ANXIETY. A malady which plagues most of us at some time in life. This emotional sensation is changeable. Causes rooted out.

ARCHITECTURE. Using techniques of visualization, the architect pictures a completed project and is better able to carry out his work.

ART WORK. Painting and drawing abilities are enhanced. Sharper sense of color and form surfaces. An unblocking of higher talents.

ASTHMA. Breathing difficulty is lessened by relaxing chest muscles and improving the respiratory system's rhythms. Reduces anxiety.

ASTRAPHOBIA. Fear of thunderstorms has limited outdoor travel for many people. Original cause wiped out of memory bank.

ATHLETICS. Through positive suggestion and imagination, ballplayers, runners, and other sportsmen perform to highest potential.

AUTOMATIC WRITING. An uncovering technique where subject answers questions put to him by a hypnotist to recall memory of past events.

AUTOMOBILE TRAVEL. Car sickness is lessened. Fear of driving overcome. Alertness at wheel and in traffic increased markedly.

AWARENESS. The ultra-depth meditative level of hypnosis puts one in touch with one's higher intelligence. Know the inside of your mind.

BARTENDING. Memory, concentration, attention to details, getting along with people without necessarily drinking. Sympathizing easily.

BEAUTY. Your mind can preserve your good looks on the outside through improved self-image from inside. Better sleep, relaxation improves appearance.

BEHAVIOR MODIFICATION. Hypnosis speeds the changeover from negative to positive attitudes and activities. Removes hang-ups.

BLADDER CONTROL. Upon medical referral, the sensation of needing to urinate can be removed from the habit reflexes assuming no illness present.

BLEEDING. To lessen loss of blood during surgery and after accidents. Also for menstrual hemorrhaging and patients with hemophilia.

BLUSHING. The rush of blood to the face is triggered by thoughts of embarrassment. Hypnotic reconditioning is extremely effective.

BOATING. Many have overcome fear of water and developed better balance. Freedom from seasickness and nausea. Improve confidence for sailing.

BOREDOM. The person who is listless, living in a rut without enthusiasm can be trained to program fun into his life. Increase interest in hobbies.

BOWLING. Posthypnotic suggestion brings great coordination. Bowler pictures himself delivering the strike just as ball leaves hand.

BRAINWASHING. Hypnosis is used to wipe out painful memories. For fresh outlook on life. Useful for victims in rape cases and child abuse.

BREAST DEVELOPMENT. Medical hypnotists report effective response by increasing circulation. Remove negative mental limitations.

BREATHING PROBLEMS. Rhythms of breathing can be corrected in a trance-state. Respiratory diseases react positively and quickly.

BRIDGE PLAYING. The ability to remember cards which have been played. A remarkable increase in concentration gained. Win more games.

BRUXISM. Describing the clenching and grinding of the teeth. This disturbance most often occurs during the night and is due to stress.

BULIMIA. A psychological disturbance resulting in an insatiable appetite for food. The patient eats constantly and anything available.

BURSITIS. Medical practitioners find that chronic pain in shoulders and elsewhere can be somewhat ameliorated through hypnotic suggestions.

CANCER. Hypnotherapists are sometimes called in by attending physicians to relieve terminal pain where the patient resists conventional drugs.

CHARLEY HORSE. Muscle spasms quickly respond to the ultra-deep relaxation which takes place under hypnotic trance. Useful for athletes.

CHEMISTRY. Students find their memories improve for learning formulas. Professional chemists also use hypnosis for creative laboratory work.

CHERAPHOBIA. Fear of gaiety, loud laughter, or boisterous behavior that results in depression and anxiety. Sometimes found among the elderly.

CHILD ABUSE. A growing problem often resulting from discord between parents who have lost their ability to cope. Hypnosis brings rationality.

CHILDBIRTH. Pain during labor can be entirely eliminated and childbirth can become a pleasurable experience rather than a fearful one. A boon.

CHILD, GIFTED. For the bright child, hypnosis offers the possibility of unlimited expansion of latent creativity. Self-hypnotic techniques used.

CHILD, SUBNORMAL. The child who is dull or less than average finds new areas of growth within the untapped potential. Sensorimotor exercises.

CHINOPHOBIA. Fear of the snow. Snowflakes terrify when they touch the skin of people with this problem. Desensitization is employed in trance.

CHIROPRACTIC ADJUSTMENT. Hypnosis is used to relax overly tense patients. The doctor combines his skill with suggestions for improvement.

CLAUSTROPHOBIA. Fear of confined spaces such as closets, elevators, and rooms without windows. One of the most common of phobias. Correctible.

CLIMACTERIUM, MALE. Thought of as analogous to the menopause in females. Fatigue, decreased sexual drive, irritability, etc. Responsive to hypnosis.

CLUMSINESS. An unconscious ineptitude which prevents the patient from performing certain acts. Poise and skill are increased through images.

COLDS. Immunity to colds is improved through proper breathing and adherence to health rules. Resistance is increased through positive suggestion.

COLOR BLINDNESS. Some cases of color blindness have responded to posthypnotic suggestion. Incorrect teaching often limits self-confidence.

COMEDIANS. Professional comics, like actors, use self-hypnosis to memorize lines and to keep their spirits high in difficult times.

COMPULSION. Repetitive motor action even though the subject wishes to change. Such as alcoholism, overeating, and smoking—all can be moderated.

CONFIDENCE. Self-image is enhanced, especially confidence. One develops greater sense of worthiness and other values, such as persistence.

CONSTIPATION. The sphincter muscles are trained to relax and elimination becomes easy. Strain and hemorrhoidal pain are greatly minimized.

CONSTRUCTION WORKERS. The need for balance, alertness, and courage. Fear of heights, tunnels, sewers, and electrical currents are areas we have helped.

CONTACT LENSES. People learn to wear contact lenses with comfort, reduce strain and excess tearing. A great aid to the ophthomologist.

CONTRACEPTION. Self-hypnosis has been found helpful in reducing the tendency of body to reject diaphragms and intrauterine devices.

CONVALESCENCE. The calming influence of the meditative practice of hypnosis and self-hypnosis reduces patient restlessness, aids in recovery.

COUGHING. Nonorganic throat irritations can be removed. Constant clearing of the throat is often due to nervous anxiety.

COURAGE. Facing the harsh realities of life takes mental-moral strength. Following through without faltering is made easier through hypnosis.

CREATIVITY. Free the hidden abilities in any and all creative areas—painting, sculpture, dance, interior decorating, writing, music, etc.

CRIME. Hypnosis is used in prisons to correct underlying anti-social attitudes. Also to discover motives and hidden information.

DANCING. Learn steps easily, develop timing, grace and rhythm. For professionals—overcome stage fright. Greater poise.

DENTISTRY. A popular practice in the removal of pain, especially in cases where Novocaine cannot be used. No fear of needles—quick healing.

DENTURES. Artificial dentures more easily accepted. Settle into the gums quickly and soon begin to work as one's own teeth. Gums heal faster.

DEPRESSION. Psychologists and analysts report remarkable results with hypnotic techniques as alternative or addition to drug therapy.

DIABETES. An aid for the diabetic in sticking to his diet. In some cases, detected early, remission of the illness has been reported.

DIETING. For people on a salt-restricted, cholesterol, carbohydrate diet, self-hypnosis is a boon, bringing control of appetite.

DIRECTED DREAM. An aid to unblocking fears and anxieties. Administered under professional direction can also be used for self-understanding.

DISCIPLINE. Hypnosis spurs the urge to do what needs to be done with decisiveness and determination. Eliminate excuses and cop-outs.

DRUG DEPENDENCY. Correct the basic insecurities which lead to drug addiction. A high euphoric feeling under hypnosis makes drugs unnecessary.

DYSMENORRHEA. Menstrual pains and cramps can be alleviated. This is done with approval of the physician after thorough medical examination.

DYSPHONIA. A relatively common disorder which appears as hoarseness. For no apparent reason, the voice becomes higher or lower than usual.

EATING. You can develop an aversion to unhealthy foods or beverages. Learn the ability to control urges and keep the proper weight level.

EDUCATION. Examinations and tests become easier. Assimilating knowledge for a better career, greater self-respect and increased income.

ELECTROLYSIS. The removal of unwanted hair from the face and other parts of the body can be accomplished without pain under hypnosis.

ELEVATORS. Fear of elevators affects many people and, fortunately, is corrected with ease by a trained hypnotist. Desensitization techniques.

ENERGY. Stamina is sometimes more mental than physical. Quick energy is suggested. "One hour's rest shall equal five or six."

ENTHUSIASM. Joyfulness in relation to work and people. The power of the mind can inject a sense of high expectation of good happenings.

ENURESIS. Bedwetting, a common problem affecting young children. Often remains into teens. Hypnosis helps when all else fails.

ESPIONAGE. The secret material codes and messages are memorized on a subliminal level to be recalled later under hypnosis. Used world-wide.

EXERCISE. The discipline to exercise regularly becomes automatic. Using self-hypnosis, one is unaware of the exertion. Results quickened.

EYESTRAIN. Nerves and muscles around the eyes relax. Circulation increases. Train yourself to come out of the trance with clearer vision.

EXORCISM. Practice of removing unwanted spirit beings. Hypnotists have been employed under supervision of priest, minister, or psychiatrist.

FAINTING. Momentary loss of consciousness, swooning or lightheadedness comes from loss of circulation to the brain. Hypnosis encourages bloodflow.

FAITH. People who lose belief in themselves can be opened up to trust and anticipation of positive happenings. Believing helps in receiving.

FASTING. For religious or health purposes, anyone can be conditioned to fast for a day or several days, depending upon the situation.

FEARS OF ALL KINDS. Fire, darkness, snakes, spiders, shadows, thunder. All respond to some degree to positive suggestion in a trance.

FEEDBACK. Reinforcement from mind to body reflexes. Hypnosis functions to strengthen inner programming to modify behavior quickly.

FERTILITY. In cases where the inability to bear children is psychological rather than organic, a reversal of attitude often brings about pregnancy.

FETISHES. Those who are dependent upon an object to function sexually can be deprogrammed, then reprogrammed in order to function normally.

FEVER. Body temperature may be elevated or lowered by hypnotic means in cases where problem is psychogenic rather than organic.

FLAGELLATION. The art of whipping as a sexual excitement. Often a manifestation of sadomasochism. Correctible if motivated.

FLATULENCE. Passing wind can be controlled with subconscious conditioning. Even in cases where there is a digestive problem. The mind can postpone.

FLYING. A popular solution to the fear of flight, hypnosis has been used by thousands. Therapy consists of sleeping through trip pleasantly.

FORENSIC HYPNOSIS. An aid to lawyers in uncovering the truth. Forgotten information, dates, names and places recalled.

FORGETFULNESS. A memory disturbance often associated with emotionally charged situations. Desire to avoid pain of the past.

FRIGIDITY. A term denoting lack of female sexual response. Difficulty in reaching orgasm. Hypnosis proves it is mental instead of physical.

GAGGING. Difficulty in swallowing pills is often habit rather than organic interference. The throat can be opened to receive medication.

GAMBLING. Compulsive habits, having been learned, can be unlearned. Suggestions for a more constructive way of life are instilled.

GENDER IDENTITY. The behavior and appearance of masculinity or femininity can be strengthened. Orientation toward assigned role sometimes accomplished.

GERIATRICS. The handling of elderly patients is simplified by the use of positive suggestion. Appetite improves as well as disposition.

GOALS. The setting of short-term and long-term goals is an important aspect of hypnotic programming. We can all benefit by planning ahead.

GOLF. Players report increased stamina, greater concentration, elimination of slicing and raising of the head. Scores improve remarkably.

GOOSE FLESH. The contraction of the small muscles surround-

ing hair follicles occurs during fright or extreme cold. The mind modi-
fies.

GROWTH. Exceptionally effective in the psychological sense.
Also, useful physically for undersized children and teenagers.

GUILT FEELINGS. Realization that one has done wrong often
exaggerated. Associated with lowered self-esteem and need for self-
punishment.

GYNECOLOGY. The physician finds hypnotic suggestion an important aid in relaxing the nervous patient in order to carry out examination.

GYNEPHOBIA. A morbid fear of contact with a woman's body
often stems from early negative experience. Regression to source brings
awareness.

HABITS. Repetitive behavior becomes entrenched in the subconscious. Get into your subconscious and exchange bad habits for good
ones.

HAIR GROWTH. Reports indicate that self-hypnosis, diligently
applied, can retard loss of hair. In some cases, even regrowth has been
noted.

HALLUCINATIONS. Imagined or false sense of perception (often
found among mentally disturbed) can be helped in a receptive subject.

HEADACHES. Even severe migraine appears to respond in varying degrees to hypnotic suggestion and deep relaxation. Throbbing
ceases.

HEADBANGING. Commonly observed during temper tantrums
in small children. Best time for induction is before bedtime.

HEALING. Psychosomatic ailments especially show improvement
with ultra-depth techniques. Faith healers often use hypnotic methods.

HEARING. Some nonorganic problems have been recorded as
highly responsive to hypnosis. Also used to develop tolerance to hearing aids.

HICCUPS. The spasms which persistently rock the diaphragm.
When all else seems to fail, hypnosis often brings instantaneous results.

HOARDING. The practice of collecting objects of a particular
kind that have no practical use. Usually a sign of emotional disturbance, need for love.

HOMOSEXUALITY. Transference to heterosexual relationships
has been successful in many cases where the motivation has been
strong.

HYDROPHOBIA. Fear of water is often encountered in the day-to-day work of hypnotists. Anyone can become a fearless swimmer with help.

HYPERACTIVITY. Excessive muscular activity, often refers to disturbed childhood behavior. Short attention span, relaxation helps.

HYPERSEXUALITY. Greatly increased sexual activity beyond one's physical needs. Persistent repetition of the sex act, yet never achieving orgasm.

HYPNODRAMA. A useful technique in which the subject cybernetically re-enacts past problems or relationships and discovers solutions.

HYPOCHONDRIA. The person who consistently fears imagined illnesses can use his imaginative powers to eliminate anxieties and face reality.

HYPERESTHESIA. Increased sensitivity to touch, sometimes excruciating. Seen in hysterics who overact to physical stimuli. Tolerance.

HYPERTENSION. High blood pressure responds favorably to hypnosis under medical and clinical supervision. Self-hypnosis self monitors.

HYSTERICS. An extremely emotional state resulting in abnormal sensations, fits of laughter, or convulsive crying. Hypnosis soothes and reassures.

IDEALIZATION. Overestimation of the love-object, which often leads to disappointment and depression. Object is exalted in the mind. Unreality.

IDENTITY CRISIS. Loss of the sense of person and social continuity. Inability to adapt to new role in society. Strong need to change personality.

IDEOGAMY. Inability to have sexual intercourse with any woman except one's wife or some individual woman. Situational impotence results.

IMAGE IMPROVEMENT. Self-analysis under hypnotic guidance leads to a more realistic self-evaluation. You can see yourself at your best.

IMPOTENCE. Most cases of impotence are mental rather than physical. Therefore, mental persuasion can revive male's sexual drive.

IMPULSIVENESS. Sudden action without forethought or rational judgment often leads to mistakes. Preventing rash decisions becomes automatic.

INFERIORITY COMPLEX. Feeling of inadequacy in relation to others and the world are changeable. Self-worth takes over. Image improves.

INHIBITIONS. Conditioned attitudes which limit one's level of fulfillment can be altered. Useful in areas of sexuality and personality.

INCOMPATIBILITY. Marriage counselors find harmony and understanding often results from a joint hypnosis session including husband and wife.

INJECTIONS. The needle need not hurt at all. Learn simple self-hypnosis method of affecting local anesthesia to any area of your body.

INTERCOURSE. Sexual interaction improves through removal of resistances and the control of sensation. Corrects psychosomatic disturbances.

INSECURITY. Irrational feelings of unprotectedness and helplessness vanish when a strong sense of independence and self-esteem is developed.

INSIGHT. Getting to know the "inner you" through repeated sessions with meditative self-hypnosis. Brings wide-range and penetrating awareness.

INTROVERSION. Common personality disturbance where the person's attention is morbidly turned inward limiting interaction with others.

INVALIDISM. The mental state of a patient who, though free of physical illness, imagines himself sick and refuses to accept healthy living.

IRRITABILITY. The testy individual who is easily disturbed by petty annoyances can be trained to remain calm and reason with logic.

ISOLATION. Fear or aversion to making contact with other people or groups. Self-inflicted loneliness can be replaced with friendliness.

ITCHING. Uncontrollable scratching, often with no organic cause, resulting from nervousness or habit. Self-hypnosis smooths and soothes.

JEALOUSY. The insecurity which underlies envious feelings about another person are lessened. Insight and understanding improve with self-esteem.

JET LAG. Plane travel can turn one's day into night. Equilibrium and balance is re-established quickly. Adjustment to new time schedule.

JOCKEYS. For extra stamina when feelings of exhaustion begin. Improve timing of trot and pacing. Think like a winner. Patience and energy.

JOVIALITY. Put your most cheerful face forward. Getting out of

218 GLOSSARY

the doldrums is easy with inner suggestion. Relate to others openly with warmth.

JUDGMENT. Think things through to logical conclusion. Recognize true relationship of ideas. Avoid snap judgments. See other point of view.

JUVENILE DELINQUENCY. Group hypnosis works wonders for young people in trouble. Hypnosis presents alternatives to anti-social behavior.

KICK-OFF. Football players report posthypnotic suggestion can increase distance and accuracy. Mental rehearsal during hypnosis builds power.

KLEPTOMANIA. Compulsive stealing because of emotional needs. Hypnosis can reveal reasons for behavior through regression and automatic writing.

LANGUAGE. The time involved in learning a new language is cut to about one-third. Recall improves. Learn to think in new language.

LARYNGITIS. Inflammation of the larynx can be lessened with focused healing. Trance-level meditation speeds return of voice.

LAZINESS. Indolence, aversion to work. Habitual resistance gives way to repetitive suggetion for improved motivation.

LEADERSHIP. Organizational and political leaders use the dynamics of mind-power to build a following. Helps in public speaking, TV, etc.

LEISURE. Program your leisure time to make the most of every moment. Develop the ability to relax quickly while on vacation. Plan your trip.

LESIONS. Wounds from injuries or surgery heal faster with hypnotic suggestion. We have also noticed less pain and signs of scarring.

LETHARGY. The listless person who feels drowsy or dull needs the psychic lift in spirits and energy only his mental energy can give him.

LIMPING. In cases of labored, jerky movements when walking, imagery helps if lameness has not completely atrophied the muscles from disuse.

LISPING. Like shuttering and stammering, speech impediments show remarkable improvement with the help of a skilled practitioner of hypnosis.

LONGEVITY. Regular sessions of relaxation, coupled with positive suggestion to improve health, adds up to extra years without ailments.

LOVE. The ability to express affection and to receive pleasure from others—ability to gratify oneself as well as others.

LYING. The habitual fabricator often is unaware of his deeply rooted habit. With guidance and training he learns to face realities of life.

MALINGERING. Simulation of symptoms of illness or injury with intent to deceive. For some people this can become an escape from reality.

MANNERS. Improve the behavior of the young. Politeness, consideration in cases of unruliness, or need for group training as in schools.

MARIJUANA. Dependency on pot for euphoric feeling is replaced with natural tranquillity and mind-control over physical/emotional self.

MARITAL DISCORD. Marriage counselors use hypnosis to bring couples closer. Communication established under joint hypnotic induction.

MARKSMANSHIP. Self-hypnosis sharpens visual concentration. Steadier nerves and muscles increase coordination for greater accuracy.

MASOCHISM. A person who enjoys inflicting pain and discomfort upon himself, as well as encouraging another to mistrust him—self-hate.

MASSAGE. Hypnotic suggestion when combined with stroking and muscle manipulation expands benefits of deep relaxation. Learn technique easily.

MASTURBATION. Excessive self-stimulation resulting in psychological dependency and exclusion of other forms of intercourse. Controlled.

MATHEMATICS. Greater insight and understanding of basic principles. Numerical formulas absorbed quickly under concentrated meditation.

MEDICATION. The administration of medicines, swallowing of pills becomes easier with a cooperative patient. Many nurses use indirect hypnosis.

MEMORY. The mental faculty of retaining information for immediate recall becomes enhanced with the improved concentration which results.

MENOPAUSE. The discomfort of "change of life" which many

women experience as hot flushes and dizziness is often more mental than physical.

METAPHYSICS. Psychics employ hypnotic techniques to enhance extra sensory perception and study parapsychological phenomena.

MIGRAINE HEADACHES. The tensions which bring on severe pain are dispersed. Diminishes throbbing at temples. Used in many clinics.

MODELS. Very useful for maintaining posture in both fashion work as well as artists' models. Also, to maintain weight. Build confidence.

MONEY MAKING. Increasing one's income comes with the organization of mind and time. Plan a positive program of action.

MOURNING. When sorrow and lamentation exceeds the normal mourning period, a hypnotist can divert attention toward other pursuits.

MUSCLE CRAMPS. "Charley horse" or other spastic muscle pains respond to the relaxing methods of hypnosis. Nerves "let go."

MUSIC. Perception of sound is sensitized and amplified. Subtler nuances of melody more easily recognized in music appreciation.

MYSOPHOBIA. Unnatural anxiety about dirt, germs, and infections. People so troubled tend to wash their hands too often or wear gloves.

NAGGING. Like other troublesome habits, this one lends itself to the deconditioning process of hypnotic suggestion. Awareness increases.

NARCISSISM. An exaggerated opinion of oneself, usually a reaction to low self-esteem. Demonstrated by constantly looking in the mirror.

NAIL BITING (or picking). A simple problem to overcome. Often a few sessions with a professional hypnotist is all that is required.

NAUSEA. Stomach distress can be alleviated if psychogenic. In cases of extreme obesity, practitioner may suggest nausea to curb appetite.

NEATNESS. Both youngsters and adults who tend to be careless and slovenly learn how to organize their belongings and improve appearance.

NECROPHILIA. A sexual perversion, real or fantasy, in which the love object must be dead in order for the disturbed person to become aroused.

NECROPHOBIA. An unreasonable terror of being in the presence of a dead person. Manifested in dread of photos of coffins, attending funerals, etc.

NEGATIVISM. A conditioning of thinking which plagues many. One goes against own best interests. Positivism replaces old attitudes quickly.

NEURESTHENIA. A nervous disorder; general decline in mental and physical energy characterized by symptoms of fatigue, aches, pains, and depression.

NERVOUSNESS. Emotional stress and anxiety respond quickly and easily. Remarkable results are witnessed after the very first session.

NIGHT-EATING. The syndrome of nighttime nibbling even when not hungry is very common. Often people wake up in middle of night for an unnecessary snack.

NIGHTMARES. Terrifying dreams can be lessened by self-hypnosis exercises before falling asleep. In many cases, pleasant dreams can be suggested.

NIGHT-WALKING. Somnambulistic strolling can be dangerous. Autosuggestions before bedtime very helpful to eliminate this compulsion.

NOISINESS. Sensitivity to sound, even when so moderate as to go unnoticed by others can seriously disturb the ultra-sensitive. De-sensitization used.

NOSE BLEEDS. Stress factor is often responsible for difficulty in conquering chronic and persistent nose-bleeding. Hypnotists report success.

NURSING. Nurses find the techniques of relaxation and positive suggestion aid in healing. Also recommended for nursing mothers. Improves milk.

NYCTOPHOBIA. Abnormal fear of nighttime or darkness. Shadows seem to move like monsters. Usually associated with traumatized young children.

NYMPHOMANIA. Used to describe a woman with uncontrollable, insatiable sexual desires. Denoting frequency of desire rather than complete fulfillment.

OBEDIENCE. Hypnosis is sometimes employed in classroom situations where turmoil and unruly behavior interferes with the welfare of the group.

OBESITY. Lose weight without hunger pangs. Weight loss is

steady and remains off permanently as new eating habits are established.

OBSESSIONS. Are emotional impulses that persistently force themselves into one's consciousness. Thoughts can be rechannelled.

OBSTACLES. Blocks and interferences to successful living can be overcome. With persistent autosuggestion under self-hypnosis, careers blossom.

OBSTETRICS. Treatment of women before, during and after childbirth. Obstetrician uses hypnosis to eliminate pain during delivery.

OCCULT. Mediums and psychics use the hypnotic trance to tap their cosmic "sixth sense." Reports of astral projection and other psychic phenomena.

OCCUPATIONAL APTITUDE. New approaches and added possibilities open up. Abilities, skills, and talents long hidden reveal themselves.

OPHIDIOPHOBIA. Fear of snakes can be so obsessive as to extend even to words and pictures as well as the letter S. Hypnosis desensitizes.

OPPORTUNITY. Recognizing opportunity when it knocks takes perception and positive anticipation. Insight and planning through meditation.

OPTOMETRY. Hypnosis is a boon to doctors in fitting glasses and contact lenses. Toleration of lenses becomes easier and adjustment time is shorter.

OPTIMISM. Positive thinking increases immediately because hypnosis is based on the concept, "make the most of the best, the least of the worst."

ORAL COMPULSION. Overeating, nail biting, smoking, alcoholism, thumb sucking, constant munching. All respond to proper suggestion.

ORGANIZATION. Work out logical plans, and learn to tie up loose ends. Neatness, accuracy enhanced. Tap your subconscious to work out a plan.

ORGASM. Sexual inhibition which retards development of feeling during intercourse. For both men and women greater control becomes natural.

ORTHODONTICS. The prevention and correction of irregular teeth. Practitioners find hypnotic suggestion helps patients tolerate braces.

OVERDOSE. Hypnotists have been called in to bring about vomiting in cases of poisoning or drug abuse. Hypnosis also helps in keeping alert.

PAIN CONTROL. In cases where continuance of drugs is harmful, hypnosis can be used to remove sensation of pain and lower its threshold.

PANAPHOBIA. A sense of panic which might be related to almost anything. The anxiety-ridden victim remains alienated from others and stays indoors.

PARAPSYCHOLOGY. Mediums and others involved in the occult often use the hypnotic trance to expand their awareness and concentration.

PASSIVITY. Nonassertiveness causes many people to live a limited life. Hypnosis builds confidence and bolsters ego to behave more assertively.

PATIENCE. A great virtue of happy living is waiting serenely for things to happen. Learning to be tolerant of others comes with inner peace.

PERCEPTION. Open your sensory system to keener awareness through sight, hearing, touch, smell and taste. Sensitize input and learn control.

PERSPIRATION. Unusual sweating, often a sign of inner stress. Sweaty palms reveal anxieties raging within. Easily corrected through hypnosis.

PESSIMISM. Because the basic premise of hypnosis is to "think positively" inevitably the practitioner becomes uplifted in his mental outlook.

PHOTOGRAPHY. Knowledge of hypnotic techniques (with approval of subject) helps in getting more relaxed poses and best facial expression.

PHOBIAS. The variety of phobias seem endless. Dust, wind, forests, birds, caves, heights, ocean, cracks in the sidewalk, etc., etc.

PHYSIOTHERAPY. Hypnosis is a dependable aid to the therapist who is retraining patients to use their muscles to function better. Aids walking.

PIANO PLAYING. Finger dexterity is improved. Memory becomes sharper. Regular practice can become a joy rather than a chore. Opens creativity.

PILOTS. In order to stay alert and attentive under all circumstances, pilots use self-hypnosis for energy stimulation. Excellent for students.

POETRY. Under meditation, listening to the still, small voice of inspiration produces elevated inner thoughts and beautiful concepts.

POISE. Inner confidence and calm attitude shines through, bringing an aura of regal pride. Useful for actors, lecturers, and politicians.

POSTURE. Slouching is bad body language. Train your body to sit, stand, and walk in a balanced, erect way. Visual imagery and muscle training.

PREMATURE EJACULATION. A sexual disorder which troubles many men. Dramatic improvement becomes evident after just a few hypnotic sessions.

PROCRASTINATION. Getting on with the tasks which need doing, rather than putting them off. Taking immediate action is programmed subconsciously.

PROMPTNESS. Some people are late for every appointment, to the annoyance of others. Punctuality can be trained into the reflexes with quick results.

PSORIASIS. Many professional hypnotists report great improvement in patients referred by doctors. Some cases of dramatic remission.

PSYCHOSOMATIC AILMENTS. Science has accepted that the mind can make one ill. Therefore, reversing the action, the mind can also help one improve.

PSYCHOTHERAPY. Hypnosis allows the doctor to open his patient to reveal hidden problems under a detached transcendent state of being.

PYROMANIA. Morbid impulse to set fire to things. Often culminates in the actual act of setting fires. Analysis under hypnosis reveals reasons.

PYROPHOBIA. Terrifying fear of fire. Victims often complain of recurring nightmares of being burned. Sometimes associated with religion.

QUALIFYING. In sports, auditions, job interviews, those employing self-hypnosis have greater confidence and stronger positive expectations.

QUEASINESS. Uneasiness and discomfort such as nausea or dizziness. Sometimes used to denote a troubled or guilty conscience.

QUERULENCE. Suspicious and unreasonable, touchy, easily dissatisfied, complaining of ill-treatment without cause. A personality disturbance.

QUIBBLING. Argumentative for the sake of arguing. Nit-picking. Such a person uses ambiguous or irrelevant language to evade a definitive point.

QUOTIENT, INTELLIGENCE. The ratio of a subject's intelligence (determined by tests) compared to average for his age group. Hypnosis removes blocks.

RACIAL RELATIONS. Hypnosis found to bring greater tolerance and acceptance during periods of racial strife. Used in group therapy sessions.

RACING. The mind makes the difference in contests of speed such as running, driving, sailing. Self-hypnosis can decide if you're a winner or not.

RADIOLOGY. Radiologists report that hypnosis facilitates diagnostic procedures. Eliminates anxieties and relaxes intestinal tensions.

RAPE. Hypnosis is imployed to great advantage for both rehabilitating the victim as well as in treating the sexual offender to understand his act.

READING SKILLS. For slow learners where remedial work is indicated, reading skill is accelerated through the help of a professional.

RECONDITIONING. Hypnotic techniques prove useful in restoring normalcy to damaged body reflexes, mental attitudes and emotional stability.

REGRESSION. A valuable tool in psychoanalytical work with disturbed people. A return in memory to earlier behavior to understand and correct.

REHABILITATION. Hypnosis used in conjunction with medication. Vocational retraining to achieve maximum psychosocial adjustment. Speeds recovery.

REJUVENATION. Mitigates pathological symptoms of old age. Good results with sexual impotence in men. Restores a more youthful appearance in women.

RELAXATION. Relief from body tension is almost immediate as progressive body relaxation is the first step toward hypnotic induction.

RESPIRATION. In cases of breathing difficulty such as emphysema and asthma, hypnosis relaxes the chest muscles, restores normal rhythms.

RHEUMATISM. A painful disorder of joints or extremities or back. A medical referral required to hypnotist who lessens pain and stiffness.

RHINOPLASTY. Plastic surgery of the nose is often painful with swelling and difficulty in breathing. Bruises diminished.

SADISM. Describing people whose sexual pleasure depends on pain, or cruelty. Humiliating another person also a personality problem.

SALESMANSHIP. The ability to convince others to buy one's product increased by direct eye-to-eye contact and persuasive tone of voice.

SCULPTURE. Greater feeling for form and design. Dexterity of hands and strength of media control. Originality of composition enhanced.

SEASICKNESS. The rocking motion of rough seas can be easily ignored under posthypnotic suggestion. Nausea and anxiety diminished.

SELF-IMAGE. Get to like yourself through deeper insight. Learn to see your best attributes. Live up to your highest potential. Succeed.

SENILITY. Characteristic manifestations of old age can be retarded with the early application of antiaging hypnotic techniques.

SEXUALITY. Overcome unsureness in relation to intimacy. Build confidence and assertiveness. Experience sexual fulfillment in every way.

SHORTHAND. Learn the symbols under concentrated meditation. Self-hypnosis makes assimilation of learning quicker and recall often complete.

SHYNESS. Socially inept people learn to become more outgoing, able to meet new people without embarrassment. Develop better communication.

SINGERS. Dry throat and tense vocal cords are relaxed. Pitch may be improved and range of sound extended. Volume and resonance increased.

SKIN RASHES. Dermatologists often send patients with nonspecific skin problems to hypnotherapists to explore for possible psychogenic causes.

SMOKING. Many lives have been saved by removing the desire. Thousands of clinics are using hypnotic-type methods to help people quit smoking.

SNEEZING. Uncontrollable spasms of sneezing have been brought under restraint when every other method has failed. Hypnosis interrupts reflex.

SNORING. Self-suggestion under autohypnosis applied just before falling asleep will alleviate this problem. Posthypnosis lasts through the night.

SOMNAMBULISM. Deepest trance level of hypnosis where there is no memory when awakened. Also observed in sleepwalkers without hypnotic trance.

SOMNILOQUY. Talking in one's sleep may not only disturb one's bedmate, but cause problems for erring husbands. Subject rouses before speaking.

SPACE TRAVEL. Astronauts as well as regular pilots find techniques of hypnotic time distortion useful in tolerating stress. Fortitude.

SPEEDREADING. Concentration and mental focus is increased. Outside distractions are transcended. Retention and comprehension improved.

STAGE-FRIGHT. Performers, politicians and lecturers rise above fear of facing an audience. Stage presence projected. Poise, charisma.

STUDY HABITS. Organization and determination to succeed on a higher level. Improves concentration and reduces anxiety about examinations.

STUTTERING. Spasmodic gripping of the vocal cords is relieved. Many children have shown remarkable control in just a few weeks of hypnosis.

SUICIDE. Those despondent souls on the verge of ending their lives can be deterred by hypnosis until proper analysis corrects the cause.

SURGERY. Your mind can bring about analgesia and anesthesia. Freedom from fear. Minimizes bleeding. Accelerates healing and recovery.

SWIMMING. Olympic champions tell us that self-hypnosis makes the difference between mediocrity and winning the meet. Improves timing and rhythm.

TACHYPHAGIA. Compulsive food grabbing and eating rapidly without regard for taste or hunger. Often found in deteriorating schizophrenics.

TALENT. Natural untapped abilities and aptitudes are discovered by reaching into the deeper areas of mind. Visualization of work completed.

TARDINESS. People who are habitually late for appointments, who dawdle or behave in a sluggish manner can be aided and trained for promptness.

TEACHING. Imparting knowledge takes patience and tolerance. Instructors use both self-hypnosis for themselves and "hetero-" for students.

TEAMWORK. In collegiate sports, group hypnosis has proven most effective. Even the "peptalk" before a game is a form of indirect hypnotic suggestion.

TELEPATHY. The exchange of thoughts or images. This faculty can be expanded under hypnotic training. Bypass conscious thoughts of limitation.

TEMPER TANTRUM. An angry, explosive state of mind can be brought back to reason. Tolerance induced. Irritability reduced. Control instilled.

TENSION. The stress and strain of everyday living troubles all of us. The immediate effect of hypnotic system is profound relaxation.

TENNIS. Learn how great your abilities are with inner tennis. Using visual images you train your mind to control your muscle reflexes.

TERMINAL ILLNESS. Helping the patient to minimize pain and emotional anxieties toward the end of life. Inner calm and acceptance of death.

TOOTHACHES. Until one is able to visit the dentist, hypnosis removes pain and discomfort. Some practitioners affect total anesthesia.

TRANSCENDENTAL MEDITATION. A highly lauded Indian technique is in reality a medium level of self-hypnosis, in which one rises above stress.

TRICHOTILLOMANIA. A morbid tendency to pull one's own hair. Often associated with anxiety-prone young children as well as adults.

TRISKAIDEKAPHOBIA. Fear of the number thirteen manifests itself in various restricting ways, such as fear of the thirteenth of each month.

TWITCHING. Involuntary spasms of muscles cause jerking movements of the face or parts of the body. Dramatic results through relaxing nerves.

TYPEWRITING. Develop speed and minimize errors through increasing your concentration and finger dexterity. Muscle reflexes become automatic.

ULCERS. Medically described as psychophysiologic in origin, this disorder of the digestive tract can be cleared up with suggestion.

UNCOMFORTABLE. The common state of uneasiness due to new or distressful circumstances can be corrected because hypnosis tranquilizes.

UNDERACHIEVING. Failure to succeed or perform up to one's ability is often based on low self-esteem. Image improved through mirror technique.

UNDERSTANDING. Comprehension can be expanded as one taps the deeper areas of inner intelligence. The power of abstract thinking enhanced.

UNREALITY. The escapist has difficulty in coping with practical problems. Under hypnotherapy reality is visualized as less threatening.

UROPHILIA. A pathological, inordinate interest in urine and urination. Often in relation to sexual preferences and perversity. Correctible.

VAGINA DENTATA. A morbid fantasy that the female vagina has teeth. Vaginal opening equated with a devouring mouth. Employ desensitization.

VAGINISMUS. Pain during intercourse is brought about by spasms of the internal sphincter muscles. Self-hypnosis loosens the tensions.

VANDALISM. A hostile compulsion to destroy the property of others. The underlying anger is uncovered and brought under control through hypnosis.

VASECTOMY. Surgical contraception for males is made more comfortable. Freedom from pain or anxiety as accelerated healing takes place.

VERBIGERATE. To repeat the same word or phrase over and over again. Often this deeply rooted habit is subconscious and needs trance level.

VERTIGO. A sensation of dizziness, a whirling in the head, feelings of imbalance are usually symptoms of aggravated stress. Hypnosis works.

VIRILITY. Manly vigor can be greatly enhanced. Sexual performance improves and mental concentration takes over control of genitals.

VISION. Many people report improved sight in cases where the problem is stress-related rather than organic or genetic in origin.

VITALITY. When energy is at a low ebb, your mind can bring you great burst of renewed power. Vibrant added stamina can result.

VOCABULARY. Extending one's capacity to use words correctly, add new words to enrich one's speech and communicate with other people.

VOCATIONAL APTITUDE. Tapping the warehouse of talents and skills to improve income and pleasure in working. Hidden abilities surface.

VOICE. You can improve the sound of your voice. Loud, soft, harshness. Speaking too fast or too slow. Getting rid of unwanted accents.

VOMITING. In cases of intestinal distress or food poisoning, vomiting can be brought about by suggestion under hypnosis with medical aid.

VOYEURISM. Inordinate desire to spy on members of the opposite sex for sexual gratification. Regression to source provides relief.

WANDERLUST. The compulsion to rove about and travel without regard to circumstances which demand staying in one place. Inner peace.

WARTS. Many hypnotists are reporting excellent results in the removal of warts and other skin growths. Check with physician first.

WEAKNESS. Lack of physical strength is often based on mental attitude. Feelings of exhaustion must first be checked by a doctor.

WEALTH. Most millionaires have adopted a mental method in visualization. They see their goals as easily obtainable and forge ahead.

WEATHER ACCLIMATION. An ability to adjust to changes in weather. Extreme heat or freezing weather can be made less stressful.

WEIGHT. The stabilization of weight can be attained for the underweight as well as the overweight. Fluctuation brought under control.

WHEEZING. Difficulty in inhaling and exhaling causes some

people to emit a whistling sound such as that associated with asthma. Ameliorated.

WILL-POWER. Self-hypnosis brings the ability to use inner mental persuasion to achieve control over one's disturbing behavior patterns.

WISDOM. Enhance your inner potential for deep creative meditation. Ancient gurus and seers have established prayer and meditation for this.

WITHDRAWAL SYMPTOMS. Chills, excessive sneezing, cramps, vomiting, and muscular twitching all respond favorably to suggestion under hypnosis.

XENOPHOBIA. An unreasonable fear and/or hatred of foreigners or strangers. To a lesser degree discomfort of anything new or unusual.

X-RAY TECHNICIANS. To quiet patients and gain their co-operation. Used indirectly, on a light trance level, for holding positions.

YAWNING. Uncontrollable, repetitive yawning can be both embarrassing and irritating. Your habit reflexes can be reconditioned to resist.

YOUTHFULNESS. A feeling of enthusiasm and freshness is more mental than physical. Therefore try mental persuasion and see the change.

ZEST. Motivational energy to set practical goals and reach them without wasting time. The listless person finds new meaning to life.

ZOOLAGNIA. Sexual attraction to animals, sometimes unconscious as in extreme adoration of pets to the exclusion of human sexual relations.

ZOOPHOBIA. Fear of all animals no matter how small or tame. Usually associated with trauma in childhood. Banish with regression to source.